THE SECRETARIAT FACTOR

Also by Thomas Kiernan:

THE INTRICATE MUSIC *A Biography of John Steinbeck*
HOW TO ASK FOR MORE AND GET IT (with Francis Greenburger)
ARAFAT *The Man and the Myth*
THE ARABS
THE MIRACLE AT COOGAN'S BLUFF
THE DOCTOR'S GUIDE TO TENNIS ELBOW, TRICK KNEE AND OTHER MISERIES
OF THE WEEKEND ATHLETE (with Leon Root, M.D.)
SHRINKS, ETC. *A Consumer's Guide to Psychotherapies*
JANE *An Intimate Biography of Jane Fonda*
OH, MY ACHING BACK *A Doctor's Guide to Your Back Pain and How
to Control It* (with Leon Root, M.D.)
WHO'S WHO IN THE HISTORY OF PHILOSOPHY

THE SECRETARIAT FACTOR

The Story of a Multimillion-dollar Breeding Industry

THOMAS KIERNAN

Doubleday & Company, Inc.
Garden City, New York   1979

ISBN: 0-385-14988-3
Library of Congress Catalog Card Number 78–20008
Copyright © 1979 by Thomas Kiernan

For Ron Turcotte . . . May you ride again.

FOREWORD

In 1970 a thoroughbred horse was born and in time was given the name Secretariat. As a result of a series of stunning performances over several race courses three years later, he became a living legend. He was then transformed into the motherlode of a potential quarter-billion-dollar industry. Which is to say that he was retired from racing and turned into a syndicated breeding stallion.

In May of 1974, I journeyed to a vast, picturesque thoroughbred breeding farm near the town of Paris, Kentucky, to see the industry at work. As I watched the fabled chestnut pump his semen into an undistinguished-looking but expensively blooded gray mare, I wondered if from that ejaculation, or from others he had dispensed in that first spring of his stud career, would one day materialize another like him.

I wasn't the only one to wonder. Much of the country had fallen under the spell of Secretariat the year before when he won, with astonishing ease and splendid style, the three contests that made up the Triple Crown of racing, and more. It was claimed by certain pundits that an ordinary, albeit extraordinary, racehorse had been elevated to national celebrity because of the tawdry goings-on at the time in the nation's capital. With our basic human corruptibility exposed by the sleazy machinations of the Nixon crowd, went the wisdom, the country was reduced to looking to a racehorse for inspiration and succor. Having been sorely disillusioned by our human heroes but still needing something to believe in, we fastened on this almost perfect animal whose heroic feats were accomplished without a hint of corruption or dishonesty. There were even those among the more theological-minded who suggested that Secretariat was an example of God's will at work. The big handsome racing machine had been "sent" to divert us from our national shame.

Others who wondered—no doubt a bit more anxiously—about

the future potency of Secretariat were those who had a large
financial stake in his procreative fluid. The great horse's lifetime
production of sperm had been allotted early the year before
among twenty-seven investors who formed the majority of what
became known as the Secretariat Syndicate. The syndicate's pay-
ing members had plunked down close to $200,000 each for a
share in Secretariat's sperm production. Eight additional free
shares were apportioned among Claiborne Farm, Inc.—the syndicator—and the family that had bred, owned, and raced Secretariat. Yet an additional lifetime share had gone to Lucien Laurin,
Secretariat's trainer. His share was free as well, a reward for his
handling of the horse's racing career.

Each unit in the thirty-six-share syndicate gave its owner the
right to no more than five emissions of the Triple Crown winner's semen per year. The five emissions, known in the breeding
trade as "covers," could be spurted into only one broodmare per
share annually. In other words, each share brought its owner the
privilege of breeding one mare to Secretariat every year; if, after
five covers, the mare failed to conceive, the shareholder had no
recourse but to wait until the following year.

As an alternative, one or more shareholders, if they chose not
to breed to Secretariat, could individually lease or trade their annual breeding rights to outside parties. The outside parties were
thereupon entitled to breed their own mares to the stallion, provided that the mares were approved by the syndicate. This rule
was established to ensure that only the highest quality mares
were sent to Secretariat's court. To breed anything less than the
best to Secretariat would compromise his chances of success at
stud and thereby reduce his value and the value of each shareholder's investment.

The total amount of the syndication was an eyebrow-raising
record for its time—over $6,000,000. Actually the figure was mis-
leading. Since only twenty-seven shares had been sold, the others
having been disbursed free of charge, the real figure was more
like $5,000,000. No matter, the amount would have been consid-
erably more had the syndicate been formed not prior to Secretariat's winning of the Triple Crown but afterward.

For those who subscribed to the syndicate, nevertheless, it
seemed a sure-fire investment even at the dizzily high per-share

price demanded. Probably no racehorse in history had accumulated more prestige as a two-year-old than Secretariat. The syndicate was put together as he was embarking on his three-year-
old campaign. He seemed certain, barring injury, to win a good
number if not all of the leading three-year-old races. If he failed
because of injury, his stud value would not be appreciably
affected since his own breeding and conformation were so impeccable. Only if he flopped for inexplicable reasons, as many
brilliant two-year-old horses do once they've turned three, would
the syndicate members have cause to regret their outlays. But so
strappingly handsome, powerful, and well-bred was he that few
expected a flop. It was true that his own sire was suspect in
knowledgeable breeding quarters as being a producer of horses
incapable of consistently sustaining their speed over the distances
of the classic three-year-old races. Other experts dismissed such
suspicions as myth.

Whatever the case, Secretariat simply looked too good to fail.
And his early three-year-old workouts gave every indication that
he was only getting better. With auction prices for thoroughbred yearlings spinning upward at a rate that even exceeded
the country's steep inflationary spiral, it was projected that the
market for Secretariat's "first-crop" offspring alone would earn
back for many their $190,000-per-share cost of participating in
his syndication. And that was if he merely performed well as a
three-year-old. Should he win the Triple Crown—the Kentucky Derby, the Preakness, and the Belmont—there was no tell-
ing what astronomical sums his first few crops would bring in
the auction market.

This pertained to those shareholders who intended from the
start to offer their first- and second-crop yearlings for sale. These
people are known in the business as market breeders. But there
are also those who breed solely for the purpose of adding superior horses to their racing stables and breeding farms. They
would not earn their investment back so quickly. Unless they
leased their breeding rights in Secretariat during the first one or
two years at the initially established rate of $100,000 a year, they
would have to wait until their Secretariat offspring began to
prove themselves as racehorses at two and three before they
could hope to recover their investments. But then they neither

needed nor wanted a quick return on their outlays. Most were so wealthy that it would have profoundly complicated their already complex schemes of income tax avoidance.

As I wondered about Secretariat's potential to, as it were, reproduce himself, and as I mused about the many others who must have been wondering the same thing, I thought it would be interesting to follow the fortunes of his first sons and daughters through their early racing careers. It then occurred to me that it would be even more interesting, no matter how they fared, to write a book about them.

This is the book.

I have many people to thank for their co-operation and assistance in my research—far too many to list here. But I do wish to single out by name a few who went above and beyond the call of courtesy to me. They are Seth Hancock, Lawrence Robinson, John Gaines, E. V. Benjamin, Jr., Jacqueline Getty, Warner Jones, Catesby Clay, Dan Lasater, Bertram Firestone, Paul Hexter, Duane Murty, Paul Mellon, William Taylor, Howard Gilman, Walter Kaufman, Raymond Guest, Victor Heerman, Mark Zervudachi, Benjamin Walden, E. Barry Ryan, Elliott Burch, John Russell, Mack Miller, John Nerud, Charles Kenney, Lazaro Barrera, Sam Kanchugar, and Ron Turcotte.

I might also say thanks to Secretariat himself, whom I got to know quite well. Notwithstanding his eventual success or failure at stud, the inimitable and unforgettable glory of his racing days will never dim.

Old Chatham, N.Y.   T.K.
1978

THE SECRETARIAT FACTOR

THE SECOND LADY

PART I

The Breeders and Their Mares

CHAPTER 1

The Source

The dappled ice-gray mare was called Irradiate. This was her fourth mating as a broodmare. Her first, to Secretariat's sire, Bold Ruler, in 1970, had a year later produced a filly who eventually became a stakes winner and earner of over $133,000 in race purses. Stakes winners were what all thoroughbred horse breeders hoped to produce when they matched their mares to stallions. The more and richer the stakes races won by a stallion's offspring, the better.

The ultimate stakes winner was, of course, Secretariat, to whom Irradiate was being bred this warm afternoon in May of 1974. Not only had he won the Triple Crown the year before, but he had also earned more money by those and his other top-graded stakes victories than any other horse in history. Which is not to say that he was the leading money-winner of all time— only that he had needed the fewest races to earn the most money of any horse, winning a number of them in record times in the bargain. Upon his retirement late in the fall of 1973, he had run in only twenty-one races during his sixteen-month career. He left the scene as the fourth richest money-earner in history, having accumulated $1,316,808 in purse winnings. The horse next ahead of him on the list, Buckpasser, had needed thirty-one races ten years earlier to earn $145,000 more. (In fairness to the brilliant

Buckpasser, it should be noted that had he not been forced to miss the Triple Crown races in 1963 because of an injury, he probably would have earned at least another $100,000.) Ahead of Buckpasser on the all-time earnings list was Round Table, who twenty years before had required sixty-six races to win $433,000 more than Secretariat. And leading the list was the splendid, fondly remembered Kelso, who had needed sixty-three races over six years to reach his pinnacle.

Secretariat's stunning earnings-per-race record was only one of many factors that had turned him into an instant legend. Infinitely more compelling was the figure of the horse himself—his record-shattering performances as the first horse to win the Triple Crown in twenty-five years, the awesome power and authority of his style of running, his versatility and grace afoot, and, not the least, his beguiling good looks. Had he never run a race or otherwise come to public attention, he was still a model of equine appearance and conformation. In the words of many grizzled veterans of the racing scene, he was almost "too good-looking" to be any good. Not even the most avuncular expert judges of horseflesh could find a flaw in his conformation. He was the perfect blend of design and performance, of form and substance. One well-known veterinary school professor had superimposed a skeletal chart, representing the ideal horse, on a blown-up photo of Secretariat to illustrate for his students an example of equine perfection in the flesh. The press dubbed him "Superhorse," and it seemed by all the evidence that for once the press was not engaging in its usual sporting hyperbole.

But now it was 1974, and the legend was being put to a new and, for some, riskily expensive test. This was to see if he could transmit his genes, through the breeding process, to his offspring. By the day in May when he was introduced for the second time to Irradiate, he had already covered twenty-eight of the thirty-six mares that had been selected to be bred to him, some more than once. Irradiate was the twenty-ninth on his schedule. The seven remaining mares would visit Secretariat over the next few weeks, plus a few more that had clearly not been impregnated during earlier covers, at the end of which time the thoroughbred breeding season would come to a close. There would then ensue

the long wait on the part of the syndicate members to learn if
Secretariat had passed the test.

Secretariat had faced another test prior to this. This test—a
clinical one—had raised doubts about whether he would be able
to produce offspring at all. Upon his retirement he had been
flown to Claiborne Farm, the handsome thoroughbred breeding
farm in the bluegrass country near Paris and Lexington, Kentucky, where he would stand as a stallion. Although the syndication had been completed nine months before, the twenty-seven
subscribers had been required to put up only 10 per cent of their
respective $190,000 payments. As was the convention with all
such stallion syndications, the formal closing of the syndicate
would not occur until Secretariat passed an independently administered fertility examination that proved he was physiologically capable of producing offspring.

In November, soon after the great horse arrived at Claiborne
with his stablemate Riva Ridge, who had also been syndicated
but for a lesser amount, Secretariat's shoes were removed and his
hooves clipped, practically down to the quick, to discourage any
desire to romp about the sloping two-acre paddock in which he
was to be turned out. Secretariat arrived at Claiborne—the very
same farm at which he had been conceived during the mating of
his dam and sire four-and-a-half years earlier—as a finely tuned,
on-edge racing machine. He had run and won his last race only
two weeks before, in Canada. He had then been returned to his
home base at New York's Belmont Park, where he was maintained
on the usual post-race feed-and-exercise regimen by his trainer,
Lucien Laurin. When Secretariat was shipped to Kentucky, he
had no instinctive sense that he was being retired; to him the air
journey was probably just another prerace trip such as he had
made before.

It takes time for the tautly strung system of a healthy, well-
conditioned racehorse to be de-energized by a decrease in
activity. Thus the clipping of Secretariat's hooves to make them
tender. Put out to pasture on his own after almost two years of
constant training for competition, his energy and exuberance
would be too great for Claiborne's stout fences to confine. If his
hooves weren't clipped, he might injure himself galloping and
bucking about his paddock.

Under other circumstances he might have been tranquilized for a time. But Helen Chenery Tweedy, the woman who headed the stable that owned Secretariat and who was commonly known as "Penny," was anxious to have the Secretariat and Riva Ridge syndicates formally concluded so that she and other members of her family could get their hands on the much-needed millions the syndications would bring. Secretariat and Riva Ridge had been bred and owned by her father, Christopher T. Chenery. He had died at the beginning of 1973 after a long illness. His lawyers informed Penny Tweedy, who had a few years before assumed the management of the breeding farm and racing stable her father had so brilliantly and successfully developed over the years, that the federal tax bite on his estate would force her, her brother, and her sister to sell the farm. Riva Ridge and Secretariat had come along at a fortunate time, however. If she could syndicate them—which meant, in effect, sell all but a minor interest in each to two groups of investors—the proceeds would enable the Chenery heirs to pay off the monumental tax on their father's estate and save the farm and stable.

It was while the estate began the tax-settlement process in February of 1973 that Penny Tweedy, through the offices of Claiborne Farm, offered Secretariat for syndication. He had just turned three. He had achieved the unprecedented by being named "Horse of the Year" as a two-year-old—the Academy Award of the racing industry and one that had always in the past gone to a three-year-old or upward. Not only that, but the horse he had edged out for the distinction was Riva Ridge, who in the same year, as a three-year-old, had won the Kentucky Derby and Belmont Stakes—two of the three Triple Crown races. Riva Ridge was a proven racehorse in February of 1973 and theoretically should have been worth considerably more than the year-younger Secretariat. But on the strength of his "Horse of the Year" award and Riva Ridge's more recent disappointing performances, the growing chestnut's syndication value was deemed appreciably higher than his fully tested bay stablemate's. Secretariat's value was set at $6,080,000, while Riva Ridge's was later established at a shade over $5,000,000. They would, it was determined, be retired to stud together at the end of 1973.

So, Penny Tweedy and the other survivors of Christopher

Chenery were anxious to get the syndications formally completed and the money in. To accomplish this meant the administration of independent clinical fertility tests as soon as practicable. Both Secretariat and Riva Ridge failed the tests. Secretariat's failure became another in the series of media hooplas that had attended his every move since the spring before.

Up to the point at which a clinical determination was made on Secretariat's fertility, the investors' down payments were protected by refund insurance. Central to the syndication agreement were clauses that guaranteed the return of the subscribers' initial outlays should the horse prove likely to be insufficiently fertile. It had happened before with fine stallion prospects and would happen again.* To the Secretariat syndicate's prospective members and—thanks to a good deal of misinformation processed by the press—to the public at large, it seemed to be happening with Secretariat.

But what was to occur with Secretariat, and with Riva Ridge, frequently occurs with other stallion prospects rushed from racetrack to breeding shed. It had most notably happened in prior years to Reviewer, a stallion who would eventually produce a number of useful racing offspring and a truly memorable one in Ruffian, who two years after Secretariat's retirement threatened to eclipse his feats with her own awesome but fragile brilliance.

Both Secretariat and Riva Ridge were young. At three, Secretariat had to that point lived only one tenth of the average equine lifespan. His physiological equivalent in human terms would be a boy just approaching the age of puberty. A lad of that age is capable of procreation, but under the microscope his semen will usually be made up of a large number of immature and unstable spermatozoa. Such was the case with Secretariat. His first fertility test, conducted by three independent veterinarians, determined that he had a condition called *spermatogonia*—the presence of immature cells in his sperm. Because it was not an uncommon condition in young, fresh stallions, it was not at first a great cause for worry. Secretariat had just come out of training

* Just a year later a celebrated European thoroughbred by the name of Cellini would be syndicated and imported to Kentucky to stand at stud. He proved not only clinically infertile but also infertile in fact. The syndicate was dissolved and Cellini was returned to the racetrack. Assault, a 1940s Triple Crown winner, had been unable to breed because of sterility.

and the likelihood was that, young as he was, his system had not yet adjusted to the manufacture of mature sperm. Yet technically, according to the fertility definitions of the syndication agreement, he was not yet ready to breed. The subscribing members of the syndicate agreed to a second test after Secretariat had had a chance to acclimatize himself to his new, less strenuous life.

In the meantime he would be test-bred to two or three nonthoroughbred mares to accustom him to the actual mating process. This was another factor in the syndication agreement. The members wanted to be sure that, no matter how fertile he might prove, Secretariat would not turn out to be what is known as a "shy breeder." The equivalent of a shy breeder in the human realm would be a man who is impotent or prematurely ejaculatory. Next to infertile or barely fertile stallions in the horse-breeding industry, the shy stallion is a less common but still occasional phenomenon. Many fine racehorses had turned into failures at stud because, in horsemen's lingo, they "couldn't raise the stick" enough. An example was the splendid Colin, who went unbeaten in fifteen races. Retired to stud, he was able to sire only eighty-one foals in twenty-three years. Prolific stallions produce that many in two or three years.

Secretariat was bred to three cold-blooded test mares during December.† Thirty-six thoroughbred mares had been lined up by the syndicate's members to go to Secretariat's court once all his tests were passed. He covered the cold-bloods well once he got the hang of it. One was an Appaloosa mare who was used on the farm to nurse foals whose dams had died. Secretariat mounted her and, with the help of Claiborne Farm's stallion handlers, got his erect penis deep into her vagina. Thereafter he left no doubt that he knew what to do. With his coppery tail twitching furiously, his teeth biting into the mare's neck and his throat emitting squeals of neurological ecstasy, he poured his semen into the coarse, spotted mare. When he withdrew moments later, one of the attending vets caught the last few reflexive spurts of semen in a cup. The cup was sent off for the second laboratory analysis.

---

† Nonthoroughbred mares were used for the test breedings so that the resultant foals, if any, being halfbreeds, would have no value other than as curios.

Although the Appaloosa, as well as one of the two other mares to whom Secretariat was test-bred, would become pregnant, the lab tests yielded the same results as before. His sperm still contained immature cells. This time the press got wind of the results and announced them to the world as though Secretariat were infertile. The legend was suddenly suspect. And most of the syndicate subscribers began to have second thoughts as they became the butts of public jokes.

They did not panic, however. Most were knowledgeable horsemen and were easily convinced that the tests' findings did not really mean that Secretariat was infertile. He had simply failed to measure up to a series of strict clinical standards in the syndication agreement. A revised agreement was proposed whereby the syndication would not become final until the following September 5. They would dispense with further lab tests and allow the horse to prove himself on his own. He would be bred to the thirty-six syndicate mares over the coming months at an additional down payment on the total cost of each share. If, by September, 60 per cent of the mares were pregnant, not counting certain technical exceptions, the syndicate would take final effect. If not, then those members who wished to could drop out with full refunds of their money.

Of the thirty-six mares, twenty-two would have to be examined "in foal" by September 5 for the syndicate to proceed. The percentage was about average for healthy, fertile thoroughbred stallions. If a less than 60 per cent impregnation rate was achieved, those members who dropped out with barren mares would receive a full refund with interest. Those who dropped out but whose mares had gotten in foal would be required to forfeit the total of $47,500 they had put up in payments on their syndicate shares. These forfeited payments could then be written off as stud fees.

When the revised agreement was circulated among the syndicate members, all but one agreed to it. The dissenter dropped out then and there. As far as the others were concerned, it was a no-lose situation. If Secretariat accomplished less than 60 per cent impregnation, those whose mares were not pregnant could withdraw from the syndicate free and clear, with no loss to them.

Those who dropped out, but whose mares were pregnant, would be even better off. For $47,500 they could behold the likely prospect of securing one of Secretariat's first offspring, an animal that would be at least worth several hundred thousand dollars in the yearling-sales markets two years later.

All the worry proved to be academic. Although the average impregnation rate of thoroughbred stallions standing in Kentucky—the heartland of the industry—was in the neighborhood of 65 per cent, the more fecund stallions were expected to impregnate about 80 per cent of their mares each breeding season. As it would turn out, of the thirty-six mares bred to Secretariat during the late winter and spring of 1974, he got thirty in foal to term. Of the other six, three were barren and three "slipped"— that is, aborted or resorbed their embryonic foals after becoming pregnant. This rate of barrenness and slippage was below average. All in all, Secretariat would achieve an impregnation rate in his first year of close to 95 per cent.

The syndication became final in September with the entirety of its original membership, save one, intact. Penny Tweedy got her money, as she did from the Riva Ridge syndication, which had undergone a similar revision. The members of the syndicate who had paid to join were:

• Ogden Phipps, the aging but fabulously wealthy heir to the steel fortune of his grandfather and one of the thoroughbred industry's foremost "improvers of the breed."

• Dr. William Lockridge, the owner of Kentucky's Walmac market-breeding farm.

• Walter Salmon, Jr., an elderly New York real-estate tycoon and owner of another large breeding farm in the bluegrass country, called Mereworth, which he had inherited from his father.

• Allaire (Mrs. Richard C.) duPont of the duPont chemical fortune, mistress of the 850-acre Woodstock Farm in Maryland, breeder and owner of the all-time money-earning horse Kelso (who, because he was a gelding, could never serve as a stallion), and avid participant in racing.

• Along with two silent partners, E. V. Benjamin, Jr., a retired Louisiana and Texas oil millionaire and the master of
Big Sink Farm near Lexington, Kentucky.

• Zenya Yoshida, who as Japan's leading thoroughbred
breeder had begun to spend enormous amounts of money in
the United States in the late 1960s for American horseflesh.

• Milton Dance, known universally as "Laddie," the husband
of an Oregon lumber heiress, the owner of a breeding farm
in Maryland, and a celebrated auctioneer with the horse-sales
firm of Fasig-Tipton, Inc.

• Richard Stokes and his wife, Diana, heiress to the Johnson
& Johnson Band-Aid and baby-powder millions, proprie-
tors of a modestly scaled breeding farm near Leesburg, Virginia.

• William Farish III, a Texas financier, rancher, and racing
stable owner.

• Paul Mellon, a philanthropist of inestimable wealth by virtue of his inheritance of much of the Mellon Pennsylvania
banking and oil fortune, and a determined breeder of racehorses at his vast Rokeby Farm in the Blue Ridge Mountains
of Virginia.

• William M. McKnight, the immensely rich retired guiding
light and chairman of the 3M Company (Minnesota Mining
& Manufacturing Co.), and the owner of one of Florida's
leading breeding and racing operations, Tartan Farm and
Tartan Stable.

• Walter Haefner, a Swiss entrepreneur, banker, and sportsman who was prominent in European racing and the owner
of large stud and breeding properties in Ireland.

• The British Bloodstock Agency Ltd. of Ireland, headed by
Anglo-Irish breeder Jonathan Irving. Irving intended to
make his annual breeding right available to English breeders.

• E. P. Taylor, an elderly Canadian whose fortune derived
from a variety of industrial sources and who, with farms in

the United States and Canada, was one of the world's leading market breeders.

• Jean-Louis Levesque, a French-Canadian insurance tycoon
known throughout Canada for his racing stable's successes.

• Mr. and Mrs. Paul Hexter, she the heiress to the Hertz
Rent-a-Car fortune whose late father, John D. Hertz, bred
and owned 1943 Triple Crown winner Count Fleet and
many other fine racehorses.

• Captain Timothy Rogers, one of Ireland's foremost
breeders, who had earlier hoped to buy Secretariat outright
and import him to Ireland for the improvement of Irish,
British, and European racing bloodlines. Rogers' principal
backer in the share was French racing and breeding figure
Jacques Wertheimer, for whom Rogers was nominee.

• Tadao Tamashima, another profligate Japanese spender the
influence of whose horses, outside of Japan, is felt mostly in
Europe.

• Warner L. Jones, a top Kentucky market breeder with a
prosperous farm between Lexington and Louisville.

• J. B. Faulconer and Hilary Boone, as partners in the prosperous Kentucky bloodstock and insurance agency of Faulconer-Boone, Inc.

• Richard Brooks, a successful Baltimore automobile dealer
and theretofore a relatively modest Maryland thoroughbred
breeder.

• Dan Lasater, a young man who made a fortune in the fast-
food business with his Ponderosa steak houses and who had
recently retired, at the age of twenty-nine, to find similar
success running what virtually became a chain of racing
stables across the country.

• George Strawbridge, a young Philadelphian, an heir to the
Campbell Soup fortune, and an avid proponent of the
steeplechase version of horseracing.

• Bertram R. Firestone, member of the Firestone Tire &
Rubber Co. family and a vigorous new breeder and owner.

• The brothers Howard and Charles Gilman, chief officers of New York's Gilman Paper Company, in the name of which they bought their share in the syndicate and operated a Florida breeding farm.

• F. Eugene Dixon, another Philadelphia sportsman and an inheritee of the fortune of the heralded, old-line racing family of George B. Widener, his uncle.

• Alfred Gwynne Vanderbilt, of the railroad Vanderbilts, who bred and raced horses from his Sagamore Farm near Baltimore and who, at the time of the Secretariat syndication, was chairman of the New York Racing Association, the corporation that owns and operates the three major New York racetracks.

This was the twenty-seven-paid-member Secretariat syndicate. Claiborne Farm, as syndicator and manager of the stallion, was awarded the equivalent of three free shares, or breeding rights, the first year, with a fourth to be added the year after. The Chenery interests, headed by Penny Tweedy, retained five shares, three in the name of the Estate of Christopher T. Chenery and two in the name of the Chenery Corporation—the family holding company that operated the Virginia farm called The Meadow, the birthplace of Secretariat and the core of Penny Tweedy's thoroughbred operations. After some ill-tempered wrangling, Lucien Laurin was given his free lifetime breeding right. To some, Secretariat might not have achieved what he did had it not been for Laurin's training expertise.

It was now time for Secretariat to meet his second, more important test. He began to cover thoroughbred mares in mid-February of 1974. On February 18, during his second cover, he successfully impregnated one of industrialist-breeder Walter Jeffords' prized mares, a thirteen-year-old producer of stakes winners named My Card. No one knew it at the time, of course, since it takes a month or more to definitely determine that a mare is in foal, but Secretariat was on his way.

He still had two more tests to face. The first would occur two years later, when the average cash value of those of his offspring put up for sale would be determined. The second and more vital one would come a year later, when the fittest members of his first crop went to the racetrack and entered competition. Would he have produced anything capable of sustaining or even expanding his initial syndication value as a stallion once the original interest in his first crop died down? It was inevitable that he would be judged as a stallion, even by people who knew better, on the basis of his first crop.

The question would not be answered for three years. Yet there were those, expert in the arcane science of breeding, who were already tendering pseudoscientific answers. Those immature sperm, they said, were not a favorable sign. He could be as fertile as any stallion and produce hundreds of sons and daughters over the years. But unless and until his spermatozoa became stabilized and unified, they would forever miss making the wondrous connection that occasionally enables a stallion to impose the majority of his dominant genes on those of a broodmare.

CHAPTER 2

The Connections

Irradiate was of special interest to Seth Hancock, and he had walked down from his office at Claiborne Farm to the black-creosoted breeding shed to watch Secretariat cover the gray mare.

Hancock, a tall, courtly, phlegmatic young man, had been the talk of the backstage thoroughbred world for more than a year. Fifteen months before, he had been catapulted into the management of the enormously successful, tradition-rich Claiborne by the death of his father, Arthur B. Hancock, Jr. Many observers, some bitten by envy and others by condescension, predicted the beginning of the end of Claiborne, the General Motors of the thoroughbred industry. Seth Hancock was only twenty-three years old, barely out of college, and without a shred of experience in the running of a wide-ranging, multimillion-dollar horse-breeding operation. Others more charitably took a wait-and-see attitude. "Bull" Hancock, as Seth's father was universally known, had been a master horseman and had turned Claiborne into what it was after inheriting it from his own father, Arthur B. Hancock, Sr.—also a master horseman who had started the farm in the early 1900s. The Hancock blood ran rich with horse-breeding instinct. Seth and his older brother Arthur B. III, who was in the process of starting his own stud farm after a falling-out with Bull, had surely inherited the instincts.

The Hancock family traced its beginnings to the Deep South of antebellum Alabama and Louisiana. Seth Hancock's great-grandfather was Richard J. Hancock, a farmboy who was conscripted into the Confederate Army at the start of the Civil War. He was sent with his brigade to Virginia in 1862 to fight under Stonewall Jackson. In 1863, while recovering from a wound, he met Thomasia Harris, the daughter of a wealthy Virginia plantation owner. After a second serious wound retired him from combat in 1864, he married Thomasia and settled in with her at her father's fifteen-hundred-acre plantation near Charlottesville, which was known as Ellerslie. Richard Hancock had always been interested in horses. After the war was over, to establish himself with Virginia's landed gentry, he decided to raise thoroughbred horses with his father-in-law's help.

For the next twenty years Richard Hancock shrewdly built up the Ellerslie Stud until one of his horses, Knight of Ellerslie, won the important Preakness Stakes. Knight of Ellerslie also went on to become a significant sire. During this time, Hancock himself sired a son, whom he named Arthur.

Whereas the Civil War had served as a boon to the fortunes of Richard Hancock, once a poor farmboy and outsider, it had a devastating effect on many of Virginia's native families. One was the Chenery family, which had settled long before on some land near Fredericksburg, halfway between Washington and Richmond. At war's end, sixteen-year-old James Hollis Chenery found himself the only male survivor of his family. James went to work after the war in a dry-goods store at Richmond, and in 1881, when he was thirty-two, he married Ida Taylor, a second cousin. The two produced five children over the next eight years, all but one of whom would go to college and carve out distinguished careers for themselves, one as a newspaper and magazine editor, another as a doctor.

Probably the most precocious and ambitious of the children was Christopher Tompkins Chenery, who was born in 1886. Growing up in an environment of genteel poverty, he too took a liking to horses and resolved to one day live the life of a wealthy Virginia horseman. To achieve his ambition, he pursued an engineering career after college and went West to make his fortune. In Oregon he met Helen Bates, the daughter of a New England family, followed her to Chicago, and married her just before the outbreak of World War I. In 1917, he joined the Army and was assigned to Fort Belvoir, Virginia, near his childhood home, as a cavalry instructor. There he was put in charge of a number of young men from wealthy families of the Northeast who had interrupted careers in finance and industry to serve their country in the traditional way—the cavalry. Christopher Chenery was a dashing, daring, and authoritative personality, and during his time at Fort Belvoir he made many useful friends and contacts among America's young financial elite. After the war he exploited his friendships, abandoning his engineering career and entering the world of high finance in New York. Ten years later he was a wealthy man on the way to becoming even richer through his specialization in organizing utilities-industry financing. He then began to reflect on his childhood ambition to become a horseman.

While Chenery was growing up in Richmond, Arthur Hancock had returned to Charlottesville, after graduating from the University of Chicago in 1895, to join his father, Richard, in the breeding of horses at Ellerslie Stud. It was the Gay Nineties, a time when great industrial fortunes had been made by the likes of the Vanderbilts, Whitneys, Carnegies, Rockefellers, and Phippses, and a time when many of the same fortunes were being used to introduce their owners to the "sport of kings." Nothing had more social cachet for the era's *nouveau riche* than to indulge themselves in thoroughbred horseracing, theretofore an entertainment reserved almost exclusively to America's old-line, English-descended, land-rich southern gentry.

Arthur Hancock, a tall stringbean of a young man, stayed at Ellerslie Stud for ten years learning the thoroughbred breeding business from his father. The arcane art of successful breeding hinged then, as it does today, on three elemental factors: an exhaustive knowledge of bloodlines, a comprehensive understanding of equine genetics, and a sharply perceptive and analytical eye for physical conformation.

Richard Hancock had been self-taught in such requisites, mostly through trial and error. But with the advantage of a university education, his son Arthur soon exceeded him in his grasp of these essential factors. He was in the process of turning the art of thoroughbred breeding into a quasi-science.

In 1907, Arthur Hancock was invited to Lexington, Kentucky, to serve as a horse judge at a local fair. There he met Nancy Clay, a daughter of one of the many land-wealthy Clay families of the region. Nancy Clay's father owned a giant thirteen-hundred-acre livestock and tobacco farm near the dingy town of Paris, Kentucky, about twenty miles northeast of Lexington in a pretty, rolling country. Arthur and Nancy married in 1908, thus linking two generously landed families. And when his wife's parents died in 1910, Arthur became the lord of twin manors, having relieved his aging father of the management of the Ellerslie plantation in Virginia the year before.

The area around Lexington, Kentucky, radiating for forty or so miles in all directions, had become celebrated for the mineral qualities of its soil and the nutritional values of the grasses that grew on it. Laden particularly with high calciate and protein concentrations, the soil nourished grazing grasses that "put quick bone" on livestock. In the immediate post-Civil War period, thoroughbred breeders from all over the East and South, ever anxious to gain an advantage, began to invade the region in order to provide their horses with the best possible natural nourishment. By the turn of the century the breeding of thoroughbreds was a thriving agricultural industry in the rural region whose hub was Lexington. Tobacco and beef farms had been converted to horse nurseries, and racetracks were built to foster the industry.

In 1912, Arthur Hancock decided to move most of his thoroughbred operations from Virginia to the land his wife had inherited in Kentucky. He named the place Claiborne Farm, using an Old English spelling to honor the role of his wife's family in his acquisition of the acreage, and began to convert it to a horse-breeding facility. Over the next few years he built barns, cleared and fenced hundreds of acres of pasture, and acquired additional land.

A horse farm is not a horse farm without horses, however. And a stud farm is not a stud farm without a stallion. The fashion in those days was for every breeder to own at least one stallion and either breed his own mares to it or trade breedings to other stallions. Hancock had brought twelve mares with him from Ellerslie. But he knew that he couldn't compete with the already well-established Kentucky stud farms until he acquired a first-class stallion.

In 1913 he laid out $20,000 to buy the young stallion Celt at an auction in New York. By so doing he set the foundation for what was to become one of Kentucky's most influential and prosperous breeding farms. By 1921, fifty-two of Celt's offspring had won a total of 124 races and $206,167 in purses, making him the country's leading sire for that year and putting Hancock on a first-name basis with the racing and breeding world's wealthiest and most active participants. It was the respect such people had for his judgment and perspicacity that enabled him to go to Europe in 1926 and, on behalf of a syndicate he had formed with three others, buy the French stallion Sir Gallahad III for $125,000. Sir Gallahad was brought back to stand at stud at Claiborne Farm. The following year he was bred to, among others, a daughter of Celt called Marguerite. The resulting male foal grew up to be Gallant Fox who, by winning the Triple Crown in 1930, was only the second horse in history to achieve that distinction. Sir Gallahad III was the leading American sire of the same year in total money won by offspring, despite the fact that he had just 16 sons and daughters running.

Sir Gallahad burst on the American thoroughbred scene with a mighty impact. He led the national sire list three more times, turned Claiborne into an internationally recognized breeding farm, and made fashionable the practice of other breeders of buying prominent horses in England and Europe and importing them to America for stud duty. The American thoroughbred had had its beginnings, of course, in England. The breed had come to this country with the early colonists, and all pure horses of the breed in 1930 were descended from one or another of a trio of English stallions. After the Revolution, the infusion of new blood into infant America all but stopped. By the mid-nineteenth century, with few exceptions, the breed had stagnated. Breeders bred the same horses over and over again to produce what amounted to a few expanded families, which were in turn bred to each other and resulted in even larger interblooded families. Arthur

Hancock perceived that almost every time a quality foreign stallion had been brought to this country and bred to mares of the stagnating inbred American families, the infusion of new blood had produced sudden improvements in racing performance. It was for this reason that he had bought his first foreign stallion, Wrack, in 1915, and that he had gone after Sir Gallahad III later. His prescience was vindicated in 1930, and soon other breeders were following suit.

But few could outdo Hancock in picking imported blood. In 1936, he formed another syndicate to buy and import England's 1930 Epsom Derby winner, Blenheim II, to Claiborne. In 1940, one of Blenheim II's first sons, Whirlaway, was yet another Triple Crown winner. By then Arthur Hancock almost annually led the list of breeders whose horses won the most money. He did not usually race his horses. He was almost exclusively a market breeder, selling his yearlings at auction or privately to wealthy racing clients and accepting large stud fees from others who wanted to breed their qualified mares to his stallions. At his side during his rise to pre-eminence in the 1930s was his son Arthur, Jr., whom Nancy Clay Hancock had produced in 1910.

Arthur, Jr., often claimed to have been born a horseman. Not as tall as his father, he was considerably more hefty and outgoing and was tagged with the nickname Bull as a youth. He had spent his school summers working on the farm and watching his father operate. After Bull graduated from Princeton in 1933 he returned to Claiborne to learn the business in earnest. The Depression had little negative effect on Claiborne's rising fortunes, but World War II did. Bull Hancock was away from the farm for a lengthy period, serving in the Army Air Corps. When he returned toward the end of the war he found his father debilitated by illness and the farm itself beginning to stagnate. Many thoroughbred breeding establishments had thrived for a time, only to fade into obscurity because their owners had chosen to rest on their laurels and failed to keep new blood coming in. Claiborne had been the country's leading breeder again in 1945, but the farm's choicest bloodstock was reaching advanced age and the senior Hancock had made little effort during the war to reinvigorate it with young stock. Bull Hancock, drawing from lessons past, knew that the farm's pre-eminence would soon fade once Sir Gallahad

III and Blenheim II, then twenty-five and eighteen, respectively —as well as the aging broodmares who had produced so many of their brilliant offspring—died.

Bull resolved to tackle the problem. One of the first things he did was urge his father to sell the still-functioning but lesser Hancock stud at Virginia's Ellerslie and concentrate all his holdings at Claiborne. Virginia had once been the thoroughbred capital of the country, but like many of its complacent breeders, had lost its position to Kentucky in importance.

Yet Virginia had a fresh and far-from-complacent breeder. In the mid-1930s Christopher T. Chenery had used his new-won riches to fulfill the ambitions of his youth. Purchasing the rundown old farmstead between Washington and Richmond that had once been owned by his father's family, he poured tens of thousands of dollars into restoring it as a horse farm and rechristened it The Meadow. Then he set out to build a breeding operation and racing stable. By the end of the war, he was well on his way.

There are a number of ways for an individual to acquire a racing stable, the quickest being simply to buy one or two racehorses, hire a trainer, and rent stall space at a racetrack. This was not the way it was done by the thoroughbred aristocracy of Virginia and Kentucky, however. So Chenery took the traditional, more difficult, and expensive route of breeding his own racehorses. His strategy was to buy a string of well-blooded mares as cheaply as he could. One of his early purchases was a three-year-old filly called Hildene. She was a daughter of 1926 Kentucky Derby winner Bubbling Over, but because she had been a complete failure as a racer, and because Bubbling Over had proved a disappointment as a sire, Chenery was able to get her for a mere $600. As with his other purchases, his intention was to breed her.

In the spring of 1946, Chenery sent Hildene to Arthur Hancock's Ellerslie Stud, which Hancock was about to sell under son Bull's prodding, to be bred to a low-priced Hancock stallion named Princequillo.

Princequillo had had an interesting history. He was an extremely well-bred European horse born in England in the spring of 1940, a fifth-generation descendant of the superior nineteenth-century English stallion St. Simon. Owned by an American movie mogul living in Europe at the time, Princequillo was shipped as a yearling to the United States in 1941. His owner leased him to a Chicagoan, who was permitted to run him as a two-year-old in claiming races. Claiming races are the lifeblood of the sport, but are contests in which only the least accomplished horses at a given track compete.

Princequillo achieved little as a two-year-old. Midway through 1943, however, after Count Fleet became the sixth horse in history to win the Triple Crown, Princequillo won a distance race of over a mile and a half. After winning two more races during the summer, he triumphed in the fall in one of the country's longest races, the two-mile Jockey Club Gold Cup at New York's Belmont Park. Suddenly he was a topic of conversation among the racing fraternity.

It was his European blood, most agreed. European horses were bred "to stay a distance of ground," as the saying went. Most high-purse English and continental stakes races were mile-and-a-half-and-up contests, whereas in America the mile-and-a-half race was an exception. Most important stakes were run at distances less than that—a mile and a sixteenth, a mile and an eighth, a mile and a quarter. Consequently, American breeding concentrated more on early speed over a moderate "distance of ground" than endurance and late speed over a longer distance.

Despite Princequillo's emergence as a quality runner—he won twice more as a four-year-old in 1944 before injuring himself at Saratoga—there was not a great deal of interest in him as a stallion. What interest there was centered mostly among breeders of steeplechase horses—steeplechases being long, grueling races over obstacles. Virginia and Maryland were still the principal centers of steeplechase breeding, and in 1945 Arthur Hancock acquired Princequillo in a partnership for the purpose of installing him at his Ellerslie Stud in Virginia, within easy access of the steeplechaser breeders.

Hancock had trouble filling Princequillo's "book" during his first year at stud. A stallion's book is the minimum number of mares to which he must be bred in a season to earn back in stud fees, his keep and the expenses of his acquisition. In 1946, Bull Hancock, home from the war, had taken over much of the day-to-day responsibility of managing Claiborne and Ellerslie from his seventy-two-year-old father. In preparing the sale of Ellerslie, he contacted a number of his father's associates in syndications and urged them to breed to Princequillo. One of these was William Woodward, another familied multimillionaire, a pillar of the turf, and one of Arthur Hancock's partners in his 1926 importation of Sir Gallahad III. Woodward, a New York investment banker with thoroughbred interests in several states and in Europe, agreed to send a mare to Princequillo. Meeting Christopher Chenery at a business conference one day, he suggested that Chenery do the same.

Chenery sent his cheaply bought Hildene. Hildene, sired by Bubbling Over, was out of the undistinguished race mare Fancy Racket, who was a daughter of Arthur Hancock's first European stallion purchase, Wrack. Although the possessor of a dismal racing record, Hildene had begun to show signs of being a producer of well-made foals. By going to a Hancock stallion, she represented the beginning of a long association between the up-and-coming Chenery farm in Virginia and the Hancock complex in Kentucky that would culminate the superhorse Secretariat.

The culmination could not occur without the participation of a third family, however.

In the years immediately following the Civil War, two shrewd young Pennsylvanians by the name of Andrew Carnegie and Henry Phipps parleyed a small joint investment in an iron forge near what is now Pittsburgh into the Carnegie Steel Company. Three and a half decades later, Carnegie Steel was transformed into the United States Steel Corporation with the help of financier J. P. Morgan. The transformation netted Henry Phipps $50,000,000 and produced the beginnings of a family dynasty that did much, among other things, to change the face of horse-racing.

One of Henry Phipps' children was Henry Carnegie Phipps, who was twenty-six when his father became one of the richest men in America. H.C., as he was known, embarked on adult life with a $4,000,000 cash gift from his father and as the beneficiary of a family financial trust that freed him of the necessity of ever having to earn a living. Like the first-generation heirs of many other patriarchal fortunes, he became a Wall Street investor and financier whose principal goal was to expand his and his family's riches.

H.C. married Gladys Livingston Mills, herself an heiress to a pair of considerably older fortunes. On her mother's side she was a descendant of pre-Revolutionary Livingstons who owned vast chunks of New York State and northern New Jersey. On her father's side she descended from the Mills family, which had grown rich from banking in California during the Gold Rush and which owned county-sized tracts of land in the Western states. With the marriage, the Phipps family ascended to the top of the list of America's wealthy.

H. C. Phipps possessed little interest in horses at the time of his marriage. Gladys, on the other hand, had grown up among horses on the various Livingston and Mills family estates scattered about the East. Moreover, her father, Darius Ogden Mills, was active in racing, as was her brother Ogden Livingston Mills—both Wall Streeters like her new husband. As a result, H.C. soon developed an interest in the turf. With Gladys and her brother as the "brains" behind it, the three launched a racing stable in 1925 and named it Wheatley, after the road that ran past H.C. and Gladys' estate on Long Island's north shore.

With the stable went the beginnings of a breeding operation. Shortly, Gladys Phipps sought out the advice of Arthur Hancock in Kentucky in an effort to acquire the best possible mares and stallions for breeding purposes. The shrewd, courtly Hancock quickly became Gladys Phipps' mentor in the matters of equine pedigree and conformation. She became his faithful student and then client. As she began to acquire mares and follow Hancock's recommendations on their breedings, she boarded them at Claiborne Farm.

In 1908, H. C. and Gladys Phipps produced a son named Ogden. After graduating from Harvard in 1931, Ogden Phipps moved into the Wall Street world of his father and began to learn the intricacies of managing the assets of the huge Phipps family trust, called Bessemer Securities, from which a seemingly never-ending stream of money flowed. A shy, stocky, bull-necked young man, Ogden had inherited most of the physical characteristics of his mother's side of the family. He inherited her love of thoroughbred horses, as well. During the 1930s he was in constant attendance with her on visits to various race-tracks to see her horses run, to auction sales to buy mares and yearlings, and to Kentucky to inspect her bloodstock. Ogden and Bull Hancock, of markedly different backgrounds but contemporaries in age, became good friends. Just as Gladys Phipps learned about the horse business from Arthur Hancock, Ogden learned from Bull. Of the horses Gladys bred during the 1930s with Arthur Hancock's counsel, the most notable—although having sold him, he didn't race in her colors—was Seabiscuit.

When Bull Hancock returned from the war determined to expand Claiborne Farm's pre-eminence as a breeding establishment, he could only do it by applying the instincts and thinking instilled in him by his father. The main feature of these was the introduction of fresh foreign blood into the American breed. Bull scoured foreign pedigrees and gradually narrowed down his interest to a single horse. The horse, a seven-year-old named Nasrullah, had recently started a stud career at a farm owned by the Aga Khan in Ireland after compiling a better-than-average racing record in England during the war years. Nasrullah was a son of Nearco, Europe's best racehorse in the late thirties and himself a stallion who had already shown signs of reproductive brilliance. Hancock was more interested in Nasrullah because of his dam, however. Also owned by the Aga Khan, her name was Mumtaz Begum, and she had been sired by Blenheim II a few years before Bull's father had brought that stallion to Kentucky. The Hancocks liked the Blenheim II blood, and with Blenheim II getting on in years, it was time to ensure its continuation at Claiborne. Mixed with the genes of the brilliant Nearco and his European forebears, which had not before been directly introduced to the United States, Nasrullah was in the Hancocks' view an excellent stallion prospect for America.

It took a few years for Bull Hancock to swing the deal. But swing it he did. In 1949, with a syndicate that included Gladys Phipps and William Woodward, he bought Nasrullah. The price was a record $340,000, with each syndicate member paying $10,000 a share.

Hancock's accomplishment marked the beginning of the era of large-scale stallion syndications. But it was the beginning of an even more significant era for Claiborne Farm and for the

Phippses and the Chenerys. Within a few years Nasrullah would become one of the premier sires in the United States, and then a premier sire of sires, particularly when bred to the daughters and granddaughters of another Claiborne stallion. His most brilliant offspring would be a colt born five years after his arrival at Claiborne from Ireland. The colt, owned by the Phippses, would be called Bold Ruler. Bull Hancock had stumbled on what is known in the breeding business as a "nick."

Bold Ruler, the son of Nasrullah, was out of a mare owned by Gladys Phipps called Miss Disco. A daughter of the very good racehorse and stallion Discovery, whose own sire was a half brother of the legendary Man o' War, Miss Disco had been a useful race mare in the late 1940s. She had been purchased for breeding purposes and to upgrade Claiborne's broodmare band by Bull Hancock in 1950. Gladys Phipps was so enamored of her, however, that she persuaded Hancock to sell the mare to her. Mrs. Phipps bred her first to Nasrullah and the year after to another stallion. Then, in 1953, she returned Miss Disco to Nasrullah. A year later the mare dropped the dark bay colt foal that would grow up to be Bold Ruler.

Bold Ruler, although a horse susceptible to illnesses and ailments from his first moments on earth, would put together a scintillating racing record two and three years after his birth. Then retired to stud at Claiborne Farm, he would follow his sire, Nasrullah, who was destined to die somewhat prematurely in 1959, in continuing the dominance of Claiborne that Bull Hancock had sought to achieve after the war. And as he approached the end of his own foreshortened lifespan, he would produce the greatest monument to his prepotency: Secretariat. Secretariat would emerge from that magical "nick" Bull Hancock had inadvertently discovered when he obtained Nasrullah. The nick was the blood of Nasrullah crossed with the blood of the stallion the Hancocks hadn't thought much of except in terms of breeding steeplechasers: Princequillo. It was a cross between the Nasrullah family's speed and the Princequillo clan's staying power.

Princequillo had already begun to reveal himself as a worthwhile stallion once the Hancocks' Ellerslie Stud was disposed of and he was moved to Claiborne. One of the early samples of his soon-to-be realized reproductive brilliance was the product of his

1946 mating with Christopher Chenery's Hildene. Chenery named the bay colt, foaled in 1947 at The Meadow, Hill Prince. Hill Prince put the Meadow stable on the racing map in 1949 by being named the best two-year-old racehorse of the year, and later by winning several important stakes races and a total of over $422,000. With his success, the value of Princequillo's stud fees began to rise as breeders from around the country sought his services for their mares.

Chenery was by no means finished with Princequillo. Suspecting that he had found a nick of his own, he sent a number of mares back to him over the next few years. In 1947, he had bought a mare called Imperatrice at a dispersal sale in Saratoga for considerably more than he had paid for Hildene. Imperatrice had been a moderately good short-distance speed filly during the early war years. Built wide and muscular, sprinting was her forte and she had earned $37,255 in 31 races. She was from a family of speed horses, and Chenery hit on the idea of crossing her with the staying blood of Princequillo. He shipped her to Kentucky in the early winter of 1951 to be bred to the increasingly popular Claiborne stallion. A year later she foaled a stocky, somewhat coarse, bay filly. Chenery's wife, Helen, who did the naming of the Meadow horses, called her Somethingroyal. It was a custom in those days, as it remains today, to run separate words in a horse's name together.

Somethingroyal did not perform well at the racetrack. But in the late 1950s she proved a promising producer. Her most prominent offspring was Sir Gaylord, who was the product of her mating with the Nearco-descended stallion Turn-to. Sir Gaylord won ten of eighteen races in 1961 and 1962, and subsequently became another fashionable Claiborne stud himself as a result of his siring of the splendid big-money-winner Sir Ivor in 1965. From various stallions, Somethingroyal produced a total of sixteen foals for Christopher Chenery. Sir Gaylord was the best of the lot until 1970 when, from a 1969 breeding to Gladys Phipps' Bold Ruler, she dropped a sturdy, big-boned, copper-colored foal with three white socks and an irregular white blaze.

By the time Secretariat was born, Christopher Chenery was suffering the effects of chronic illness and senility. Riva Ridge had been produced by his stallion First Landing, whose dam had been Hildene, Chenery's bargain purchase of years before. But when Riva Ridge won the Kentucky Derby in 1972, Chenery was already disabled mentally and unable to appreciate what his breeding theories had wrought. He was even more oblivious to the stunning promise Secretariat showed during the same year.

As Chenery was losing his powers in 1970, Gladys Phipps was approaching death. She was fated never to see Secretariat. Bold Ruler, his father and her prize stallion, had contracted cancer in the same year at the still-young age of sixteen and would barely outlive her, dying in 1971. And Bull Hancock would die a year later.

Penny Chenery Tweedy, Christopher's middle-aged daughter, married to a Denver lawyer and an attractive matronly woman without a shred of firsthand experience in thoroughbreds, had assumed responsibility for the operation of The Meadow well before her father's death early in 1973. Ogden Phipps, who had long been in racing and breeding on his own and in partnership with his mother, Gladys, had inherited her rich equine assets upon her death, including the dying Bold Ruler. And the twenty-three-year-old Seth Hancock, by the default of his older brother Arthur III, had taken over the management, and with his widowed mother the ownership, of the legendary Claiborne Farm. The times were changing with a rush.

CHAPTER 3

The Completion

Seth Hancock watched intently as the whinnying Secretariat, his great muscles knotted and straining against his taut, burnished skin, his long, trumpet-headed penis already flopping half erect beneath his vein-swollen belly, was led by his elderly black groom down the sloping asphalt lane from the white and yellow stallion barn to the Claiborne breeding shed. Behind him nickered and wheyed such proven and priceless stallions as Round Table, Buckpasser, Bagdad, Bold Reason, Damascus, Forli, Drone, Nijinsky II, Sir Gaylord, Sir Ivor, and Tom Rolfe. Seth Hancock had truly inherited a dynasty. The question was: Could he sustain and possibly even expand it, much as his father had done? Secretariat and, to a lesser extent, Riva Ridge, also syndicated by Seth, were to be his answer.

The gray, Irradiate, had been well prepared for this her second cover by Secretariat. Her last heat, a month before, had timed itself wrong. On the day she was ripe Secretariat had been busy with two other mares, and when he had been rested enough to service her the next day she had lost her estrus. But now the timing was right. She had spent the morning in an adjoining barn being "teased" by one of the farm's cold-blooded teasing stallions. A coarse old plow horse, his only function was to act as a surrogate for the high-priced studs, to sexually arouse, through smell and sound, the mares in heat who were being readied for copulation with Claiborne's hot-blooded studs.

As Secretariat was led in on a stout shank, Irradiate nickered nervously, her large eyes rolling in a combination of fright and feral anticipation. Her forelegs stood in a depression in the earthen floor of the shed, and her head, up against a creosoted wall, was held immobile by a leather twitch twisted cruelly around her nose by one of the breeding crew. Her tail, wrapped in a white sterilized bandage and raised, revealing a seeping, quivering vagina. Another assistant wrapped a rope around the pastern of her left foreleg and tugged, doubling the leg upward and causing Irradiate to struggle, whimpering, for balance.

The stud groom brought Secretariat quickly around to Irradiate's rear, but well away from it, passing his shank to Lawrence Robinson, the stud manager. Robinson, dressed in a crisp navy-gray denim work uniform, cooed to the stamping Secretariat. Dr. Walter Kaufman, the farm veterinarian, thrust his rubber-gloved arm into Irradiate's vagina, swabbing it out with an anti-septic solution. Then, wiping his hands on his rubber apron and kicking a clod of manure off his floppy rubber boots, he grabbed another cloth out of his vat and advanced on Secretariat. He swabbed the highly charged chestnut's thickening penis with it, and out of the trumpet head appeared a puslike blob of cream-colored substance. Secretariat, snorting and rolling his eyes, was ready. Irradiate, wiggling her rump and seeming about to collapse on her foreknees, was ready.

Robinson led Secretariat to the mare's rump, another groom on his opposite side helping to keep the stallion straight with a second shank attached to his halter. As he advanced, Kaufman ducked under his belly and quickly coated his now fully erect penis with a lubricating salve. Secretariat sniffed at Irradiate's vagina for a moment, trembled at Kaufman's touch, let out a bellowing whinny, and then tucked his rear legs under himself in short, chopping steps. His mighty rump muscles bunching, and emitting a tattoo of snorts and grunts, he rose up on his hind-quarters, his forelegs pawing the air. Robinson's arm went up with him, then jerked on the shank once or twice to move the chestnut forward. There was nothing "shy" about this stallion. Secretariat danced ahead, his penis glancing off the top of the mare's rump. He came down hard on her back, his front hooves raising puffs of dust from Irradiate's dappled coat. The mare gave a shriek and tried to kick out with a hobbled rear leg as Robinson backed Secretariat up a few inches. The stocky Kaufman grabbed the slippery, twitching penis with two hands and quickly guided it into Irradiate's vagina. He let go as Secretariat tippled forward once again on her back, sinking his penis, its full almost-yard's length, inside her. Now both horses joined in a cacophony of grunts, squeals, and screeches. Secretariat sank his teeth into the mare's withers as her handlers held her bulging-eyed head straight. Secretariat, his own eyes seemingly about to explode, began to gyrate his rump under prancing rear legs. With his teeth still fastened on the mare's neck and his shrieks turning to ecstatic groans, his luxurious coppery tail quickly raised and began to twist and twitch in spasmodic bursts. He was ejaculating inside the mare.

Ten, perhaps fifteen seconds passed. Then, with a shudder that coursed through his entire body, Secretariat's knotted muscles went flaccid. His coat, soaked by sweat, was an oily ocher color. He released the clamp of his teeth on Irradiate's withers and, ever so briefly, laid his muzzle against the side of her neck in what might have been, in a human, a postcoital, cuddle of gratitude. The mare was now quiet, her eyes glazed and sleepy. Robinson's gentle tugs at his shank brought Secretariat slowly rearward and off Irradiate. As he came off, his still semierect penis slipped out of her, dripping fluid. Kaufman caught the penis in one hand and held it over a cup he grasped in the other, letting the cup fill with the stallion's residual semen.

As Secretariat was backed away from the mare, Kaufman scooped up a fistful of the ejaculate in his gloved hand and thrust the hand, now balled into a fist, elbow-deep into Irradiate's vagina. This was what is known as the "human service." Kaufman then put the cup aside—its remains would be sent to a laboratory for examination for any viral or bacteriological contaminants and also for attestation that a "cover" had taken place—and swabbed the mare's vagina again, taking a culture smear in the process. He then moved quickly back to Secretariat with another sterilized swabbing cloth and bathed his increasingly limpid penis. When the vet was finished, Lawrence Robinson gave Secretariat an affectionate pat on the neck and handed his shank back to the groom. The groom led his charge, his great head lowered now, looking almost sheepish, out of the shed and back to the stallion barn. Irradiate's lip twitch had been released and she followed in a different direction—to be returned to the panic-stricken foal she had dropped a few weeks earlier as a result of her mating a year before to another stallion.

The entire covering process had taken a total of three minutes between the time Secretariat had entered the shed and when he was led out of it. Everyone present—Seth Hancock, farm manager Bill Taylor, stallion manager Robinson, broodmare manager Mike Clay, veterinarian Walter Kaufman, and their assistants— quietly congratulated each other on another in the long series of successful equine couplings that had taken place with assembly-line ease and regularity that spring. More than eight hundred covers had been accomplished in the Claiborne breeding shed since the first of the year, an average of almost seven a day involving Claiborne's twenty-two active stallions. Nothing marked this one as unique to the farm personnel except possibly for the fact that it was a Secretariat cover. But then the staff had grown used to Secretariat in the preceding months. He was "just another stallion here," in farm manager Bill Taylor's words, although "one of the nicest and easiest we have . . . a real eager son-of-a-gun who makes all our jobs easier."

To Seth Hancock, nevertheless, the cover had a more than routine significance. He acknowledged it when he laconically nodded in response to a groom's "Hope you get a good one outta her, Mr. Seth." Leaving the breeding shed to return to the brick one-story Claiborne office building, he had it in mind to call Ogden Mills Phipps in New York when he reached his office. Young Phipps, the son of Ogden Phipps, the grandson of Gladys and H. C. Phipps, was the nominal owner of Irradiate. He would want to know that the cover had gone well. Hancock himself was particularly pleased because, although Irradiate was not his, he would be Phipps' partner in the resulting foal—should, of course, the mare become pregnant by that day's cover.

In his treatise *Meditations on Hunting*, Spanish philosopher José Ortega y Gasset claimed that the reason the rich and the aristocratic of the Western world engage in the breeding and racing of horses derives from their need to fill up otherwise empty lives. Through the hunt and the horse race, Ortega said, the rich, insulated by their money from the harsh realities of the world, are able to vicariously experience the feral dangers and risks that to ordinary people are the woof and warp of life.

American social critic H. L. Mencken took a more jaundiced view. He claimed that the American financial aristocracy has pre-occupied itself with the breeding of thoroughbreds—the "im-provement of the breed"—precisely because they have been for so many generations preoccupied with their own breeding and have made such a botch of it. There had been such a great degree of inbreeding within the social aristocracy in America, said Mencken, writing in the 1930s, that it was no wonder the Ameri-can thoroughbred was in the process of being inbred to extinc-tion. Only when the aristocracy recognized the folly of its pat-tern of intermarriage would the thoroughbred horse be rescued from genetic stagnation.

Another more waggish commentator insisted that a kind of counterbalancing equation existed between the rich and the re-sults of their thoroughbred breeding pursuits. The equation was that the more the aristocracy breeds the fine physical, intel-lectual, and character traits, which were what enabled it to prevail, out of itself through successive generations, the more splendid do its horses become in physique and character. It is as if the aristocracy has given up on itself in the ambition for human beauty and intelligence, and has invested all its energies in these areas in its horses by way of compensation.

These theories cannot be proved. One could point to Ogden Mills Phipps, nevertheless, as evidence in support of their efficacy.

As I have noted, Henry Carnegie Phipps and his wife, Gladys Mills Phipps produced, in 1908, an only child—a boy—whom they named Ogden after her brother Ogden Mills (Ogden, be-sides, being an old Mills family name). H. C. Phipps had grown up with his father's family's sinewy Scottish physique. His wife, Gladys, had inherited the lean and willowy conformation of the maternal Livingston side of her family. Her father, Darius Ogden Mills, was the carrier of the traditional Mills family stockiness, and he passed it on to Gladys' brother Ogden Mills. Although Ogden Mills and his sister Gladys Phipps were physical opposites—he stocky and athletic, she slim and fragile—she must have retained strong traces of the Mills breadth in her genes because Ogden Phipps, the son she produced with the also lean H. C. Phipps in 1908, grew up to be the spitting image of her brother and father.

Ogden Phipps married twice in his life. His first union was soon after his graduation from Harvard, and it produced an eccentric son, Henry Ogden, who was to die of a drug overdose thirty-one years later. His second marriage was to Lillian Bostwick, the daughter of another dynastic American family active in the world of polo and steeplechase racing. From this union issued two children in the 1940s—Ogden Mills Phipps and Cynthia Phipps. Both children, born to such wealth and tradition that no other pursuits interested them, have carried on the family vocation of horse breeding and racing. Ogden Mills Phipps is today the youngest chairman of the New York Racing Association in history, having succeeded in that post, among others, his father. Moreover, barely out of his teens, he was the youngest member ever admitted to the Jockey Club, the autocratic governing body of thoroughbred breeding and racing in America, of which there are no more aristocratic organizations in the world except, possibly, Britain's House of Lords and the English Jockey Club.

Ogden Mills Phipps is known universally as Dinny. The nickname is a diminutive variation on Ogden, of course, but there are those who have worked with or have otherwise associated with him who insist that his nickname should really be "Dimmy." Be that as it may, Dinny Phipps is a largely guileless, amiable, and accessible fellow who bears so little resemblance to one's image of a dynast and aristocrat that he appears to be the opposite. Porcine rather than equine in physique, blond and almost bald, he looks more the son of a Bavarian bratwurst butcher than a man worth countless millions in inherited cash and trust funds.

Dinny's father, Ogden Phipps, reached the apex of his career in racing with Buckpasser, the "superhorse" of the 1960s. Since Gladys Phipps' entry into racing in the late twenties, the business of horses had always been a family affair with the Phippses, with various horses owned in different combinations of partnerships

with her husband, her brother, her son, even her grandchildren
and other relatives. Gladys had always remained the "brains," as
well as the principal financial resource, of all such partnerships,
however. But Buckpasser was Ogden's pride and joy, since it was
he who had recommended the breeding of his dam, Busanda, a
Phipps family mare, to the splendid racehorse and stallion Tom
Fool in 1962. Buckpasser turned out to be that ever-desired but
rare combination of flawless conformation and giant heart that
resulted in a winner of over $1,460,000—even more than Secre-
tariat was to win almost ten years later, although it took
Buckpasser ten more races to outdo Secretariat. Buckpasser might
have won considerably more, and sooner, had he not suffered an
injury that kept him out of some key races. Nevertheless, like
Secretariat in 1973, when he was syndicated by Bull Hancock
and Phipps to stand at stud at Claiborne Farm, his $4,800,000
value was a record for its time.

Buckpasser, although a flawlessly put-together horse, was a
bay, which is to say that his body color was a plain dark brown
that extended to black in his lower legs, tail, and mane. Bay is by
far the most common color among thoroughbreds, and perhaps
for that reason Buckpasser did not excite the public in the manner that Secretariat, a horse the color of an autumn sunset, did.
Ogden Phipps felt bitter about that in 1973 when Secretariat
landed on the covers of three national magazines in the same
week. He believed that Buckpasser had been every bit as good if
not better than Secretariat. His bitterness was sharpened by the
fact that, but for the flip of a coin, Secretariat would have been
his.

The story is well known by now, but here it is again in its
briefest details. When Gladys Phipps acquired Bold Ruler from
the breeding of Nasrullah and Miss Disco and then retired him to
stud after his racing career, she was not particularly interested in
making money from the stud fees he could command. She had
become knowledgeable about equine pedigrees under the Hancocks' tutoring, and she had a number of friends in the thoroughbred industry who owned mares she admired and believed
would produce consistently superior offspring when crossbred to
Bold Ruler. She thereupon devised a stud-fee arrangement—a
kind of pick-of-the-litter deal—whereby a select few mare

owners would be invited to breed a qualified mare to Bold Ruler for free two years in a row. One year the owner of the mare would get to keep the resulting foal; the other year the foal would become the property of the Phippses. The method of determination of which foal went to whom was a coin flip. By this device Gladys Phipps created an ongoing source of foals from a procession of the finest mares in the country—mares that she didn't own and whose offspring she would otherwise have had to pay hundreds of thousands of dollars each year in the yearling auction markets to acquire.

Christopher Chenery had risen into the top ranks of turfdom with the achievements of his Hill Prince in 1949 and 1950. He had already become friendly with the Hancocks and the Phippses and had retired Hill Prince to stand at stud at Claiborne Farm rather than at his own Meadow. When Bull Hancock and Gladys Phipps invited him to participate in the Bold Ruler arrangement, he gladly agreed.

Chenery at first, in the early sixties, sent a single mare to Bold Ruler each year and came away every other year with a foal. The first mare he sent, at Bull Hancock's insistence in 1959, was his aging Imperatrice, who seven years earlier had produced the Princequillo-sired Somethingroyal. By then Princequillo was in great demand as a stallion, having sired at Claiborne the splendid Round Table in the very same year that Nasrullah had produced Bold Ruler. From her breeding to Bold Ruler, Imperatrice in 1960 produced a colt foal. Having won the coin toss and elected to keep the foal, giving Gladys Phipps the following year's foal, Chenery named the colt Speedwell. Prophetically, Speedwell would go on to become the first stakes winner produced by Bold Ruler.

In the mid-sixties, Chenery began to send two mares a year to Bold Ruler, and the coin agreement was revised accordingly. Now the winner of each semiannual coin flip would get first choice of one of the first pair of foals. The loser would automatically get the foal the winner did not choose. But the loser at the same time, also automatically, would have first choice with respect to the following year's pair, with the winner to receive the remaining foal of that duo. The coin toss would not be made until the first pair of foals had been born and the mares had been "bred back" to Bold Ruler. The mares did not have to be the same for each breeding.

In the next few years Bold Ruler matings to pairs of Chenery mares produced little of note—this despite the fact that, beginning in 1963, Bold Ruler was at or near the top of the leading sire lists (this meant that he was consistently producing offspring who were accumulating more money in total annual purse earnings than the offspring of any other stallion).

The year 1968 marked the beginning of another two-year cycle in the Phipps-Chenery breeding arrangement. Chenery sent two mares from Virginia to Claiborne to meet Bold Ruler. One was called Hasty Matelda. The other was Somethingroyal, the daughter of Imperatrice and Princequillo. In the early spring of 1969, Hasty Matelda produced a colt foal by Bold Ruler. A little later Somethingroyal dropped a healthy filly foal.

A month later Somethingroyal was bred back to Bold Ruler. Instead of sending Hasty Matelda back to the stallion to fulfill the final notch of the breeding agreement, however, Chenery substituted another of his mares, a splendid racing filly called Cicada. The two mares were examined in June by Dr. Floyd Sager, then the chief Claiborne veterinarian. Somethingroyal was found to be pregnant again, and if all went well she would drop another foal early in 1970, making the first of the second pair whose ownership would be decided by the coin flip. Cicada was discovered to be barren, however—her covers by Bold Ruler had failed to take, and it was by then too late to have her reserviced. There would only be one foal to choose from the second year's breeding, which meant that the winner of the coin toss would end up with only one horse, while the loser would get two—the foal the winner didn't choose from the first pair and, automatically, the sole foal from the second paired breeding.

The coin toss was arranged for August of 1969 during the annual New York Racing Association's summer meeting at the ancient but pleasantly bucolic Saratoga race course in upstate New York. By this time Penny Tweedy had taken over her ailing father's thoroughbred affairs. Ogden Phipps had been deputized by his mother to execute the coin flip for her. The two met, along with the Phipps family trainer Eddie Neloy, and tossed the coin.

Both knew the consequences. The winner would end up with only one horse. Neither therefore wanted to win.

Into the air went the coin. When it landed, Ogden Phipps was the winner. He and his mother got Somethingroyal's 1969 filly foal by Bold Ruler. Penny Tweedy got the Hasty Matelda colt, plus the second Bold Ruler foal still being carried by Somethingroyal. As fate would have it, this was the foal that would become Secretariat.

So, then, but for the wrong side of a coin, Secretariat would have belonged to the Phippses and raced in the name of Dinny Phipps' sister Cynthia. If it was any consolation to Ogden Phipps, he could still privately revel in the fact that Bold Ruler belonged to his family instead of to the Hancocks, as the great stallion would have been had Gladys Phipps not persuaded Bull Hancock to sell Miss Disco to her a few years before that mare produced Bold Ruler.

Such were the quirky fortunes of the thoroughbred breeding business. Bloodline experts such as the Phippses and Hancocks spent hours every day, through deep concentrated study of equine genetics and thoroughbred pedigrees, in search of the most ideal matings, only to have their successes and failures turn on simple twists of fate or flips of coins. Despite all the pseudo-scientific breeding theories that had been developed over the years, the first axiom of breeding seemed to forever obtain. This was: "Breed your best mare to the best possible stallion you can afford, and hope for the best." This was as close to science as one could really get in horse breeding, and it had been proved time and time again. But it had likewise proved widely fallible. Much depended on pure luck—luck in the stallion and, perhaps even more so, in the mare.

One would think, on superficial reflection, that the breeding of horses could be mathematically quantified so that if a single breeding of Stallion A to Mare B produced Racehorse C, and if Racehorse C turned out to be an exemplary performer, then subsequent breedings between A and B would produce a series of identical C's. Such, of course, is not the case. No one knows why a series of identical stallion-mare breedings result in a superior horse one year, a mediocre horse the next, a useful horse the following, and a complete dud the year after that. Experience had

long ago proven in general that superior bloodlines provided a
better chance for the consistent production of superior racehorses, but no bloodline carried with it a guarantee that it would
reproduce, or even better, itself with anything approaching unerring consistency. This was where luck came in.

Yet no one could define the considerable luck factor. Perhaps
it had to do with the state of molecular balances in the sperm and
ovum of the stallion and mare, respectively, at the moment of
conception. Perhaps it had to do with their respective "moods"
during copulation. Perhaps it was merely a matter of timing—
should copulation and impregnation occur just a few seconds before or after, a completely different horse might be the result,
in character, conformation, even color. Or perhaps it was simply
a question of the stallion and mare's astrological balance at the
moment of fertilization. All these theories were subscribed to
along with many more, but no one knew the real answer. So the
answer reverted simply to the all-purpose category of "luck."

Ogden Phipps had known this well enough. There was no way
on earth by which he could predict the differences between the
1969 Bold Ruler-Somethingroyal foal he had won by the coin
toss and the foal by the same union to be born the following
year, which he had lost. All he was concerned about at the time
was the fact that Christopher Chenery had gotten two horses by
Bold Ruler to his one. Later, when the filly he won, to be called
The Bride, turned out to be a failure as a racer, and the unborn
colt he lost turned out to be Secretariat, he would good-na-
turedly suffer the jokesters who jibed him for his "breeding expertise" as well as his coin-flipping dexterity. The lesson he
learned, however, and that he tried to pass on to all who would
listen, was that in the end there was no accounting for luck in the
horse-breeding business.

The question of luck had been on Phipps' mind as well when
he was asked both to assist in and to join the Secretariat syndication early in 1973. Bull Hancock had not thrust Claiborne Farm
on the inexperienced Seth without safeguards. Three years before his death, after his older son and namesake had struck out on
his own in the rich Kentucky breeding world, Bull had revised
his will so that on his death, Seth would take over the farm only
on the condition that he agree to submit all management deci-

sions to a committee of overseers made up of three of Bull's trusted friends—a committee that would function until Seth reached the age of thirty-five. One of the members of the committee was Ogden Phipps. When Penny Tweedy, acting on behalf of her family, approached Claiborne for the syndication of Secretariat and Riva Ridge, she was approaching Phipps as much as she was the young Seth Hancock. Indeed, Seth had to receive Phipps' permission, as well as that of Charles Kenney and William Haggin Perry, the other members of the overseeing triumvirate, to commit Claiborne to the dual syndications. By then, the Phippses were practically principals in Claiborne Farm.

It was clear from the outset that Seth not only could not embark on the syndications without Ogden Phipps' permission, but also that he could not accomplish them without Phipps' help. Seth was a greenhorn, a bit on the reticent side and without the wide circle of personal contacts in the breeding business, outside of the immediate area of the farm, that Phipps enjoyed. Phipps liked Seth, however, and thought he had it in him to continue his father's proven methods and traditions at Claiborne. Reflecting on the luck factor in breeding, he might otherwise have been reluctant to invest the unheard-of price of $190,000 in a Secretariat share. He wondered for a while if there was any wisdom in investing such an amount in a horse that, but for an ironic twist of luck, would have been his. His investment and breeding sense told him to stay away from Secretariat now. He and his family had been supremely lucky with Bold Ruler, with Buckpasser, and with a number of other stallions over the years. The loss of the coin toss four years earlier had possibly been a portent of a change in the Phippses' luck. If it was, Secretariat would not amount to much at stud. On the other hand, on Claiborne's continuing good fortunes as a stud farm hinged his own as a breeder and racing owner. And, with Bold Ruler now dead, Claiborne could only continue to flourish with the introduction of young, fresh, top-blooded stallions. So in order to help Seth Hancock get the syndication off the ground, Phipps bought the first share. Then he proceeded to use his contacts to assist Seth in quickly completing the record syndication. Ogden Phipps remained suspicious of Secretariat's breeding potential, however, and refused to allow his son Dinny—by then very much in the racing and breeding business—to buy in. One Phipps risk was enough.

This was what Seth Hancock wanted to call Dinny Phipps in New York about that May afternoon of Irradiate's second cover by Secretariat. Since the day in mid-February when Secretariat began his formal breeding career under the terms of the revised syndication agreement, there had been a good deal of trading in the shareholders' "seasons."

The very first mare bred to him was My Card, owned by another utilities magnate and Kentucky breeder, Walter Jeffords, Jr. Jeffords had acquired George Strawbridge's season, or annual breeding right, for two years at a sum that easily got Strawbridge back the money he had invested. Strawbridge had a theory that fine racehorses do not begin to produce well as stallions until they had been at stud for at least two years, and he had bought a share in the syndicate with a view to recouping his money over the first two years and thereafter breeding his own mares to Secretariat free and clear. He had found a willing buyer of his first two annual seasons in Jeffords, who was primarily a market breeder and who believed that Secretariat's first two crops would bring enormous prices as yearlings. There would not have been time to learn anything about the superhorse's ability as a racehorse sire, so people would be buying those of his early offspring offered for sale solely on pedigree and promise, plus the "romance of being able to have one of the first Secretariats." Jeffords was sure that he would make a tidy profit if he put the two Secretariats he bred on Strawbridge's share up for sale as yearlings in 1976 and 1977. He would not be wrong.

By May, it had already been long determined by veterinary examination that My Card was in foal. Secretariat had covered her twice, the second time on February 18, and it was guessed that the mare had "caught" on the second cover. The stallion, whose ability to breed had been questioned, had gotten in foal the first mare he was bred to, not counting the earlier cold-blooded test mares. Syndicate fingers began to uncross.

Since My Card, a number of other mares bred in February and early March had been pronounced in foal. Indeed, Secretariat had successfully impregnated his first nine mares, most on only one cover. Prospects looked almost too good.

In the meantime, more breeding rights had begun to change hands. Allaire duPont sold her season to Texas breeder Roger Braugh. The Faulconer-Boone agency sold its first two seasons to Jacqueline Getty, a rich California daughter-in-law of J. Paul Getty; her husband had recently died, leaving her with his racing stable. Richard Brooks sold his to Texas oil tycoon Nelson Bunker Hunt, who had extensive racing interests in America and Europe. F. Eugene Dixon sold his season to Kentucky breeder Catesby Clay. The Chenery-Tweedy interests sold three of their five breeding rights to others. And Claiborne Farm, in the person of Seth Hancock and with the permission of Ogden Phipps, dispensed with two of its three seasons. The recipient was Phipps' son Dinny, and the deal was that in exchange for the two seasons, enabling Dinny Phipps to breed his own mares to Secretariat, he and Claiborne, again in the person of Seth Hancock, would become partners in the resulting foals.

Hancock was particularly agreeable to the arrangement because the tenth mare bred to Secretariat, the Claiborne-owned Iskra, appeared to be barren—ironically, the first mare Secretariat had been unable to impregnate. There were no other qualified Claiborne mares available to go to Secretariat by the time Iskra's barrenness was discovered, short of sending mares of the same immediate blood, which would be dangerous inbreeding. Many of Claiborne's broodmares descended from the Nasrullah-Princequillo nick discovered by Bull Hancock in the early 1950s. Other qualified Claiborne mares had already been bred to other stallions. Iskra was of completely different bloodlines than Secretariat, going back several generations. One of the Hancocks' most valuable "outcrosses" to Bold Ruler blood, she had been bred to Bold Ruler and had produced a colt foal in 1972 who, in the summer of 1973, had been sold at auction as a yearling for a then-record $600,000. (This yearling would later race brilliantly under the name of Wajima and be retired to stud in 1975 at a syndication price that would break Secretariat's record.) Iskra's barrenness to Secretariat was a singular disappointment. Hancock had been entertaining visions of the first $1,000,000 sales yearling in history.

The Phippses had several mares that had not yet been booked to particular stallions. One, called Broadway, was formally owned by the senior Phipps and was a good outcross to the Bold Ruler line. Phipps was all but decided on sending her to Secretariat. Another was Lady Be Good, nominally owned by Dinny Phipps. She was sent on one of the Claiborne seasons late in April and seemed to have caught. And then there was Irradiate, who the year before had produced a promising colt by 1969 Kentucky Derby winner Majestic Prince.

Irradiate was by the magnificent Italian racehorse and stallion Ribot, the sire in America of such splendid performers as Arts and Letters, Tom Rolfe, Graustark, and many others. Irradiate's blood traced back through her sire to the paternal blood of Secretariat, to be sure, but it was at such a remove—four generations on both sides—that there was no concern about inbreeding. Many fine horses were inbred that far back in their pedigrees; it was only first- and second-generation inbreeding the most horsemen sought to avoid.*

Irradiate was not new to Bold Ruler blood either. After racing usefully for the Phippses' Wheatley Stable in the late 1960s, she had been retired to their broodmare band and bred to Bold Ruler in 1970. A year later she had produced a filly who became Celestial Lights, stakes winner of $133,000 for the Phippses. Her own dam, High Voltage, had been both a superior racing filly in the mid-1950s and later, as a broodmare, a producer of several excellent racehorses from matings with Bold Ruler and other stallions.

Altogether, Irradiate seemed a highly desirable mate for Secretariat. If only she had taken to the chestnut's cover. Seth Hancock had a good feeling about it as he returned to his office. The prospective partner in the foal, he was sure Irradiate had "caught." And that is what he told Dinny Phipps when he reached him on the phone.

* It should be mentioned that close inbreeding is not frowned upon by all. A number of breeders have had short-term success over the years with close inbreeding. Today, however, it is generally avoided except in experimental ways.

CHAPTER 4

Hope

Unlike Ogden Phipps, the first of the shareholders in the syndicate, Alfred Gwynne Vanderbilt, the last, had no reservations about Secretariat's potential as a stallion. Vanderbilt, although the great-great-grandson of Cornelius Vanderbilt, founder of the most powerful railroad fortune in America, derived most of his personal riches from his mother's family, whence came the miracle drug of its time, Bromo-Seltzer. Born in 1912, he grew interested in the thoroughbred as a teen-ager. At the age of twenty-one he was presented by his mother with Sagamore Farm, a lush six-hundred-acre breeding and racing operation near Baltimore, her hometown. (Vanderbilt's father had died in the sinking of the *Lusitania* in 1915.)

Vanderbilt's first great horse was one he purchased in 1933—Discovery. Discovery was to play two important roles in Vanderbilt's future as a breeder. The first was his siring of a mare who, when Vanderbilt bred her to a stallion named Polynesian in 1949, produced the magnificent Native Dancer. The mare's name was Geisha, and her 1950 gray son became, between 1952 and 1954, the nation's most universally revered horse until the advent of Secretariat twenty years later. Native Dancer won twenty-one of twenty-two races, losing only the Kentucky Derby by a head in a controversial upset after being interfered with by a rival.

The second of Discovery's most important contributions was his siring of Miss Disco, the mare who eventually ended up in the hands of Bull Hancock and then Gladys Phipps, and became the dam of Bold Ruler. Despite this breeding connection to the Hancock-Phipps constellation of the thoroughbred universe, and despite the fact that he and Ogden Phipps saw each other regularly in their various roles as Jockey Club and Racing Association officers, Vanderbilt and Phipps maintained a long-standing coolness to one another. Their mutual dislike was compounded by Vanderbilt's frequently iconoclastic initiatives while serving as the head of Pimlico racetrack in the 1930s and later as president of Belmont Park, the Phippses' home turf and, to some of them, their private kingdom.

Vanderbilt had been one of Secretariat's most enthusiastic boosters during the chestnut's two-year-old season. For that reason and others he was deeply insulted when he learned that he was not to be invited to join the syndicate. Only a good deal of roundabout pressure on his part after one of the original subscribers dropped out got him a leftover last share. The fact that he took offense at his initial exclusion from the syndicate might have been justified. He knew, as did others, that if it had not been for him, there would have been no Secretariat. Indeed, there would have been no Bold Ruler.

When Vanderbilt left the Navy at the end of World War II, he decided to cut back on his racing and breeding operations by selling most of his young bloodstock. One of the yearlings he sold was Miss Disco. Bought by Sidney S. Schupper, she developed into a fine stakes winner before being bought by Bull Hancock and then the Phippses. Had Vanderbilt not sold her, she would probably never have been bred to Nasrullah and would thus not have produced Bold Ruler. By another of those twists of fate that haunted the business, Vanderbilt concluded, Secretariat would not exist had it not been for his decision in 1945.

Unlike Ogden Phipps, Vanderbilt had no qualms about Secretariat's breeding potential. It was true that the eight previous Triple Crown winners, from Sir Barton in 1919 to Citation in 1948, had for the most part produced nothing out of the ordinary at stud. Indeed, three of them—Citation, Assault, and Omaha, himself the son of a Triple Crown winner—had been enormous disappointments. Vanderbilt was sharply aware of the jinx that seemed to haunt Triple Crown winners. But he attributed it to poor breeding practices, claiming that most of the great winners had been bred to inferior mares. In Vanderbilt's mind his own Native Dancer should have been a Triple Crown winner, having missed by a whisker when he was unfairly muscled out of a Kentucky Derby victory. Native Dancer had been bred by crossing the speed and sprinting blood of Polynesian with the staying power under heavy weights of Discovery. Bold Ruler's breeding had been similar—the speed of Nasrullah crossed with the endurance of Discovery. Secretariat's had been a refinement of this, with the even greater Princequillo staying blood added to the mix.

Native Dancer had gone from gifted racehorse to equally gifted sire in the almost twenty years following his retirement, particularly in his ability to sire horses, both male and female, that themselves became important sires and producers. Native Dancer's blood figured significantly in the pedigrees of a number of top-flight broodmares and stallions at the time of the Secretariat syndication. Vanderbilt believed that Secretariat, even before he began his three-year-old campaign, was the greatest horse to have come along since Native Dancer. As chairman of the New York Racing Association, at whose racetracks Secretariat had performed so promisingly in 1972, he went out of his way to promote the big red chesnut to the press and the public as the fondly remembered Native Dancer's equal. And he believed that if Secretariat won the Triple Crown in 1973, as he was predicting, he would escape the stud jinx that had affected most of the other Triple Crown winners in history. Like Native Dancer, Vanderbilt would say, Secretariat had been the product of an ideal if accidental breeding combination. Even if he didn't transmit his own racing abilities to his progeny, he was still sure to produce sons and daughters who, when they were sent to stud, would succeed in doing so to theirs, just as many of Native Dancer's offspring had.

Partly because Native Dancer had proved an even more gifted sire of sires and dams of racehorses than a sire of racing performers themselves, Vanderbilt subscribed to the theory that the genes of grandparents are a more significant factor in successful equine breeding than those of the parents. Although the theory was unprovable, there was enough evidence in breeding history to make it plausible. As a result, not just Vanderbilt but also many other breeders practiced it, seeking breeding matches not through particular stallions and mares but through their parents. To this kind of breeder, Stallion A and Mare B, both superior racers in their running careers, might seem at first blush an ideal mating prospect. But if the racing or blood qualities of at least one of the Stallion A's parents did not match up well with those of Mare B's parents, the likelihood was that A and B would produce nothing worthwhile. The breeder would thereupon pursue a mating of more favorable grandparental influences.

Vanderbilt had to concede that Native Dancer's ultimate value as a stallion had been as the grandfather of racing performers, not as the father. He saw the same value in Secretariat in the event that the chestnut did not succeed in stamping his own "get" with his varied racing gifts. If Secretariat did not produce a long list of stakes winners and classic horses over the coming years, the likelihood was, based on history, that he would at least produce horses who themselves would do so. For this reason alone, Vanderbilt maintained, Secretariat was worth every penny of his syndication price. And this was why Vanderbilt so urgently wanted into the syndicate. By being able to breed over the years several of his fine mares sired by Native Dancer to the greatest horse sired by Bold Ruler, he might happen on a grandparental nick that would produce for him a succession of racing horses, then breeding horses, that would establish a new dynasty for his Sagamore farm and racing stable.

Once in the syndicate, Vanderbilt began to prepare his first breeding to Secretariat. He had a number of qualified mares, but settled on a seven-year-old granddaughter of Native Dancer named Cold Comfort. The mare had been sired by Nearctic, another astoundingly successful son of Nearco and thus a half brother to Nasrullah, Bold Ruler's father and Secretariat's paternal grandfather. Cold Comfort possessed a strong dose of Nearco blood two generations back, and it would be joined by Secretariat's strain of it three generations back. Certain anti-inbreeding purists would have said that the combination was a bit too close for comfort. But Vanderbilt had a logical defense in Cold Comfort's Native Dancer blood. Native Dancer-Nearco line crosses had been carried out with great success in the late fifties and sixties, the most successful result having been the fabulous Northern Dancer, another near winner of the Triple Crown in 1964. Northern Dancer was sired by Nearctic, the Nearco son, out of an excellent mare called Natalma, sired by Native Dancer. Nearco and Native Dancer, then, were Northern Dancer's grandfathers. Vanderbilt believed that mixing the Nearco-Native Dancer blood of Cold Comfort with the Nearco-Princequillo blood of Secretariat, he had a good chance to obtain an exemplary foal from his first-year's syndicate breeding right. What's more, Cold Comfort had been a splendid racing filly in her career, winning several important stakes and earning nearly $320,000.

Cold Comfort was the mare that immediately followed the Phippses' Irradiate in Secretariat's breeding schedule. And like Irradiate, she caught on her second cover in mid-May of 1974.

It was clear from the beginning that a number of other syndicate members had designs similar to Alfred Vanderbilt's. Native Dancer was a proven grandsire, particularly when his sons and, especially, his daughters had been crossed to Nearco daughters and, especially, sons—as witness Northern Dancer, who was not only the best racehorse of 1962–63 but who also had become one of the two or three leading stallions in America thereafter.

Several shareholders in the syndicate owned mares who had either been sired by Native Dancer or whose dams had been sired by the Vanderbilt-bred stallion. One was a mare named Show Stopper. A gray like Native Dancer, she was seven and on the small side. Her dam was Raise You, a good stakes-winning filly in the late 1940s and a granddaughter of the premier French foundation stallion Teddy. Native Dancer and Raise You had been bred several times, their most valuable product having been the precocious Raise a Native, who was Northern Dancer's principal rival for best-racehorse honors in 1963 before his career was ended by injury. Raise a Native thereafter went on to become a superb stallion, siring among others Alydar and Exclusive Native, the sire of Affirmed. Alydar and Affirmed would become the top horses of 1977–78.

HOPE 49

Show Stopper was Raise a Native's full sister,* but she had been unable to distinguish herself as a racehorse. She was owned in 1974 by the brothers Howard and Charles Gilman, chief executive officers and owners of the Gilman Paper Company in New York. They operated a thoroughbred farm in northern Florida as a subsidiary of their company. Called Wild Oak Plantation, the farm housed a number of splendidly blooded mares who were bred each year to top stallions under various syndicate shares held by the Gilman Paper Company. The Gilmans were almost exclusively market breeders, and each year they sold as yearlings at public auction the choicest product of their breedings.

The Gilman brothers had leaped at the chance to buy into the Secretariat syndicate for the same reason other market breeders had. They were interested in short-term profit and cash flow, the lifeblood of breeders who don't have access to mighty fortunes and trust funds. They ran their breeding operations as businesses, much like any other corporate pursuit, but with the added advantage of capital-gains relief. Most of their investment money came from short-term corporate bank loans, which enabled them to make large and varied equine expenditures but that had to be paid off within a few years. With a $190,000 investment in the Secretariat syndicate, the Gilmans were certain they would at least double their money with the sale of their first Secretariat yearling—presuming, of course, that Show Stopper, the Native Dancer mare they were going to send to Claiborne Farm in 1974, became pregnant and successfully foaled a Secretariat colt or filly the following spring. As it happened, Show Stopper, bred late in March to Secretariat, the eleventh mare to go to his court, caught on the first cover. Her breeding followed that of Iskra, the Claiborne mare who would be the first not to catch.

Another shareholder with a Native Dancer mare was Bertram R. Firestone. The year 1974 was to be a busy one for the diminutive, amiable, and articulate Firestone. Still a young man, he was a scion of the Firestone tire and rubber clan who had compounded his riches by profitable New York real-estate investments and through his marriage to an heiress of the Avon cosmetics empire.

* A "full" sister or brother means that the horses the term is applied to were produced by the same stallion and mare. A "half" sister or brother means that two horses have the same dam but different sires.

He was now in the process of divorcing his wife, who did not share his recently discovered enthusiasm for the horse business, and planning to marry yet another heiress—this one the wife of Richard Stokes also a shareholder in the Secretariat syndicate. Diana Stokes, soon to become Diana Firestone, was the Johnson & Johnson heiress whose passion for all aspects of the thoroughbred industry matched Bert Firestone's. She would bring the Stokes share in Secretariat to the marriage with her, and as the new Firestones planned the acquisition and development of breeding farms in Virginia and Ireland, they found themselves in the likely position of acquiring two first-crop Secretariat foals in 1975.

Diana Stokes' mare was Exclusive Dancer, a modestly successful stakes winner in the late 1960s and the daughter, by Native Dancer, of Exclusive. Exclusive was best known for having produced Exclusive Native in 1965, the son of Native Dancer, and Raise You, who was also the dam of the Gilman brothers' Show Stopper. Exclusive Dancer was sent to Secretariat on April 1, 1974. When, during the first week in May, she was examined and determined not to be in foal, she was covered again by the red stallion on May 17. This time she caught.

Bert Firestone's mare had been sent to Secretariat two weeks prior to Exclusive Dancer's service. The mare, a four-year-old named Gamba by the popular stallion Gun Bow (no immediate Native Dancer or Nearco blood here), was covered twice by Secretariat in early March during her foal heat, but missed.† When she came into heat again at the beginning of April she was covered once more by Secretariat and this time caught. As the Firestones would soon learn, they had two Secretariat foals in their future. Since they both market-bred and bred for their own racing stable, they planned to keep one and sell the other when the time came.

The final daughter of Native Dancer to be bred to Secretariat in his first season (although not the last mare with Native Dancer

† A "foal heat" is the first heat a mare comes into after giving birth and usually occurs about nine days of foaling. Many breeders believe that servicing a mare during her foal heat results in better foals the following year. Others believe the opposite, and prefer not to bred a mare until her second heat, which usually comes another twenty to thirty days later.

blood running in its veins) was probably his most celebrated one. Her name was Natalma, and at seventeen she was most notable in the thoroughbred world as being the dam of Northern Dancer, who along with Bold Ruler had been one of Nearco's best racing grandchildren. Natalma had been born from a 1956 breeding of Native Dancer and a mare named Almahmoud, whose pedigree, although distinguished, had nothing in the way of immediate blood connections to the Nearco-Nasrullah-Bold Ruler line of Secretariat or the Discovery-Polynesian cross of Native Dancer. For some reason her mating to Native Dancer produced a breeding foundation that "nicked" well with that of the Nearco line, the proof being their daughter Natalma's breeding to Nearco's son Nearctic, which produced the incomparable Northern Dancer, who himself has turned out to be a priceless sire of racehorses and producers.

Natalma, then, owned by Canadian multimillionaire, industrial tycoon, and breeder E. P. Taylor, who also owned Northern Dancer and several other nonpareil racehorses, appeared the best match of all the Native Dancer mares to be sent to Secretariat, despite her age. She was the last mare to be bred to him in 1974, having been vanned from Taylor's Windfields Farm in Maryland to Claiborne late in May. Taylor was both a market breeder and a breeder for his own stable, which raced mostly in Canada. As a market breeder, the owner of Northern Dancer and several other top-rated stallions, the yearlings he put up for sale average some of the highest prices of any breeder's. In a Natalma-Secretariat breeding, he too visualized the prospect of selling the first million-dollar yearling in history. Unfortunately for him, and possibly for Secretariat's subsequent reputation as a transmitter of his racing class, his delicious dream was dashed. Natalma would turn up barren after five covers, the last of which took place on June 29, the day before the end of the breeding season.

Iskra and Natalma, both for different reasons ideal crosses to Secretariat's Bold Ruler-Princequillo blood—a bloodline combination that by 1974 had saturated the American racing breed to the point of threatening to stagnate it—were barren. As it would turn out, four other mares were to fail to produce foals from Secretariat's first season at stud.

One, ironically enough, was Ogden Phipps' Broadway. A six-teen-year-old, she had been bred on several occasions to Bold Ruler and produced a series of fine racehorses, including Reviewer, who had recently sired the filly who would become the ill-fated Ruffian. (It should be noted that Ruffian's dam, Shenanigans, was a daughter of Alfred Vanderbilt's Native Dancer.) Since Broadway had produced so well from her services to Bold Ruler, then almost three years dead, Phipps thought it would be appropriate to breed her to his most accomplished son. It would be a gamble, though. Broadway was due to drop a foal late in the spring by the Phipps stallion Buckpasser. Secretariat would have to catch her in her foaling heat, or else she would likely be barren, since the thoroughbred breeding season would be over before she came into heat again. Phipps took the gamble and lost. Secretariat covered Broadway several times during her foaling heat late in May, but she failed to catch.

The Phippses had another fine elderly mare in Lady Be Good, who had been a stakes winner and had produced a number of further stakes winners for them over the years. Bred on a Claiborne breeding right, she would get in foal but then abort during the summer. So it was, then, that the Phipps family would end up with only one prospective foal out of three separate breedings, that one to be owned in partnership with Seth Hancock and Claiborne Farm.

This was not the only irony that attended Secretariat's first year at stud. The Chenery-Tweedy family interests had sold three of their five breeding rights, hoping to get two good Secretariat offspring for the Meadow racing stable and make some immediate money in the bargain. (Individual seasons were selling for $100,000, half the amount refundable if a mare failed to produce a live foal.) One of Penny Tweedy's pet ideas that first year was to breed the dam of Riva Ridge to Secretariat and the dam of Secretariat to Riva Ridge. Not only would such matings represent good outcrosses, they would also offer splendid possibilities for the ultimate in pleasant irony should both the resulting foals go on to stardom.

The dam of Riva Ridge, Iberia, was sent to Secretariat in early April, to be followed immediately by Hopespringseternal, another Chenery mare, by Ogden Phipps' Buckpasser, who carried a strong dose of Princequillo blood. Iberia would turn up barren from her Secretariat covers, thus destroying Penny Tweedy's hopes for a successful breeding switch between her two famous horses. Hopespringseternal would catch, however, and be pronounced in foal in June.

Although it was entirely acceptable within the breeding rules of the syndicate, a number of people criticized Tweedy for sending Hopespringseternal to Secretariat. Her dam, Rose Bower, had been sired by Princequillo. Thus her dam was a half sister to Secretariat's dam, making Hopespringseternal and Secretariat blood cousins of sorts. Such close inbreeding was not at all unusual in the industry, yet many believed that the Bold Ruler-Princequillo connection had been vastly overworked and that breeders such as Tweedy should endeavor to infuse it with new blood rather than continue repeating it. In fact, a number of her critics were upset at having been excluded from the syndicate. Others were people in the thoroughbred business who had been offended by what they viewed as her attempts to commercialize Secretariat during his final racing year by hiring a large show-business talent agency to handle the horse's appearances and exploitation. They interpreted the Hopespringseternal breeding as a naïve and unrealistic desire on her part to instantly get another Secretariat, and some tagged her with the name "Greedy" Tweedy. It was a disparaging moniker that would be whispered behind her back until she divorced her husband and remarried, taking on a new, unrhymable surname. Whether her critics were justified or not, Penny Tweedy and the other Chenerys would end up with only one foal from their great horse's first year at stud.

There were to be even further ironies. One of the seasons to Secretariat sold by Penny Tweedy was to Raymond Guest, a first cousin of Ogden Phipps and a multimillionaire in his own right as a result of his inheritance, with his brother Winston, of his father's English fortune. Guest presided over a large international breeding and racing operation from his baronial Powhaten Plantation in the foothills of Virginia's Blue Ridge Mountains. Guest owned a ten-year-old mare named Belle Foulee by Tom Fool out of a dam by Christopher Chenery's Hill Prince, the Hildene-Princequillo horse that had catapulted Chenery and the Meadow Stud into the thoroughbred world's top ranks. Tom Fool, one of the top sires of the 1950s, was the carrier of bloodlines unrelated to the Nearco-Nasrullah-Bold Ruler line for seven generations. Belle Foulee was a promising mate for Secretariat. Although never raced, she was closely related in blood to a number of fine runners, including the champion filly Shuvee. The only trouble with all this thinking was that she would turn up barren after being covered by the freshman stallion three times in late May.

In the meantime, Albert Stall, a New Orleans breeder, had acquired another of the Chenery seasons to breed his mare Color Me Blue to Secretariat. Sired by The Axe II, a ranking stallion in the late sixties, the five-year-old Color Me Blue also carried Tom Fool blood, had been a useful facing filly, and was a complete outcross to Secretariat. She caught easily to Secretariat's only cover in mid-April and was pronounced in foal in early June.

Stall had already devised a plan to send Color Me Blue to auction in the fall with her *in utero* foal. His wish was to try to capitalize early on the big-money interest in Secretariat's first crop. He was not the only breeder with such a strategy in mind. Raymond Guest, who liked Color Me Blue's pedigree, decided to keep his eye on the mare, as well as any others that might be consigned to auction sales while in foal. He was confident that he could obtain a first-crop foal after all, although it might cost him considerably more than if Belle Foulee had gotten in foal to Secretariat.

The final Chenery share was taken by none other than Seth Hancock, acting not for Claiborne but for his own personal account in partnership with Fred Foster, a friend from Tennessee. The two shared a six-year-old mare called Levee Night, a former stakes winner they had acquired from Seth's father's estate when tax considerations forced a dispersal sale of Bull Hancock's personal mares in 1973. Although in the racing end of the business in a minor way, Hancock was at heart a market breeder like his father. If Levee Night got in foal, he planned to sell the pregnant mare once Secretariat was pronounced fertile in August and the syndicate was formally closed. He knew the announcement that the beloved Triple Crown winner had turned out to be a proper stallion would bring dozens of other breeders out of the woodwork anxious to have a first-crop foal, and that Levee Night, carrying such a foal, would be worth countless times her ordinary value. There was no end to the ways one could make money from a $100,000 season to Secretariat in his first year.

CHAPTER 5

Anticipation

Between mid-February and the end of June, then, Secretariat had serviced the thirty-six thoroughbred mares of his first book. Most were superbly bred in their own right, many were proven racehorses and producers, and few were "blue hens"—a term that signified a mare who had consistently produced superior stakes-winning offspring. In all the talk about Secretariat's ability to stamp his progeny with his own incomparable racing ability and heart, many had overlooked the fact that the mares to which he was bred would have as much if not more to say about the final results. In the view of many experienced horsemen, the broodmare is the pivotal figure of any breeding. It is her ability to capture the genetic qualities of a stallion, mix them with her own genetic combinations, and then produce a foal containing the best of both that is the determining factor in breeding.

A rule of thoroughbred breeding, there are always exceptions to it of course. A number of gifted male racehorses in history were never able to reproduce anything like themselves, no matter how many top-flight mares they were bred to. Similarly there have been well-bred mares who have been unable to produce anything of quality no matter how many different proven stallions they were serviced by. Conversely, undistinguished stallions have occasionally produced superior offspring when mated with top-flight mares. And even top stallions bred to top mares have frequently produced inferior horses, when the same stallions have produced superior horses out of inferior mares. "It's all a crap game," most experienced horsemen agree, and all one can realistically hope for is that "by breeding the best to the best," one will get something worthwhile.

There are a few, more specific, guidelines breeders follow, however. One, generally accepted today, is the one that cautions against inbreeding too closely—two generations' separation of common ancestry is considered the proper minimum. Another is a rule that seeks to cancel the bad features of one horse with the good features of another. If a mare, say, has a conformational defect that is common to her family, it may be bred out of her foals by mating her to stallions who are without the defect and whose families have never evinced it. Dispositional and character idiosyncrasies are viewed in the same light. For instance, the blood of Secretariat's sire, Bold Ruler, was long thought to carry with it defects in disposition—alternating combinations of moodiness and fractiousness—that negatively affected otherwise superior racing ability. This was believed to have been bred out of Secretariat and a number of other Bold Ruler offspring through the latter's consistent mating to the mares of Princequillo and others who were generally even-tempered and therefore capable of concentrating on their training and racing tasks. Heart and character, as well as racing class, were what breeders sought above all in their lengthy cogitations over stallion-mare pairings, and much of their planning had to do with outbreeding negative characteristics and capturing from the stallion and mare the positive traits, both physical and spiritual, that would produce the most desirable horse.

But even this strategy never worked with unerring consistency. Indeed, no breeding strategy had ever proved even remotely infallible. There were simply too many unknown variables. All one could do in the end was to fall back on the "best to the best" guideline and hope that one's money would not have been ill spent.

Of course, the Secretariat syndicate members and the breeders who bought seasons in 1974 really did not have to worry about ill-spent money, particularly the market breeders. Secretariat's prestige was such that most knew they would easily make their money back in the marketing of his first offspring before the horses had a chance to race and thus prove or disprove the stallion's inherent ability to reproduce himself. It was this thought that dictated the breeders' strategies in selecting mares for Secretariat. The "home breeders," the term used to describe those who intended to keep their first Secretariat offspring for their own racing and subsequent breeding purposes, were looking for one thing—mainly, effective racing outcrosses. The market breeders were looking for another—crosses with other proven and fashionable pedigrees that would bring top dollar for the offspring in the marketplace.

Of the thirty-six mares sent to Secretariat in 1974, the fifteen discussed so far represented a mix of home breeders' and market breeders' strategies. The rest were bred from similar rationales.

Walter Jeffords' My Card was the first to meet Secretariat. The second was a mare owned by Mr. and Mrs. Paul Hexter—she of the Hertz empire. An aging, well-preserved, whiskey-voiced blonde, Helen Hexter's greatest moments in racing had come when her father's Count Fleet won the Triple Crown in 1943. When her father, John D. Hertz, died, most of his thoroughbred holdings were dispersed. Mrs. Hexter, inheriting the rest, continued the family racing and breeding tradition. She and her husband acquired a stud farm in Ireland to take advantage of that country's tax subsidies on horse breeding, and divided their thoroughbred interests between Europe and the United States. She was knowledgeable about thoroughbreds, had been captivated by Secretariat, and gladly bought into the syndicate when she was advised to by Charles Kenney, the Kentucky horseman who had been the manager of her father's Stoner Creek Stud and was a member of Seth Hancock's committee of overseers at nearby Claiborne Farm.

Kenney acted as a breeding consultant to the Hexters, and it was he who recommended sending Scaremenot, one of Helen Hexter's mares, to Secretariat. Scaremenot was eight, had never raced, but had produced two foals out of three breedings to other stallions in prior years and had dropped a foal early in January of 1974. A bay, her pedigree was exemplary, particularly in view of Helen Hexter's wish to get a Secretariat first-crop foal for her racing stable. She was by Bagdad, a big winner as a race-horse in California in the late fifties and a better-than-average stallion since. Her dam was Not Afraid, who had produced the fine midfifties runner and even better stallion, Prince John, from a mating with Princequillo. Not Afraid's own sire had been Helen Hexter's father's Count Fleet, an extraordinary runner but over the course of his stallion career a disappointing sire. Never-theless, Scaremenot's pedigree represented a potentially effective outcross to Secretariat's.

What Kenney had particularly eyed in his advice to Helen Hexter was the success both Count Fleet's and Bagdad's blood had had when mixed with Princequillo's, which Secretariat car-ried by half. The addition of the other half, Bold Ruler's, might make an even more potent mix. Scaremenot was bred to Secre-tariat during the first heat after her foal heat in mid-February. She would become "settled," another term for conceiving, on her second cover.

Secretariat's third mare was Rotondella, a four-year-old who had just been retired after a racing career in England. Owned by Japanese breeder and industrial tycoon Tadao Tamashima, she was to be bred on the share he had bought in order to eventually introduce Secretariat's blood into the Japanese breeding industry. Tamashima had sent Rotondella from England to the man who acted as his agent in Kentucky, E. Barry Ryan, owner of the large Normandy Farm a few miles away from Claiborne. Ryan would supervise the breeding of Rotondella and the mares of two other foreign clients who had acquired seasons, French breeder Jacques Wertheimer and Britain's Earl of Suffolk.

Rotondella's service by Secretariat was to be her first by any stallion. Like the Phippses' Irradiate, she had been sired by the brilliant racer and stallion Ribot. Her dam, Fantan, was by the important European and later American sire Ambiorix. Most of her blood went back through European lines and did not cross Secretariat's for several generations. (Ribot, Ambiorix, and Bold Ruler all had descended in part from the early twentieth-century English foundation stallion Phalaris.)

Rotondella, inexperienced at breeding, was first serviced by the still barely experienced Secretariat on Washington's birthday of

1974. She would need the full complement of five covers over the next two months before she caught.

The day after Rotondella's first cover, E. Barry Ryan had Jacques Wertheimer's mare Gleam II vanned over to Claiborne. It was not unusual in recent years for Britons, Europeans, and other foreign breeders to send mares to the United States for breeding. Two factors encouraged this. One was the fact that so many superb European stallions had been imported to America by breeding syndicates since the time Arthur Hancock, Sr., had started the practice in the 1920s. Now the European bloodlines had begun to stagnate, and European breeders rich enough were bent on getting some of the new American blood back by breeding to the best American stallions. Not only that, but the even wealthier Europeans and syndicate organizers were arriving in America in increasing numbers to pay top prices for completely North American-bred yearlings. In the case of Secretariat, the introduction of several of his offspring could be a boon to Ireland, England, and France, which were the three most active countries in racing and breeding, as well as personal triumphs to those who managed to acquire such horses.

The other factor was the development of the jet cargo plane, which made transatlantic horse transportation fast and easy, although expensive. For people rich enough to be in the foreign thoroughbred business, however, the expenses were minimal and just another write-off cost.

Jacques Wertheimer's Gleam II, a seven-year-old, had been a stakes winner in France. Her breeding, by Spy Well out of the mare Glamour by Djebe, was completely European. Wertheimer's plan was to bring the Secretariat foal to France, race it if possible when it came of age, and then use it to improve the local breed. His preference was for a colt foal that he would eventually be able to stand at stud—the quickest way to introduce and spread desired new blood. But he knew like every breeder that the laws of equine genetics made his chances of getting a colt only fifty-fifty at best. He would not be overly disappointed by a filly, for her breeding usefulness, though different, might be just as valuable in the long run.

The office building at Claiborne Farm in Paris, Kentucky, where Secretariat stands at stud.

The breeding shed at Claiborne Farm.

Secretariat with Claiborne stud manager Lawrence Robinson, a few minutes before being taken to the breeding shed to cover Fiji II.

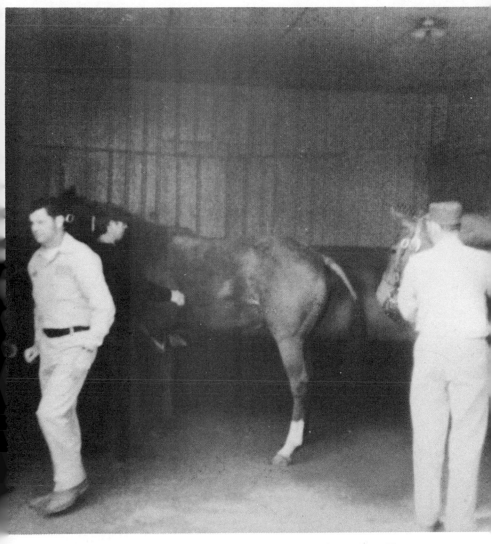

Fiji II is readied for Secretariat's cover as the big red stallion con-
templates her.

Secretariat, assisted by Lawrence Robinson, covering Fiji II while farm veterinarian Walter Kaufman (quilted jacket) looks on with cup he will use for the "human service."

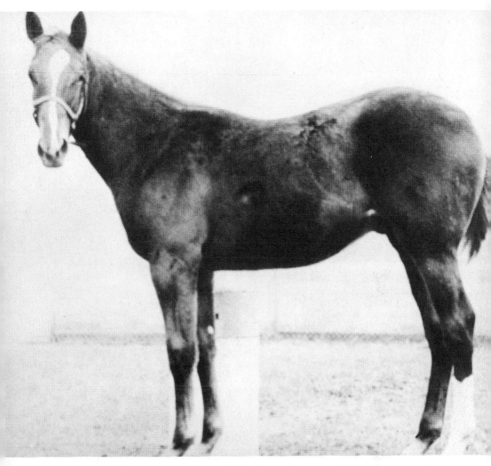

The result of the Secretariat-Fiji II breeding was this chestnut colt, pictured at ten months of age. The colt would be sold privately by its breeder, Walter Salmon, and named Acratariat. *(photo courtesy Mereworth Farm)*

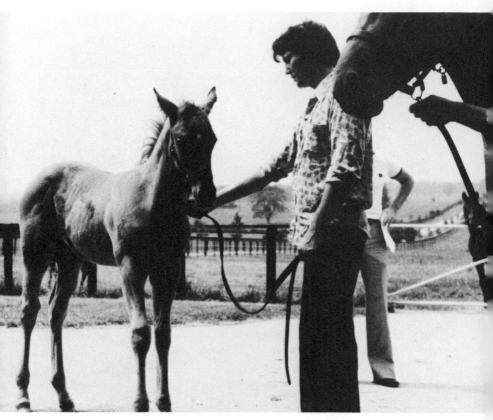

Secretariat's chestnut filly out of Windy's Daughter, shortly after being foaled. Bred by Jacqueline Getty and Mrs. Paul Blackmun of California, she would be called Centrifolia. She would be sold at auction to a principally Irish syndicate of which Mrs. Getty is a member.

At six months of age, the roan colt foaled by the Gilman brothers' mare Show Stopper (in background). Later named Grey Legion, the colt would be sold at auction at Saratoga a year later for $550,000. *(photo courtesy Howard Gilman)*

Paul Mellon's chestnut colt out of All Beautiful, photographed with his dam two days after his birth at Mellon's palatial Rokeby Farm in Virginia. *(photo courtesy Paul Mellon)*

Gleam II would catch to Secretariat on her second cover, almost a month before Rotondella would settle.

Next for Secretariat was Fiji II, another English-bred mare of impeccable blood credentials. She had been purchased and then imported to the United States by Walter Salmon, Jr., the New York real-estate magnate and market breeder who operated in the latter function from his large Mereworth Farm near Lexington, Kentucky. Fiji II, by the English sire Acropolis, was totally English and European in her paternal pedigree; Rififi, her dam, was as well, being a daughter of the excellent English sire Mossborough who himself was a son of Nearco. Fiji II, then, a great-granddaughter of Nearco, was to be bred by Salmon on his syndicate share to a great-grandson of Nearco. It was certainly an acceptable generational spread. The outcome would be particularly interesting to observe because Secretariat's Nearco blood came down from his father's side, whereas Fiji II's came from her mother's. What effect if any, Salmon wondered, would the outcross of Secretariat's Princequillo and Fiji II's Acropolis blood have on the conjoining of the Nearco line?

Fiji II went over to Claiborne from Mereworth Farm on March 4. It would take a second cover three weeks later for Secretariat to settle her.

Of all the fine mares selected for novice stallion's court in 1974, few had more credentials as a genuine blue hen than shareholder Paul Mellon's All Beautiful. Her blood flowed thickly with the genetic influences of Fair Play, one of the great foundation stallions of the modern American breed. Fair Play had sired both Man o' War and Display, among others. An inbreeding of a son and daughter of each in 1947 had produced the high-earning Battlefield, who won important stakes in the early 1950s and, in 1959, became All Beautiful's sire. Her dam was Parlo, a champion racing filly of the midfifties who came from the classic English line of Gainsborough by way of that stallion's son and grandson, Hyperion and Heliopolis. Which meant that All Beautiful's genetic matrix would be, theoretically, a splendid outcross to Secretariat's. What's more, from a breeding to Ribot, All Beautiful had produced the great distance horse and Horse of the Year of 1969,

Arts and Letters. The Italian-bred Ribot, one of the most brilliant running horses of modern times anywhere and a stallion of great achievement, carried a small strain of the blood of Secretariat through his Italian dam. The Ribot line had been one largely of stout distance horses, as had the family of All Beautiful, which undoubtedly accounted for the brilliance over a distance of ground of Arts and Letters. In 1969 he won the Jockey Club Gold Cup, a race of two miles, by fourteen lengths, as well as the similarly grueling Belmont Stakes of one-and-a-half miles. Paul Mellon hoped that a mating of All Beautiful and Secretariat would produce something on the same order as Arts and Letters, since Secretariat's staying blood seemed to have been as potent in his racing performance as his Bold Ruler speed blood. (Secretariat's record-shattering Belmont Stakes triumph had gone down in history as one of the most unforgettable races of all time. Although he didn't run in the Jockey Club Gold Cup, in many ways his Belmont and other mile-and-a-half races were tougher than two-mile races because the paces were never as slow; in the longer races the early pace was invariably more restrained in order to "save" the contestants for the final run to home.)

Arts and Letters was only one of a number of classic horses Paul Mellon had bred over the years for his Rokeby Stable. The racing stable and its breeding foundation, the elegant Rokeby Farms in Upperville, Virginia, were reflections of his taste and of the money that enabled him to indulge that taste. Mellon, an intellectual blessed with fabulous wealth, has devoted much of his philanthropic career to cultural pursuits, particularly in the field of art. A reticent man—one sometimes feels that he is almost embarrassed by his wealth—he is also one devoted to the intrinsic, soul-elevating value of excellence in a diversity of pursuits. He thinks of the thoroughbred not just as a potential profit-loss tax device but also as a genuine aesthetic gift to mankind from the gods. He therefore treats his racing and breeding operations with a certain mystic reverence and approaches all matters pertaining to his horses with an intellectual and spiritual commitment that is rare in the industry. Even his trainer was a college graduate, a rarity among the racetrack fraternity. And not just a graduate of any college—he was a Yale man, a man with whom Paul Mellon, a fellow Old Blue, could commune.

Mellon had been suitably dazzled by Secretariat and bought into the syndicate without a qualm. To reject a share in Secretariat would have been akin to declining the opportunity to buy a Rembrandt. He approached the matter of which of his mares to first breed to Secretariat probably with more seriousness than he had ever brought to a breeding before. Together with Elliott Burch, his Yale-graduate trainer, and Bernie Garrettson, his farm manager, he decided on All Beautiful. All three were aware, of course, that All Beautiful was not-too-distantly related to Secretariat through the Display connection—Display was the father of the dam of All Beautiful's sire, Battlefield; he was also the father of the sire of Bold Ruler's dam, Miss Disco. But if anything this was what sold them on the prospective mating. Basically the blood of Display, like that of Princequillo, was considered to be of the late-maturing variety. Perhaps a combination of All Beautiful's early-maturing Hyperion blood and Secretariat's even more early-maturing Bold Ruler strain would produce a youngster who would mature early as a racer and still have the wherewithal to become a classic staying horse at three.

"Early-maturing" and "late-maturing" are terms that refer to horses that develop good racing form as two-year-olds and ones who do not come into their own until they are three or four. A number of factors go into the determination of when a horse matures sufficiently to run at its full potential. Among them are physique, bone and muscle growth, the ability to concentrate, temperament, responsiveness to training, inherent character and "personality" development, and so on. Breeders believe that all these determinants are transmitted genetically and therefore take them into serious account when plotting mating strategies.

Market breeders are especially desirous of obtaining both speed and early maturity in their breeding programs, for this is what usually brings top dollar in the sales arena. People who buy yearlings are generally looking for horses that have the pedigree potential to perform well on the racetrack at two so that they can begin to recover their investment as soon as possible. Most two-year-old races are run at distances of under a mile to avoid extensive stresses on the juveniles' still developing legs and hearts. They are, in other words, sprints, and it is sustained speed from post to wire that wins such races. Usually it is only early-maturing or "precocious" horses who can be depended on to perform consistently well in two-year-old races.

Home breeders desire early maturity and speed as well, but they are not so preoccupied with it as they plan their matings. They can afford to give their horses time to mature through their two-year-old years.

Nevertheless, many home breeders are also market breeders— that is, they will cull out yearlings from a particular year's crop, for tax reasons or others, and offer them for sale. In these cases they too would like to show speed and early maturity in the pedigrees of the yearlings they are discarding.

Paul Mellon had no intention of selling his first Secretariat foal. But he was not unaware of the additional prestige that would accrue to him and Rokeby if he managed to breed the first Secretariat to show class as a two-year-old. Hence his breeding strategy in selecting All Beautiful. The fourteen-year-old mare went to Secretariat on March 5, the day after he first serviced Fiji II. She would catch on her first cover.

And so followed a series of further syndicate breedings throughout the remainder of March. All but that of Claiborne's Iskra would result in pregnancies. Following All Beautiful came Crimson Saint, sent by Texas rancher Roger Braugh on the season he had acquired from shareholder Allaire duPont. Crimson Saint was a daughter of the high-class early-1960s racer Crimson Satan, descended on her dam's side from the fine stallion Menow. She had been recently retired after a profitable racing career in California and was considered by Braugh to be the best of a "best-to-the-best" type mate for Secretariat.

After her came Bertram Firestone's Gamba, who was followed by the ten-year-old Bright New Day, a mare owned by Lucien Laurin, Secretariat's trainer and the holder of a free lifetime annual season to his former charge. Like Seth Hancock and his partner Fred Foster, the truculent Laurin, a Canadian by birth, planned to sell his mare while she was in foal to Secretariat and had already located an eager buyer in Canada. Bright New Day, sired by the imported French *chef de race* Ambiorix,* had been a

---

* *Chef de race* is a French term signifying a stallion that has become the progenitor of a distinguished racing and breeding family.

modestly successful racer and a producer of better horses than herself.

Bright New Day was followed on Secretariat's schedule by the fated-to-be-barren Iskra, who was followed in turn by the Gilmans' gray Show Stopper. Then came Barely Even, a five-year-old owned by shareholder William Lockridge. A stakes winner, she was related to Secretariat through her sire Creme dela Creme, whose dam was a daughter of Nasrullah.

The first day of April brought Diana Stokes Firestone's Exclusive Dancer to the breeding shed at Claiborne. She was followed by Zest II, an English mare owned by that country's Earl of Suffolk, who had entered into a partnership arrangement with Texas billionaire and international racing owner Nelson Bunker Hunt. Hunt, who had not been invited to join the syndicate despite his extensive breeding interests and enormous investment capital, had decided to gain access to Secretariat by buying seasons. He put up the money to acquire the season held by the British Bloodstock Agency Ltd. (Ireland) under its share, and in exchange took a half interest in Lord Suffolk's mare, whose English bloodlines he liked. His strategy was to sell the resulting offspring as a weanling in order to test the market for Secretariat's first offspring. He had acquired another Secretariat season through shareholder Richard Brooks and planned to breed his own blue hen mare, Charming Alibi, on it. He too thought that in Charming Alibi he had a mare who would produce a foal that would be worth a million dollars as a yearling, since she was the dam of Dahlia, Secretariat's filly contemporary and rival as a money-winner. But before deciding to consign the yearling to auction, he wanted another well-bred Secretariat foal with which to test the financial waters.

Zest II, fourteen years old, had proved an outstanding producer in England despite having accomplished nothing as a racehorse. The BBA season required that the breeding be carried out with an English-owned mare. So Hunt made his deal with Lord Suffolk. With English, French, and other foreign breeders invading the American market with huge sums to buy well-bred young horses, Hunt even thought that the English would go after the Secretariat-Zest II offspring, at a high price, in order to get its outcrossed blood back on their breeding ground. Hunt paid the expenses of flying Zest II to Kentucky for her date with Secretariat. She would be settled by him on two covers.

Next came a mating that would be the case of the closest inbreeding of Secretariat's book. The mare was Arctic Dancer, owned by French-Canadian insurance tycoon Jean-Louis Levesque. Arctic Dancer was the dam of La Prevoyante who, before she died prematurely, had earned some $570,000 in purses and was the champion two-year-old filly of 1972. Arctic Dancer was also full sister to the amazing Northern Dancer, which meant that she had been sired by Nearctic from a mating with Native Dancer's splendid daughter Natalma—who, ironically, was also scheduled to be bred to Secretariat and would turn up barren.

Arctic Dancer would have no such problem, conceiving on Secretariat's second cover during the afternoon of April 7. Despite or possibly because of the close confluence of Nearco blood in the breeding, many on the scene at Claiborne predicted that her foal might well turn out to be the most accomplished of Secretariat's first lot.

CHAPTER 6

Success

The breeding season was half over, but no one knew yet how many of the mares covered by Secretariat had gotten into foal. The first two—My Card and Scaremenot—had been medically determined in foal during the first week of April. But the third, Rotondella, had not yet caught, and it was too soon to make a judgment about the mares that had followed her. None had come back into heat, however, and that was a hopeful sign that Secretariat was probably operating at an impregnation rate of 60 per cent or more.

Iberia, Riva Ridge's dam, was the next to meet him in the breeding shed. She would come up barren after a full five covers over her next two heats, but Hopespringseternal, who followed Iberia and was the other of Penny Tweedy's choices to go to Secretariat, would settle without difficulty on her first heat during the second week of April.

Central Kentucky's frigid winter had given away to spring by then. The lengthening days brought with them pleasantly warming airs that were at once a relief to the winter-weary citizens of the region and a reminder of the sweltering summer that lay ahead. The grass carpeting of Claiborne's rolling fields and paddocks was lush and green again, a bright emerald green that belied its "bluegrass" name. Stoner Creek ran fast and clear, spilling over watering dams as it coursed its way through the farm's vast acreage. Leaves were already halfway to their full growth on the many tall maples and sycamores that stood like random sentinels around the breeding barn, dappling the asphalt walkways in a jigsaw puzzle of sun and shade. The distant wire-fenced fields were filled with horses—mares with gamboling foals at their sides, barren mares, and pensioners, some belonging to the farm, most boarders, and that year's "book" mares—while in the black-board-fenced paddocks nearer by, the farm's stallions lazed and grazed.

Claiborne Farm is really four separate but integrated horse-farming operations. The first, without which the others could not exist, comprises the operation and maintenance of the physical plant itself—the barns and other buildings, the land, the miles upon miles of fencing, and the 400-plus beef cattle that are tended both as a cash crop and as a source of natural fertilizer.

The second consists of the management and care of the brood-mares, of which there are usually about 350 in residence at any given time during the breeding season. During the season the mares there to be bred are teased each morning. The ones that respond to the several teasing stallions spotted about the farm are then examined by Dr. Kaufman, who makes his rounds in a large station wagon equipped with veterinary paraphernalia. By examining the mares' cervixes, Kaufman can tell which mares have come fully into heat and are ready to be bred. The information is sent to the Claiborne offices and the mares are prepared for their trips to the breeding shed to meet the appropriate stallions that afternoon or the next morning. "We breed some mares on their foal heat," says Kaufman, "but not a great many. We won't breed a mare that has just dropped her maiden foal on her foal heat, which usually starts about seven or eight days after foaling. We won't breed any mare on her foal heat if she has dropped a placenta weighing more than fourteen pounds—she needs time to reorganize her system. Nor will we breed one who has retained her placenta for more than three hours, or if she has had a difficult delivery. Of those we do breed on their foal heat, an average of about 60 per cent catch on the first cover. I have no opinion as to whether foal-heat-bred mares produce sturdier foals or not."

Along with caring for the broodmares goes the responsibility for foaling. Hundreds of thoroughbred horses are born between the beginning of January and the end of May in Claiborne's two large and antiseptically clean foaling barns. Among the more celebrated racehorses foaled there over the years have been Granville, Seabiscuit, Nashua, Bold Ruler and Round Table (in the same year), Dedicate, Kelso, Moccasin, Tom Rolfe, Buckpasser, Ruffian, and Forego—all champions in their time. Other notables born at Claiborne include Riva Ridge, Wajima, Ridan, Numbered Account, Misty Morn, Gamely, Crafty Admiral, Cicada, and Canonero II.

The reason the breeding season, and therefore the foaling period (a mare's normal gestation period is eleven months), is limited to the winter-spring period is because by the rules of the Jockey Club, the overseer of all matters having to do with the thoroughbred, all horses become officially one year old on the January first following their birth. Although physiologically only seven months old, a horse born in May is technically a year old the following January. A horse born in January is physiologically a year old the following January. As horses technically become one year old, or yearlings, those born earlier the preceding year, say in January and February, have a physiological advantage over those born in April and May. This advantage loses its importance the following year, when all horses officially become two, except that those that are born in January and February tend to begin racing as two-year-olds sooner than those born later in the spring. If a race-bred thoroughbred were to be born later than May, however, he would have little hope of catching up until he was three and would not be fit to race against his more mature contemporaries at two. Therefore, to encourage as much two-year-old racing as possible, breeders do not breed stallions after the middle of June save in the occasional exceptional case. This ensures that no foals will be born later than May. Naturally, many mare owners endeavor to have their mares bred as early in the breeding season as possible so that they can get "early" foals the following year—that is, foals born in January. Other owners prefer to breed later in the season, in the belief that "late" foals grow better and are healthier because of being born in the warmer months of springtime.

The third arm of Claiborne's operation is its yearling division. Here, on a separate segment of the farm, one-year-olds are introduced to the saddle-breaking and training process, and some at the same time are prepared for the summer and fall yearling auction sales in Keeneland, Saratoga, and other places. Sales yearlings particularly are rushed along nutritionally so that they are abundant in flesh and bone by the time of the sales. The physical differences between two yearlings born on the same day the year before—one destined for the auction rings, the other to be retained and trained—is usually marked by late spring. The sales yearling, fed intensively with special fattening feed mixtures, comes close to looking like a nearly full-grown horse, while the other still retains its foalish characteristics. These artificial-growth practices, which are often abetted by hormonal injections, are frowned on by many purists in the thoroughbred business on the ground that such yearlings give misleading impressions of maturity—which is exactly why it is done. The mature-looking yearling, his rump and girth filled out handsomely and supported by pedigree and a lack of obvious conformational defects, fetches top dollar in the yearling market. Naïve buyers tend to be captivated by the look of maturity and robustness of such horses. What they overlook is the fact that the fat will have to be melted off before the horses can be put into serious training. Otherwise their excess weight puts stresses on their still-forming bones, tissues, and joints, which can cause severe injuries or a pattern of chronic ailments that will render the grown horse useless.

The fourth component of the Claiborne operation is the stud itself, which centers around the stallion barns and the breeding-and-teasing barn situated at the administrative center of the farm. It was here that Secretariat continued his cover assignments through the second half of his first season at stud.

The two mares to follow Jean-Louis Levesque's Arctic Dancer were Iberia, Riva Ridge's dam, and Hopespringseternal, the two Chenery-Tweedy selections. After them, at the end of the first week in April, came Arrangement, a ten-year-old owned by Tartan Farms of Ocala, Florida. Tartan was a combined breeding farm and racing stable owned by William M. McKnight, retired multimillionaire chairman of the 3M Company. He had gone to work for the company as an office clerk in 1907 when it was a small sandpaper-manufacturing organization, became president in 1929, and helped guide and expand it into the industrial colossus it is today. He became chairman in 1949, when sales were in the $1,000,000,000 range, and retired in 1966 with $200,000,000 in personal stock after developing Tartan Farms in 1960.

McKnight was the money behind Florida's Tartan, which was a relatively young facility compared to many of Kentucky's breeding farms and racing stables. The "brains" belonged to John Nerud, who had spent most of his adult life as a race trainer, his later years for the Tartan stable, and had recently given up training to become president of Tartan Farms, Inc., and the expanding organization's corporate umbrella. Nerud was and is a colorful, sharp-minded, outspoken horseman and is celebrated in the racing world for being the author of sentiment that would seem to sum up the attraction that world holds for so many people. After a day at Belmont Park in which his Tartan horses had performed dismally in several races, a friend had commiserated with Nerud. "Just wasn't a good day at the races, 'at's all," Nerud had responded, undaunted. "But I'll tell ya one thing: I'd rather have me a bad day at the track than a goddamn good day anywhere else."

The two most noted horses Nerud had been associated with in his training career were Gallant Man and Dr. Fager, the latter named after a surgeon from Boston who had saved Nerud's life after a training accident resulted in a blood clot on Nerud's brain. The equine Dr. Fager, owned by McKnight, had won more than $1,000,000 on the racetrack and was Horse of the Year in 1968. When he was retired to stud, there was a great deal of skepticism about his potential as a future sire. Except for his dam, who had turned out to be somewhat of a blue hen as a producer, his pedigree was without distinction or cachet. Dr. Fager had proved to be an extraordinary sire, however, producing a long line of important stakes winners from his first few crops in the early 1970s. Nerud had been the one to select the breeding cross from which Dr. Fager himself was produced, and the horse's success led him to fasten on a breeding theory that puts emphasis on matching a stallion of good racing performance to a mare of good pedigree, despite the fact that she might have had a mediocre racing record. Dr. Fager had been produced by the good racing but unfashionably bred stallion Rough 'n' Tumble out of Aspidistra, a mediocre runner but herself from a money-winning family, if also an unfashionably bred one. "Aspidistra had the foundation," says Nerud, "and Rough 'n' Tumble had the performance. A lot of breeders look for mares loaded with black type,* but that don't mean much to me because a mare who's won a couple of third-class stakes on some dinky track in the Southwest will get black type on her catalogue page. I've always believed that if you're a market breeder it helps to have a stakes-winning black-type pedigree, but if you're breeding for your own use you'll take a mare with a good-producing pedigree. She's as valuable to you as having a stakes winner. My own experience is to breed a mare from a strong family, whether she's black type or not, to a black-type stallion. This is where you got your best chance to get a good horse. At a sale I buy at, for instance, I look for a filly from a foundation line. If she got foundation in her pedigree, she's good enough for me."

Dr. Fager had been bred from such a mating. When Dr. Fager went to stud, Nerud bred him to a number of nonblack-type mares and had good results. So his theory was more or less set in his mind as he mused over the question of which of Tartan's mares to send to Secretariat. After some indecision, he settled on Arrangement, who had been a modest winner but more importantly was proving to be a promising producer from her earlier breedings to other top-flight stallions. Arrangement was by Intentionally, Tartan's excellent foundation sire who was a big-money stakes winner in the late fifties. Her dam had been Floral Gal, a winning performer. In Nerud's phrase, Arrangement possessed "good foundation," and her previous foals provided evidence to support his selective-breeding theory. He was not a believer in simply matching the best female performers to the best male performers and hoping for the best result. Arrange-

---

* "Black type" is a horseman's phrase indicating superior racing performance. It derives from the practice of sales-auction firms of putting the records of the better-performing antecedents of a sales horse in bold face, or "black type." The best performers among the antecedents are put in all capitals bold face.

ment would not catch until her fourth cover at the beginning of
June.

Following Arrangement came a nine-year-old mare called
Guest Room, owned by breeder-auctioneer Milton "Laddie"
Dance and his wealthy wife. Guest Room was by Hail to Reason,
a well-bred, highly successful stallion who had been a splendid
track performer in the early sixties.

Guest Room settled on her first cover on April 18 and was followed by Aphonia, owned by the young fast-food king, Dan
Lasater. Of all the shareholders, Lasater had been in racing and
breeding the shortest time—three years. In those three years he
had developed a vast racing stable split into several geographic
divisions, each under the management of a trainer gifted at
"claiming" horses.

Claiming races are the bread and butter of the racing industry.
A claiming race is one in which every horse entered is for sale to
another qualified owner at the race's stated claiming price. The
claiming figure of a given race can range from as little as $1,000
to as much as $50,000. Such races are so numerous because they
tend to equalize the competition and they are the most expedient
way for those who organize and program races—the racing
secretaries at various tracks—to put together nine and ten race
cards day after day.

Claiming races have the effect of equalizing competition because an owner with a horse worth $30,000 is discouraged from
racing him in a race in which the competition is worth less. A
well-conditioned horse worth $30,000, experience shows, will
nine times out of ten win races in which the competition, on the
basis of past performances, is worth less. Normally, an owner
would prefer to run his horse against lesser competition in order
to make the likelihood of winning as favorable as possible. But
an owner who races a $30,000 horse in a lesser-priced claiming
contest would also face the likelihood of having his horse
claimed from him by another owner—that is, bought—for less
than he's worth. Owners are therefore encouraged to race their
horses in races in which the competition is, by past performance,
the equivalent or higher in value. This, theoretically, gives every
horse in a race a fair chance to win under the claiming and

other conditions determined for the race by the track's racing secretary.

Claiming races are also useful sources of racing stock. Many an owner will start out in racing with only one or two horses and then, through the vehicle of claiming horses that appeal to him at the prices set under race conditions, gradually expand his stable. This is how Dan Lasater started. Spending liberally to claim at tracks around the country under the tutelage of several shrewd trainers who could step up the claimed horses in class, he managed in three years to become the country's leading purse-winning owner at numerous tracks around the country. Then he expanded into breeding, buying farms in Kentucky and Florida, and bought a share in the Secretariat syndicate among others. "This is a business to me," says the handsome Lasater. "That's one of the reasons it has been so successful so quickly. You see other people come into racing with a few million dollars and they hire some society trainer they wouldn't let run an elevator in their real business. I like horses, but I don't get sentimental about them like some of these idle-rich old-timers. I just plain like to make money at business, and this is one way to make money."

The twelve-year-old Aphonia was a mare Lasater had purchased the year before at a broodmare auction. By the fine Tom Fool-sired racer Dunce, who had been a disappointment at stud after being retired from competition in the early 1960s, she was out of the classically bred mare Gambetta. Aphonia had been an easy breeder and useful producer, and she caught to Secretariat's first cover on April 19, the day after Guest Room conceived.

The next day Secretariat serviced two mares, one in the morning and the second in the afternoon. It was his first such double cover, and it caused some controversy around the farm. Most stallions are known to produce considerably less sperm when an ejaculation follows so quickly upon a preceding one. The first mare to be covered that day was Aladancer, a premier six-year-old daughter of Northern Dancer owned by Swiss banker Walter Haefner. Following her in the afternoon came Jo Dan, an unraced four-year-old daughter of Buckpasser and Cosmah, a black-type mare who had produced a number of first-class runners in her time. The worry on the farm, which was based mostly on breeding myths, was that Jo Dan, receiving a reduced amount of sperm on Secretariat's second cover of the day, might, if she caught to the cover, end up with a lesser foal than she would otherwise. Warner L. Jones, a longtime Kentucky breeder and the owner of Jo Dan, was consulted by phone. He dismissed the misgivings of some of the Claiborne personnel and gave the go-ahead. As it happened, Jo Dan would catch to Secretariat's cover that afternoon, as would Aladancer from the morning cover.

Next on the schedule was the superb race filly Windy's Daughter, who was being bred for the first time. The mating came about because no breeders from the West Coast segment of the American racing world had been given an opportunity to join the syndicate. California racing and home breeding had for a long time been considered by the thoroughbred establishment as inferior to what was conducted east of the Mississippi. Californians, tired of laboring for so long under this prejudice, had accomplished a great deal in upgrading the quality of their home-grown racing and breeding stock during the 1960s. At a meeting of the California Thoroughbred Breeders Association during the summer of 1973 after Secretariat's record syndication had been announced and he had won the Triple Crown, several participants vented their resentment at having been excluded. There were any number of high-class mares in California qualified for breeding to Secretariat. By being excluded, the California racing scene was being denied an opportunity to establish a foundation of Secretariat blood for later breeding purposes in the state. The only way it would be possible to ensure getting the blood would be for a local breeder to buy one of the yearlings when it came up for sale. However, such a purchase would undoubtedly be exorbitant in price. And even if it was accomplished, the yearling would not carry the blood of any of the exemplary breeding stock already headquartered in California. It would be much more desirable if Secretariat was bred directly to a mare who carried such blood.

Jacqueline Getty, the handsome blond widow of George Getty III, who was the son of Jean Paul Getty and a wealthy principal in one of his father's oil companies, came up with a solution. She had inherited her late husband's racing and breeding interests, which had spread from California to New York and then to England and the Continent, and was well connected to the Kentucky thoroughbred establishment, owning shares in four other stallion syndicates. Friendly with Duane Murty, who with his brothers was a well-known breeder and bloodstock agent, Jackie Getty arranged through him to obtain seasons for Secretariat's first two years at stud under the share owned by Lexington's Faulconer-Boone bloodstock agency. The price was stiff, however. Faulconer-Boone at first asked $300,000 for the two seasons, an amount that would have given them an immediate 50 per cent-plus profit on their $190,000 investment in the syndicate. After some convoluted negotiations through the brothers Murty, the two-year price was reduced to $175,000—$75,000 for the first season, $100,000 for the second, an average of $87,500 per year simply to breed to Secretariat. The average was about $10,000 below what other breeding-right buyers were paying, but it carried with it a potentially ruinous condition for Jackie Getty. Whereas other breeders would only have to pay half their fees should their mares not give birth to a live foal,† she was required to risk all of her investment on what essentially was a biological hope. Used to dealing in vast sums of money, her misgivings were few. She was delighted to become a part of the Secretariat legend.

With her breeding rights in hand, all she needed was a mare. She owned a number of well-bred mares, but most were non-California breds and were booked to go to stallions in which she already owned shares. A friend, Mrs. Paul Blackman, owned with her father California's best 1973 racing filly, Windy's Daughter. California-bred by the popular local stallion Windy Sea out of the local mare Fleet Judy, whose grandsire was Nasrullah, Windy's Daughter had been unbeaten in seven starts as a two-year-old in 1972. In 1973 she won a California stakes before being sent to New York to race. There she proved that her Cali-

---

† The convention in the matter of stud fees is that the total fee is refundable to a breeder whose mare does not produce a live foal from a breeding to a particular stallion. There are exceptions to this, as with certain fashionable, expensive, in-demand stallions whose owners are required to refund only half the fee should a mare fail to produce a live foal.

fornia form was up to eastern standards by winning three major stakes races out of four. Two of them were components of the Triple Crown for three-year-old fillies, and in one she equaled the track's time record for the race. She was beaten in the third Triple Crown race, the Coaching Club American Oaks, and in her next start injured her ankle and was retired. She was returned to California with $304,682 in winnings, the third-leading California-bred money-earner of all time. She was a popular local heroine in California racing circles for having performed so well against the allegedly superior eastern horses, and a number of breeders wanted to see her go to Secretariat. Consequently, Mrs. Blackman offered her to Jacqueline Getty as the mare to be bred under the Getty 1974 breeding right to Secretariat in exchange for a half interest in the resulting foal, if any. Getty now became a bit nervous, knowing that when fillies are bred for the first time they often have difficulty getting in foal. She yielded to the pressure of other Californians, however, and agreed to the deal.

With Duane Murty handling the transportation and breeding arrangements, Windy's Daughter was shipped from California to Claiborne Farm and first introduced to Secretariat at the beginning of the last week of April. As Jackie Getty anticipated, she proved difficult to settle. She needed four covers, the last at the end of May, before she would catch.

Albert Stall's Color Me Blue followed Windy's Daughter on April 28, and was followed a day later by Artists Proof, a mare owned by the second of the two Japanese members of the syndicate, Zenya Yoshida. Yoshida, who had recently gained public notice for his record-breaking auction purchase of the yearling who would become Wajima, had quietly bought a bluegrass farm a few years earlier in order to become active in the American thoroughbred market. Artists Proof was, like the Rotondella of Yoshida's countryman Tadao Tamashima, a Ribot-sired mare and was the second of the three Ribots—the third being Irradiate—to be bred to Secretariat in 1974. Her dam was Be Ambitious, sired by *chef de race* Ambiorix, and she had been a good stakes winner.

Artists Proof would catch from her first cover, as would, the same day, William Farish III's fourteen-year-old Ran Tan.

Strong in the blood of Hyperion on her sire's side, her maternal grandfather had been the sire of Gallant Man and the grandsire of numerous top performers. Ran Tan herself, fourteen years old, had already produced a champion, Top Knight, and several other superior runners from breedings to the Bold Ruler blood of Secretariat.

After Ran Tan, except for three second and third covers to earlier mares, Secretariat was given a week's respite from his stud labors. Then, on May 8, shareholder E. V. Benjamin's champion sprinting filly of a few years before, Chou Croute, was brought to him. Chou Croute descended on her father's side from a different strain of Nearco-Nasrullah blood than Secretariat. Despite the undistinguished ancestry of her dam's family, she had been the best speed filly of her generation and an earner of close to $300,000. Except for her color, which was bay, she physically resembled Secretariat in many ways. Like many a brilliant sprinting horse, she possessed a wide, heavily muscled rump, was thick in the neck, and had a massive chest and forearm (the forearms of a horse are the tops of the forelegs between the shoulders and the knees). Benjamin had anticipated sending her to Secretariat from the moment he first considered buying into the syndicate in February of 1973. The year before, when Secretariat was named Horse of the Year as a two-year-old, she had won the award as the nation's best sprinter in the same poll. She was the best horse Benjamin had ever had (he had raced her in partnership with his son and several friends). More because of her sprinting brilliance than her pedigree, he was sure her Secretariat foal would bring upward of $500,000 when offered at the yearling sales, which he planned to do. The mare had already more than paid for herself. Her first foal, he was convinced, would make his and his two partners' combined $190,000 share in the syndicate the most lavishly profitable investment they had ever made.

Chou Croute would catch on her first cover.

After Chou Croute came Irradiate, the gray mare the Phippses had agreed to breed in partnership with Seth Hancock and Claiborne in exchange for one of Claiborne's seasons. Irradiate was followed to the breeding shed on May 13, the day after, by

Alfred Gwynne Vanderbilt's Cold Comfort. Then came the mare that Nelson Bunker Hunt had been preparing the way for when he joined forces with England's Lord Suffolk to breed the Earl's Zest II.

The mare was Charming Alibi. She had been bred by Hunt and had been a stakes winner and good earner as a race filly. Her immediate pedigree, however, far from matched in distinction those of most of the other mares booked to Secretariat. Her sire was Honey's Alibi, an unremarkable stallion despite the fact that he was a son of the distinguished English sire Alibhai. Her dam was Adorada II, the daughter of the ordinary European stallion Hierocles. Yet when Charming Alibi had been bred by Hunt in 1969 to his classic French-English racehorse and champion stallion Vaguely Noble, she produced the filly who would grow up to be Dahlia. Dahlia, spending most of her racing career in France and England, was a contemporary of Secretariat and was almost as celebrated a runner in those countries as he was in North America. Indeed, when retired at the age of five, she would place ahead of Secretariat on the total-earnings list.

Hunt had discovered a gold mine in the combination of Charming Alibi and Vaguely Noble. By breeding the dam of Dahlia, a million-plus winner in Europe and a legend there, to Secretariat, a legendary million-plus winner in the United States, he was all but guaranteed of having the first million-plus sales yearling in history if he sent it to auction. To a breeder, this was almost as beneficial from the point of view of prestige as winning the Triple Crown, a feat Hunt was unlikely to accomplish since for tax reasons he concentrated most of his racing assets in Europe and England.

Charming Alibi would catch on the second cover of her first heat. It was mid-May and Secretariat was approaching the end of the breeding season. Of the five remaining mares who had not yet been covered by him, only two would conceive. They were Levee Night, the Hancock-Foster mare bred for its prospective foal's market value while still in the womb, and Spa II, who was owned by Kentucky market breeder and master of Runnymede Farm, Catesby Clay. The other three—the Phippses' Broadway,

Raymond Guest's Belle Foulee, and E. P. Taylor's Natalma—
were destined to be barren.

Spa II, the last booked mare to catch, was first covered by Secretariat on May 29. Clay had obtained the season from shareholder F. Eugene Dixon of racing's famous Widener family.
Dixon did not have a suitable mare to breed to Secretariat. Clay
offered him a partnership in the resulting foal in exchange for the
season to his Spa II. Spa II was an unremarkable imported mare
by the mediocre French stallion St. Crespin III out of the equally
unaccomplished French mare Pange. St. Crespin III's main claim
to fame was that he had produced a winner of France's premier
race, the Prix de l'Arc de Triomphe. Clay's aim with Spa II was
to see if he could successfully "breed up" by using Secretariat—
that is, increase the value of Spa II's dull pedigree by crossing it
with the brilliance of Secretariat's. If he could, Spa II would be
worth considerably more as a broodmare in years to come. He
planned to offer the foal for sale as a yearling in order to test his
ambition. Spa II would catch on June 20 during one of Secretariat's last covers of the season.

The novice stallion was withdrawn from duty at the end of
June and turned out to pasture for a few weeks with an antimas-
turbation device wrapped around his genitals. By then almost 40
per cent of the mares he had covered had been examined in foal.
Another 20 per cent would be showing shortly. There was no
doubt from the signs that most if not all had caught.

It was not until the end of July, though, that the minimum 60
per cent was examined in foal. At the beginning of August Seth
Hancock and Penny Tweedy were able to announce that, with
all conditions met, the syndicate had formally taken effect. Not
only had Secretariat impregnated his minimum, but also, from all
indications, it appeared that most of the late-bred mares were also
in foal. Hancock's projections were: a minimum of thirty-one
mares definitely in foal, three mares as yet undetermined by
outward sign or clinical test, two definitely barren. If the three
indefinites were later proved to be pregnant, it would mean that
he had gotten thirty-four of thirty-six mares in foal for a percentage of well over 90 per cent. And even if the three indefinites were not in foal, his rate of thirty-one out of thirty-

six would still constitute a percentage of close to 90 per cent, comfortably above the average of most of the best stallions.

There could be no doubt about it: Secretariat was a genuine stallion. The per-share value of his syndicate, which had floated in a state of limbo during the breeding season as a result of the publicity over his fertility, suddenly shot from the original $190,000 to nearly $300,000. Nonshareholding breeders began to clamor for the next year's seasons, a few offering even to buy out existing shares in order to get them. And President Gerald Ford, visiting Minnesota, was forced to apologize for a remark he had made earlier in Louisville. Laboring under the common misconceptions about Secretariat's fertility that had been fostered by the media, he likened his political critics to the stallion, saying that they were "fast on their feet but unable to produce." In offering his apology, he said, "Obviously, Secretariat suffers a similar problem to all of us in public life. The actual facts seldom catch up with the mistaken first impressions in the public mind." To which one wisecracking Democratic presidential hopeful responded, "Even Secretariat in the White House would be better for the country than Gerry Ford."

PART II

The Sons and Daughters

CHAPTER 7

The Foals

The occasion for Ford's apology was the birth of Secretariat's first offspring. Many who were waiting, still skeptical, to see the outcome of his first season at stud had forgotten the test breedings he had had with Claiborne's three nonthoroughbred mares late in 1973. One of the mares, the elderly Appaloosa* nurse mare named Leola, who had been barren the season before, caught to one of Secretariat's first test-and-training covers early in December, when his sperm first evidenced immaturities. Appaloosa breeders are a parochial and tight-knit lot. Word soon got around that Secretariat had successfully covered an Appaloosa. Enterprising breeder Jack Nankavil of Winona, Minnesota, thereupon traveled to Kentucky and made an offer to buy the mare at well over what she was worth. Appaloosas were often bred to thoroughbreds or half thoroughbreds in order to increase their racing stamina (Appaloosa racing, like quarter-horse racing, is popular in the western states). An Appaloosa producing a Secretariat foal, thought Nankavil, would be a tremendous boon to the breed and to himself, if he owned her, as a breeder.

Leola's prospective foal was worth nothing to Claiborne except

* Although considered a separate breed by their fanciers, Appaloosas are really quarter-horse offshoots of a different color. It is their markings that distinguish them from ordinary quarter horses, a blanket of varicolored spots around the rump. They are bred for these spotted patterns.

in terms of its souvenir value as Secretariat's first offspring. A cost-accounting corporation such as Claiborne did not have an entry page in its books for the care and feeding of equine souvenirs, so Hancock sold the mare to Nankavil. During the summer of 1974, Nankavil transported Leola to his backyard barn in Winona, where he worked as business manager of St. Mary's College. A few minutes after midnight on November 15, with the anxious Nankavil and his family in attendance, Leola gave birth to her foal, a strapping 125-pound dark-chestnut colt with a broad white blaze down the middle of his face and three tiny white socks at the juncture of his pasterns and hooves.

The birth was heralded by the press. Nankavil soon received name suggestions by letter and telegram from all over the world, which underscored the continuing universal interest in the foal's father. Within a week the thickly coated colt was romping around Nankavil's small snowy pasture and was the daily object of curiosity-seekers from hundreds of miles away. Although also born with the Appaloosa's dappling on his spacious back, he seemed the spitting image of his sire, with unusually thick-muscled forearms, tremendous shoulders, an arched neck, and of course that rump.

The colt was taken even by thoroughbred experts as another good sign of what could be expected of Secretariat as a stallion once his thoroughbred foals started to drop a few months hence. There was a widely held belief that the stallions most successful in transmitting their racing and breeding form were those who sired foals that looked like them in color, markings, and physical features. Such stallions are called prepotent. If Leola's colt, which Nankavil quickly named "First Secretary," was an accurate harbinger, Secretariat would be prepotent.

Well before "First Secretary" was foaled, the status of the thirty-six syndicate-bred mares had become definite. Five had turned up barren, and Dinny Phipps' Lady Be Good had aborted after an illness during the summer. Actually, two or three of the barren mares were believed to have gotten in foal. But they had aborted so early that there were no traces of embryos, which is what made them technically barren. That left thirty mares, several among them blue hens and the rest, with one or two exceptions, proven first-class producers. With the announcement of the Appaloosa foaling in Minnesota in November, the wide world of Secretariat fanciers began to look with pleasant anticipation toward the new year of 1975, when his first thoroughbred offspring would start dropping, as did knowledgeable thoroughbred horsemen, mostly Kentucky hardboots,† who were predicting failure on Secretariat's part because, in their view, the prepotency of Bold Ruler and Princequillo had been exhausted by the excessive saturation of the breed with their blood. Other more vindictive observers were hoping for Secretariat's failure because they had been denied a chance to breed to him or couldn't afford to.

Give or take a day or two, most pregnant mares foal exactly eleven lunar months, or 328 days, after they have conceived. The first of the syndicate mares to have conceived was thought to be Walter Jeffords' My Card, who had been the first to be bred to Secretariat in 1974. After her initial cover on February 18 she had not come back into heat, thus indicating that she had caught to the cover. That being so, she was expected to give birth on or about January 18, 1975, and thereby produce the first Secretariat thoroughbred offspring.

One can imagine the consternation at Jeffords' Faraway Farm, a few miles from Claiborne, where My Card was due to deliver, when on New Year's Eve morning of 1974 she began to show signs of imminent foaling. Because of the rule that a thoroughbred officially becomes a year old on January 1 of the year following the year of its birth, if My Card were prematurely to drop her foal on New Year's Eve of 1974, the foal would be a year old the following day—which would mean that when it was

---

† "Hardboot" is a term that dates back to the early days of Kentucky cattle and horse breeding and is used today to describe those native Kentuckians who can trace their lineage back to the pioneers. Syndicate breeders and long-time Kentucky farm owners such as Catesby Clay (Spa II) and Warner Jones (Jo Dan) qualify as hardboots. Such breeders as Walter Salmon and E. V. Benjamin, Jr., although they also owned large farms, are not native Kentuckians and therefore do not qualify. The term derives from the custom of old-time horse and cattle men walking into the best and most sumptuously appointed homes in boots that were coated with the hardened manure of the barn and stable. These were the men who ran their operations not from offices in Louisville and Lexington but on the spot.

physiologically a year old twelve months later, it would technically be a two-year-old. Seven to twelve months behind in maturity than other two-year-olds, it would not be able to race at
least until it was technically three. But even then, all other three-
year-olds would still be seven to twelve months more mature.
Thus it would always be at a marked disadvantage, and for all
practical purposes would never be able to race at all. Consequently it would have little value as a sales yearling, which was
Jeffords' plans for it. The fee he had paid for the breeding right
would have gone for naught.

On the other hand, if My Card could be artificially induced to
delay her foaling for a day, the foal, born on the first of January,
would grow up as the first and chronologically most mature of
Secretariat's initial crop of offspring. Its value at auction would
be appropriately enhanced. Buyers would likely fall over themselves to acquire the first Secretariat with the earliest physical potential to race as a two-year-old.

Jeffords was in his offices on New York's Fifth Avenue when
the desperate call about My Card's birth signs came to him from
his farm manager at noon of New Year's Eve. An experienced
breeder, he knew that if he ordered My Card's foaling process
extended pharmacologically, he ran a strong risk of ending up
with a defective or dead foal, and perhaps even a dead mare.

He was ready to take the risk and began calling veterinarians
in the Lexington area to get opinions on the odds of getting a
healthy foal if he ordered My Card to be extended. As it happened, he would not have to take the chance. A few hours later,
as he was preparing to call Harry Scott, Faraway Farm's manager, to authorize artificial extension, Scott called him to say that
My Card seemed to have settled down. She had waxed,‡ but all
other signs of an impending delivery had disappeared and she was
calmly munching hay in her foaling stall.

With that crisis averted, Jeffords now had to worry about
what would occur if My Card delivered the next day, as she most
likely would. The foal would still be close to three weeks premature. Was My Card aborting? Would the foal be stillborn? If it

‡ When a mare approaches foaling, the first sign is the production of a
milky substance from her teats. The substance, exposed to the air, hardens
and is like wax to the touch. Hence the term.

lived, would it have enough strength to survive? Would, in fact, the valuable My Card? Again Jeffords reached for the phone to get expert opinions.

Statistically, one in every 2.3 foals that are born more than two weeks premature, assuming they live to stand on their feet, eventually die or must be destroyed. Fortunately for Jeffords, although My Card did deliver the following evening, January 1, her foal, on the small side, arrived safely and in the bloom of health. It was a filly. Like her celebrated father, she was a chestnut, with three white stockings and a Secretariat-like white star and narrow blaze running down her face to her nose. When farm manager Scott took an appraising look at her after she gained her feet after a number of failed attempts, he remarked to an observer, "Couldn't be more like her pappy if we'd ordered it." She appeared piteously small, nevertheless. "Nah," said Scott, "nothin' to worry about. She'll catch up once spring comes. A little light of bone, but look at those nice straight legs. And the neck. She couldn't be better."

In accordance with the custom of naming one of the first fillies of a famous stallion, the My Card foal would eventually be called Miss Secretariat by the man who would buy her as a yearling. Among the functions of the Jockey Club is the control of the thoroughbred naming process. All registered thoroughbreds must have their names approved and certified by the Jockey Club. An owner may register a horse by any name he wishes so long as it conforms to the Jockey Club's regulations, which include restrictions against names that have been used before, names that are the same as living persons' (unless such persons give their approval), names that could be construed as advertising for individuals or organizations, names that are considered to be in bad taste or "otherwise objectionable to public sensibilities," and names that exceed eighteen print-characters in length (this is another reason so many thoroughbred appellations of two or more words are run together without spaces between the words, such as in a name like "Herecomesthebride"). Horses, especially well-bred ones, are often named from a combination of their sire's and dam's names, as in "Exclusive Dancer," who was the product of Native Dancer and Exclusive. Others are given names that combine elements deeper in their pedigrees. More imaginative and fanciful names are chosen on the basis of word plays, puns, *double-entendres*, and other conceits that breeders and owners draw from combinations of names in a horse's pedigree. There are many other methods used in naming horses, but almost invariably a first-crop filly from a well-known stallion will have reserved for it the stallion's name preceded by a "Miss" or followed by a "Lass," "Daughter," "Girl," or the like. From the very beginning, My Card's filly had reserved for her the name Miss Secretariat, and her buyer would, more than a year later, endorse it.

The birth of Miss Secretariat once again shone the light of public attention on her sire and revived the question of how his foals would turn out. If Miss Secretariat was any indication, the likelihood of Secretariat's prepotency—the first thing most experts look for in initially judging a stallion's potential to transmit his racing form—was reinforced. He appeared to have "thrown" something like himself in color and physique from a cold-blooded mare, and now had repeated it from a thoroughbred.

Realistically, however, it was too early to objectively tell on the basis of My Card's foal. My Card was a chestnut too, and to many experienced eyes her tiny foal more resembled her in conformation than Secretariat. Miss Secretariat's legs were straight and sturdy enough, to be sure, but she lacked the breadth of chest and rump that had been Secretariat's hallmark as a newborn foal five years earlier. In temperament, though, she seemed stamped from her sire. Once on her feet, she took no nonsense from her mother when she went for her milk.

Next to make an entrance into the world, this one a week or so premature, was a bay filly out of Helen Hexter's mare Scaremenot. She arrived at exactly six o'clock of a frigid evening at Stonereath Farm, between Lexington and Paris. The Hexters boarded their mares there under Charles Kenney's supervision, the original Hertz Stoner Creek Farm having been converted to the breeding of trotting horses. Scaremenot foaled easily, and the foal, "of medium size, good bone, and no conformation deficiencies," according to Kenney, was "on her feet and sucking in no time, as though she knew what it was all about." Two white socks covered the tiny pasterns of her left hind and right foreleg, and she displayed another of those Secretariat stars on her forehead with a narrow white stripe descending from it halfway to her nose.

Helen Hexter remembers being disappointed to learn that the filly was a bay. Various brown and bay gradations are together the most common color in the thoroughbred, with chestnut a distant second. Scaremenot was a bay. But Mrs. Hexter was sentimental about horses, particularly about Secretariat, and had fervently hoped that the foal would emulate Secretariat in color. She knew better, of course, or she wouldn't have sent Scaremenot, whose immediate family were all bays and browns, to Secretariat. Since Secretariat's sire, Bold Ruler, and his maternal grandsire, Princequillo, had been bay and brown respectively, the laws of equine genetics were clearly against Secretariat throwing a chestnut foal from Scaremenot. That knowledge did little to assuage Helen Hexter's disappointment. However, at least she didn't intend to consign the filly to the auction sales. Nonchestnut Secretariat yearlings would almost certainly have less value in the sales markets than those that carried their sire's color and markings.

Mrs. Hexter's disappointment soon abated as she turned with her husband, Paul, to the at one pleasant and ticklish task of settling on a name for the filly. She was one of those breeder owners who believed that the names of her horses were reflections of her high social tastes. She thought—but only briefly because it was too long—of "Countess Secretariat," such a name being a way to honor both the filly's famous sire and the great horse that had helped make her father's fortunes as an owner and breeder, Triple Crown winner Count Fleet. She then toyed with such names as "Fleet Secretary," "Ruler's Secret," and "Secret Count." Her husband finally persuaded her to abandon her namesake pursuit on the ground that horses so named would inevitably be compared in the public mind to Secretariat and suffer as a result. He suggested a more democratic name than names containing "Counts" and "Rulers"—one that would tie in with the filly's royal pedigree but be an expression of the more egalitarian realities of the American system. The name they would eventually settle on was Senator's Choice. It not only related in a modern democratic fashion to the great names in the filly's pedigree, but it had topical humor as well. It was a time of political scandal in Washington focused on certain congressmen and senators and the typing abilities of their secretaries. Because thoroughbreds' names are reserved but cannot be registered formally until the horses are at least yearlings, the world would not hear of Senator's Choice, or any of the other foals by their eventual names, for a while.

The third foal to arrive, this one a week late, was another bay. The first colt to be born, he was delivered by Frenchman Jacques Wertheimer's mare Gleam II at E. Barry Ryan's Normandy Farm, near Claiborne. He emerged an oversized, unco-ordinated youngster with the Secretariat forehead star, but bore little resemblance to his sire in any other way. Lean of flank and scrawny of neck, he obviously carried a dominance of Gleam II's genes. Yet his basic conformation was promising and he had no visible idiosyncrasies of physique that would prevent him from being a runner. He would be named Sociologue by Wertheimer and would be flown to France a year later to be trained and raced in Wertheimer's silks.

Roger Braugh's mare Crimson Saint, long before returned to the Braugh ranch near Riviera, Texas, was the next to foal. She delivered a compact, athletic-looking sorrel chestnut colt of which little could be told except that he was handsome and seemed to have the foundation of his sire's remarkable musculature. This was of no wonder to Braugh, since Crimson Saint was a heavily muscled, wide-bodied mare in the Secretariat mold. Her colt, which would eventually be named Reportage, was all health and vigor and stoutness.

Following Reportage came another colt, this one from the Gilman brothers' Show Stopper at their farm in northern Florida. Show Stopper was a gray, so the brothers were not surprised when the colt, a massive foal, emerged with a grayish hue over his chestnut undercoat. The hue would predominate as the colt grew, and he would be officially declared a roan.

According to the *American Stud Book*, which is administered by the Jockey Club, a roan horse is one that carries a mixture of white and chestnut or red hairs in his coat. The rarest of the thoroughbred colors, the roan is often confused with the gray.

Most horsemen dislike roan coloring in a horse because it generally gives the animal a muddy appearance and, because of the splotchiness of the coat, hides muscle definition. History shows that racegoers also think poorly of the roan. Track surveys have shown that when all betting odds are more or less equal in a race and the race features a roan starter, the roan will be by far the least wagered-on horse in the field. Roans are most commonly produced by matings of chestnut and gray, and for this reason many horsemen also dislike them. They feel that since the color genes of neither horse in the breeding were able to dominate, the same will hold true with regard to the other important genes, resulting in an ineffective racing or breeding mixture. But for exactly the same reason there are horsemen who *are* attracted to well-bred roans: the fact that no particular genes dominate suggests to them that the roan, having captured the qualities of both parents in color, might have done so with respect to all of the other desirable qualities of sire and dam.

The Gilmans themselves disliked roans and were therefore unpleasantly surprised by the Show Stopper colt's color. Their disappointment was sharpened by the fact that they planned to sell the colt as a yearling; they could already picture buyers being scared off by his "dirty suds" color. But then, when the colt struggled to his feet, their bile sweetened. He was a magnificent specimen and, except for his oversized head and his color, he seemed the infant image of Secretariat. His neck was thick and boldly crested; his breast was wide and his girth was deep; and his back tapered smoothly into the broad Secretariat rump. He had a white star on his forehead and his dam's extra-long ears, which, with his large head, gave him a mulish look. But the Gilmans were assured by their farm manager that the colt would grow to his head in no time. The Gilmans remained doubtful but encouraged. The colt would eventually be named Grey Legion.

Grey Legion was foaled on February 22. Three days later, at Walter Salmon's Mereworth Farm in Kentucky, Fiji II foaled an undersized white-blazed chestnut colt that in two years' time would be registered under the name of Acratariat. Another foal whose destiny was the sales ring, despite his color he seemed to have little of Secretariat in his physique and was generally a disappointment to the Mereworth personnel.

It was now six live foals dropped, four colts to two fillies. Four had been foaled in the bluegrass, and as reports came in from Florida and Texas in late February on the ambiguous qualities of the other two, the rumor began to travel along the Kentucky grapevine that "the big red stud" was not "stamping his get."

By the end of February the Secretariat foals began to appear with greater frequency. Penny Tweedy and her Chenery interests got their only offspring on the twenty-fifth at The Meadow when Hopespringseternal delivered a flashy but tiny white-marked chestnut filly. She was conformed more like her dam than her sire and would be named Hope For All.

The beginning of March brought a rash of youngsters. The Earl of Suffolk's Zest II produced a chestnut filly on March 3, to be called Superfast. Jean-Louis Levesque's blue hen mare Arctic Dancer shortly thereafter delivered another filly, this one a bay. She would be called Feuille d'Erable, French for maple leaf, which is Canada's national symbol. (Two years later, as Feuille d'Erable was being readied for the racetrack, Arctic Dancer would die in an accident at Claiborne Farm after being bred to Buckpasser.)

Later in March came a bay colt from Tadao Tamashima's Rotondella at E. Barry Ryan's Normandy Farm. Tamashima planned to ship the foal as a yearling to Japan for breeding purposes. And at Kentucky's Hurstland Farm, where auctioneer Milton Dance boarded his mares, his Guest Room produced a nicely proportioned chestnut filly with the look of her sire. Or was it just wishful thinking? Dance, a yearling-market expert, entertained visions of a $500,000 sale when he consigned the filly to the auction ring a year hence. She would acquire the name State Room.

The jury was still out on the question of Secretariat's prepotency. But, perhaps affected by the mumblings he heard around Claiborne, Seth Hancock remarked privately to a visitor that from all the signs so far, Secretariat's first crop would not be a good one. Hancock was speaking more from emotion than from horseman's judgment. He conceded for the first time a prejudice against Secretariat. When Secretariat and Riva Ridge had first arrived at Claiborne, his sympathies were drawn to Riva. An unprepossessing-looking bay when compared to Secretariat's spectacular features, Riva Ridge had been ignored in all the media hoopla that surrounded Secretariat when the two arrived at the farm to take up stud duties. In Hancock's eyes, the homely Riva had almost visibly sulked in humiliation, and for that reason he became first in Hancock's heart. Riva Ridge foals had begun dropping concurrently with those of Secretariat. "You mark my words," said Hancock. "There's no way Secretariat's gonna live up to everyone's expectations. And nobody expects anything from Riva. But I'm willin' to wager, on the evidence so far, that Riva will have an exceptional crop and Secretariat's will be ordinary. I've seen some of the Riva foals and I can tell you he's stampin' his get. As far as I can see Secretariat isn't." After saying this, a look of dark chagrin passed over Hancock's face. "But listen," he added, "that's jes' between you and me, okay? Please don't start spreadin' it around, least not yet. The damn shareholders'll be after my neck."

A note of sadness crept into the rumblings about Secretariat. William Lockridge's mare Barely Even had foaled a colt on March 12 at his Walmac Farm. It had been the first difficult delivery of a Secretariat. The colt emerged in a breech position. As he was squeezed through the mare's birth canal, one of his doubled-up hooves had fractured several of his fragile, barely formed ribs. Later, as the colt struggled to its feet, one of the floating ribs pierced his heart, killing him instantly. Lockridge, though a veteran horseman, was desolate for several days. A big investment and eleven months of work and care had gone for nothing.

But live and healthy foals kept coming. There was only one more death, that ironically of the foal born of Lucien Laurin's free-serviced mare Bright New Day, whom he had privately sold in foal to his Canadian friend. Through the end of foaling season in May, nineteen additional foals were dropped—nine fillies and ten colts. By the end of the season, Secretariat had produced thirty live foals. Sixteen were colts and fourteen were fillies, a slight reversal of the usual 51 per cent filly–49 per cent colt average. Since one colt and one filly had died, his percentage ratio remained virtually the same with respect to the twenty-eight surviving foals.

The owners of the new foals rejoiced, generally ignoring the dark note that continued to creep into their optimism in the form of occasional statements issuing from Claiborne Farm. While the foals were aborning, Secretariat had been busy at Claiborne servicing his second year's book of syndicate mares. Seth Hancock was heard by a newspaperman to say that he hoped that the second crop would be better than the first. When further probed, he confessed publicly for the first time his disappointment in the first crop. He was a believer in the theory of color and physique prepotency as a harbinger of a stallion's ability. "There's no doubt about it now," he said in the summer of 1975, "Secretariat has not reproduced himself with anything like the consistency we hoped for. Riva Ridge, on the other hand . . ."

Many owners of the foals, especially those to be sold at auction, did a slow burn. Messages were sent to Claiborne strongly suggesting that Hancock shut up. But he wouldn't. He was proving that he was his own man as a breeding expert, and there was nothing in the syndication agreement that required him to keep mum. Other owners, especially those who also had an interest in the Riva Ridge syndicate, were elated. They knew what Seth Hancock was up to. He was trying to upgrade the value of Riva's foals by comparing Secretariat's crop unfavorably to them.

CHAPTER 8

The Weanlings

Seth Hancock's criticism of the first Secretariat crop might also have been encouraged by the fact that his own foal—the one that Claiborne Farm owned in partnership with Dinny Phipps from the Phipps mare Irradiate—had turned out to be a disappointment. By midsummer, the splotchy gray colt with a barely discernible white blaze had started to take physical shape. To Hancock's dismay, he was a swayback.

Foals are usually weaned—removed from their mothers' milk—at about six months after birth. The weaning process is a terrifying one for the youngsters. Attached for six months to their dams by the umbilical cord of powerful instinct, they are abruptly and terminally separated from them. This is done at six months, or earlier, for two reasons. One is that their dams are usually in foal once again and need the chance to begin building up their stamina without the continued draining presence of their sucklings. The other is to get the foals off their mothers' milk so that they can be placed on a growth-oriented feeding program, and also to give them the opportunity to begin competing with their contemporaries in the pasture so that they can develop their characters and competitive instincts.

Thoroughbreds are usually weaned in one of two ways. The first and more traditional is to lock the animal up on its own in a closed stall, then remove its dam to a spot on the farm so distant that she will be unable to hear the foal's frantic cries. This method is used seldom today because of a history of so many valuable foals injuring themselves in the weaning stall as they flail about trying to escape back to their dams.

The popular way to wean today is called silent weaning or field weaning. By this method a group of mares and their sucklings are placed together during the day in a pasture. The next day two of the mares are removed and taken out of earshot. With the other mares and foals present, the weaning foals, although they might fret for a while, quickly become accustomed to the absence of their mothers. The next day two more mares are removed, and the same influences work, including the fact that the band already contains two weaned foals.*

Claiborne Farm used the silent weaning technique. The Secretariat-Irradiate foal, which Seth Hancock would name Brilliant Protégé, was weaned in September and sent out with a group of other colts to develop muscle and character. Immediately Hancock found a second criticism to make of him. Besides his swayback, he was a shy and unassertive colt—the opposite of what Secretariat had been as a yearling. Brilliant Protégé did his share of galloping and exuberant bucking about the weanling paddock, but he was always a tagger-along. The rest of the weanlings had little regard or respect for him. "Nobody told them that he was a son of Secretariat," Hancock remarked wryly.

Weaning time is when breeders begin to take stock of their weanlings' conformation, appearance, and growth patterns. Brilliant Protégé, despite his swayback and mottled color, at least had the head of Secretariat and would possibly even grow into the rump of his sire. Secretariat had a relatively short head. The shortness was accentuated by his size—by the massiveness of his cheeks, by his thick crested neck, and by his forequarters (his chest, girth, and shoulders). Brilliant Protégé had the same type of face and it was the one single thing that distinguished him as his father's son. Otherwise he was a trifle more Irradiate in ap-

---

* Once a foal is successfully weaned, which usually takes no more than a few hours by this method, it has no desire for its dam. Often, two days after a weaning, the weanling will not even recognize its mother when reunited with her.

pearance than Secretariat. Seth Hancock did not hold out much hope for him as a racer. He was awkward galloping about the paddock, showed little desire to compete with his peers, and in the bargain he had an odd two-beat gait that was obviously caused by his swooping back.

The basic conformational traits one looks for in a horse are straightness of leg and thickness of bone; wide-set eyes (which are arguably believed to denote superior intelligence and therefore good training and racing potential); a bold neck blending into powerful, obliquely angled shoulders; well-muscled forearms and straight knees; straight, polelike cannons (the bones and tendons between the knees and fetlock, or ankle, joints); smartly angled pasterns from the fetlocks to the hooves; properly formed hooves; chest with naturally well-developed pectoral muscles (the sign of a potential speed horse, since much of a horse's thrust comes from his forehand—his chest and forearms particularly); a deep girth and "well sprung" barrel or rib cage, which signify lung capacity and therefore staying potential; a short, relatively flat back that joins forehand to rear in pleasing proportion; a well-developed rump and hind thighs; and straight hind cannons with well set-in rear pasterns.

Most thoroughbreds possess all of these features to one degree of desirability or another. Secretariat had them in what many claimed was a perfect combination, one they credited as being responsible for his immortal racing class. Of course, many superior racehorses have gotten by with considerably less than perfect overall conformation. Other perfectly conformed horses "couldn't outrun a pregnant woman going downhill," as the saying has it. Conformation therefore is not a vital function of racing class, at least within certain latitudes. Nevertheless, it is believed to be an almost absolute gauge of racing potential in young horses, particularly in the case of sales yearlings. A fashionably bred yearling will bring considerably less if he has one or more visible conformational anomalies than will one with no apparent defects. Similarly, a cheaply bred but pleasingly conformed horse will bring much more than a badly conformed one. And a well-conformed cheap horse will often bring more than a poorly conformed expensive one.

What experienced horsemen look for when first assessing a

young horse's conformation are the forelegs, the horse's most fragile mechanical component. They look for a straight vertical line from the top of the forearm, through the knee, to the fetlock. A line that wavers or jogs indicates that the horse is "over at the knee" or "behind in the knee," which means that the knee is set too far forward or to the rear at its junction with the cannon bone. Such anomalies indicate the potential for knee instability, which will place more than normal racing stresses on the fragile cannons and lower joints.

When examining the legs from the side, the horseman also looks at the slope of the shoulder (the more acutely angled toward forty-five degrees it is, the better, since the shoulder is an important driving force and producer of speed; the more the angle, the more the forelegs are free to extend stride). He examines the pasterns as well, also looking for a roughly forty-five-degree angle between fetlock and hoof. Numerous horses are born with more upright pasterns, others with flatter ones. These are conformational defects because they do not provide the horse with the optimum spring-and-cushion support necessary to prevent injuries to the complex, delicate pasterns and fetlocks, not to mention the cannons.

Horsemen like to see a nicely dished face when looking at the horse in profile, but this is not a conformational requirement. Many, however, will reject as a racing prospect a horse that has a dished neck or back—"dished" meaning an excess of concavity. A dished or "ewe" neck suggests that a horse, which uses its head and neck to counterbalance the action of his hindquarters, will be directionally unstable during a race. A swayback suggests that the horse will have difficulty co-ordinating the action of forehand and hindquarters, and that he suffers too low a center of gravity for effective long striding.

One last item horsemen will assay when viewing a young horse laterally will be the hindquarters, particularly the hocks, rear cannons, and pasterns. What they look for here are, again, straight, well-boned cannons. The most common defects here are what are known as "sickle" or "cow" hocks. This means that the hocks are bowed concavely, much in the manner of a cow, drawing the horse's rear hooves too far forward under his hips. Such an offset not only limits the mechanical action and thrust of the hind legs but also tends to promote "curbs" (tendon swellings along the hock that further limit mobility and cause lameness).

Severe sickle hocks are considered an "unsoundness" in a horse, as is any other defect, however slight, that experience shows to promote lameness. Slight defects are not unsoundnesses per se, but are to be avoided whenever possible. Particular equine bloodlines carry with them a tendency to certain conformational defects, and many breeding programs are at least partly designed to "breed out" such defects. Today, except for an occasional occurrence, gross defects are rare in thoroughbreds. But slight defects such as sickle hocks and knee irregularities remain common. Secretariat was thought to be without any defect. His sire, Bold Ruler, carried a pattern of slight defects from his ancestry, as did many of the mares to whom Secretariat was bred his first year. As the summer of 1975 dissolved into the weaning time of early fall, more and more reports came in of visible defects in many of his offspring—more apparent evidence of the inability of his genes to consistently dominate over those of the mare to whom he was mated.

Another slight conformational defect is seen when viewing a horse from straight on. This is the tendency of one or both forefeet to "toe in" or "toe out" as the horse's legs are planted in a straight position. Many fine racehorses have been noted for these defects, most recently 1975 Kentucky Derby winner Foolish Pleasure, who toed out markedly in one foot. A slight splayfootedness or pigeonfootedness is not objectionable, although a normal stance is desired.

The horseman also looks for straight knees from the front view and generosity of chest. He examines the horse's "throatlatch" or "throttle" with his hands to ensure that the windpipe contains no obstructions or growths that would impede normal breathing. Since a horse breathes only through his nose, the expert then looks for ample nostrils. Finally, he steps away and considers the horse as whole, looking for such intangibles as overall physical balance, center of gravity both laterally and vertically, general musculature, and "way of going." The set of eyes and ears are taken into account as well, since these are thought to be indicators of intelligence.

At the weanling stage, a horse's basic conformation is subject to fairly accurate assessment, with even minor defects visibly discernible. The horse's eventual overall appearance, aside from his or her color and markings, is much more difficult to judge, however. At six months of age the foals have lost their "cuteness" and, as their forehands begin to catch up with their high rumps they take on an awkwardness and unsightliness that is the worst stage of their growth aesthetically. At six months, Brilliant Protégé, faultible on his swayback, had little else to recommend him in appearance but his fine Secretariat head.

Nor did E. V. Benjamin, Jr.'s small weanling colt out of the fine bay sprint mare Chou Croute. Eventually to be named Confidant, he could not even boast of a fine head. Of frisky temperament, he was light of bone and muscle in the forelegs, had inherited much of his dam's blocky physique in the hind, and from where no one knew, had a markedly coarse and heavy head that was accentuated by a pronounced "Roman nose." Despite his decidedly non-Secretariat color and appearance, Benjamin and his partners had decided in August to put him up for auction as a weanling during the coming November's annual breeding stock sales at the Keeneland racetrack near Lexington. They might get more for him the following July at the Keeneland select summer yearling sale, but then again they might not, given the competition they would face from a number of other Secretariat first-crop yearlings. Weanlings traditionally sold for less at auctions than did yearlings, mainly because they were less developed, still foalishly awkward, and more of a risk. Benjamin, however, was anxious to recoup his and his partners' investment in the syndicate. What with the weanling's insurance costs and the other expenses of maintaining his security at Big Sink Farm, they had already spent $30,000 over the $190,000 of their original investment. Despite the colt's less-than-brilliant appearance, Benjamin was sure he would bring at least $500,000 at auction on pedigree alone. The highest price ever paid for a weanling had been $202,000. The sale of Confidant, who Benjamin had taken to calling "Triple Sec," would set the horse world on its ears and would make the market even better for the owners of the yearlings to be sold the following year. "I'm doin' a lot of folks holdin' their Secretariats for sale next July a big favor," said the sixty-six-year-old Benjamin in his raspy Louisiana drawl. "This colt'll send up the yearlin' market like a goddanged Apollo rocket."

The four annual horse auctions at Keeneland—the July select yearling sale, the September yearling sale, the November breeding stock sale, and the January mixed sale—were the financial heartbeat of the Kentucky thoroughbred industry. The November sale attracted buyers from all over the world to bid on valuable broodmares, many in foal to celebrated stallions, and weanlings. The year before, three of the mares carrying Secretariat first-crop foals had been sold for prices far beyond their intrinsic value, thus heralding the market that awaited Secretariat's first offspring.

One of the mares was Seth Hancock's Levee Night, which was taken down by neighboring bluegrass breeder Tommy Gentry for $225,000. Asked why he was willing to pay so much, Gentry said, "Because next year the first crop by Secretariat will be magic in the yearling sales." Levee Night had produced a colt foal on April 30, 1975, which Gentry planned to send to the July yearling auction the following summer.

Another was Artists Proof, whose owner, Zenya Yoshida, consigned to the November 1974 sale certified as in foal to Secretariat. She was bought by Greek shipping billionaire Stavros Niarchos for a whopping $385,000. Vanned to John Gaines' (of the dog-food Gaineses) Gainesway Farm outside Lexington, she had foaled a bay colt on April 21, 1975. Niarchos intended to ship the colt to his own farm, Haras de Piencourt, in France's Normandy.

The third in-foal mare to pass through the ring at the 1974 November broodmare auction was Albert Stall's Color Me Blue, bred on the season Stall had purchased from the Chenery Estate. This was the mare Raymond Guest had been following since his own mare, Belle Foulee, had turned up barren on a season he too had gotten from the Chenery interests. Guest bought Color Me Blue after spirited bidding for $220,000 and shipped her to his Powhaten Plantation near King George, Virginia. Guest was in Europe when she foaled a chestnut colt on April 9, 1975. When Guest returned the first thing he did was go look at the colt. He believed that the foal resembled Secretariat—one of the few to be born up to that time who did—for he had seen the Triple Crown winner at The Meadow as a month-old foal in 1970. His foal even had the three Secretariat stockings rising up above the fetlocks. By the time Guest saw him, however, his bushy coat had begun to fill with white hairs. He too would be a roan. Guest intended to keep and race him, and would name him Sacrebleu.

When Sacrebleu was weaned he was, according to Guest, "a perfect individual with no conformational idiosyncrasies, but he has a charming personality. I must say, I think I am lucky enough to have gotten one of Secretariat's best if what I hear about some of the others is true."

E. V. Benjamin, Jr.'s Chou Croute colt, Confidant (or "Triple Sec," as he was informally known then), was not among the best. Yet as Benjamin prepared him for the 1975 weanling and brood-mare sale at Keeneland, he refused to acknowledge it. He went on record as boasting that he expected the bay weanling to take down in excess of $500,000. "And if some pinhooker gets him, he'll be able to get a million for him next year."

"Pinhooker" is the horsemen's term for someone who buys a weanling with the intention of reselling it as a yearling at a con-siderably higher price. Yearlings are also pinhooked to be sold as race-trained two-year-olds, but the pinhooker's principal markets are the weanling auctions. Benjamin, of course, did not expect a pinhooker to acquire his Chou Croute colt. Pinhookers were no-torious for buying cheap. If a pinhooker did go after the colt, it would mean that he "weren't worth a plug nickel, and that jes' ain't gonna be the case." Benjamin remained firm in his expecta-tion of at least $500,000, and although some of his bluegrass breeding colleagues seriously doubted it, others thought that on pedigree alone, the way auction prices had been spiraling upward in recent years, he just might pull it off.

The Keeneland sales management and publicity people made the most of the fact that there would be not one but two Secre-tariat weanlings in the November auction, the first of the Secre-tariats to be offered for sale. The sporting press and the media in general picked up the cues and, a week before the sale, began to banner it to the public. The other weanling would be the nicely made but unspectacular filly foaled by the Earl of Suffolk's Zest II. E. Barry Ryan, acting as agent for Lord Suffolk and his partner in the foal, Nelson Bunker Hunt, was to handle the arrangements. Ryan was curiously close-mouthed about the filly compared to Benjamin, particularly about its ownership. Few could understand why Lord Suffolk had invested so much to breed to Secretariat only to sell the product as a weanling. What few knew was that Hunt was the one who had dictated the sale, at the same time wishing his ownership in the weanling concealed. He feared that because of his reputation as a highly successful international breeder, potential buyers would interpret his selling the filly as a sign that something was wrong with her.

As the sale approached, publicity over the two weanlings spread across the country. E. V. Benjamin suddenly became so nerve-wracked that he was forced into the hospital for a week. His attack of nerves was clearly justified, since on the night of the sale, under the tightest security ever provided for a Keeneland auction, the Chou Croute colt was knocked down for $250,000—a record-shattering price, to be sure, but well short of Benjamin's expectations.† "That was horrible," he wailed when it was over. "Four hundred thousand would have been dirt cheap."

Benjamin might have had a foreboding of what the colt would fetch from watching the previous night's auction, when the hammer fell on the Bunker Hunt-Lord Suffolk filly for $200,000. Weanling fillies traditionally sold for more than colts, even colts by the most fashionable stallions, because the fillies were considered less of a risk. A filly was statistically much more likely to be useful as a breeder than a colt over the long term, and at their weanling stages the fillies were too immature for objective judgments to be made about their racing potential.

The bidding on the filly, which started at $100,000, was over almost as it began. There was a quick raise to $150,000, and that was jumped to $200,000. There it stopped, despite frantic efforts by the auctioneer to boost it farther. When he finally gaveled the proceedings to an end it turned out that Bunker Hunt had inad-

† The previous record was held by Secretariat syndicate member Paul Mellon, who had paid $202,000 for a weanling filly by the stallion Sir Ivor two years before.

vertently bought his own filly. It was his agent, under his orders, who had started the bidding at $100,000. When it instantly went up by $50,000, he raised it to $200,000 in the belief that the raises would continue. When they didn't, he had the horse on Hunt's behalf, although no one was yet sure that he was representing the rich Texan. Hunt, in effect, had bought out his partner and now owned the filly outright.

The bidding on Benjamin's coarse-headed colt, after a lengthy introduction of his bloodline credentials (as if anyone had to be reminded), was even briefer. The opening bid, set by Benjamin, was $200,000. A call for $250,000 followed immediately. And there it stopped as the auctioneer needled and cajoled for a topper. The packed sales pavilion fell into an oppressive quiet. Then the gavel shattered the silence. Benjamin could be heard to cry "Oh no!" as a wave of applause rose out of the seats in recognition of the record-breaking price.

The buyer was Benjamin P. Walden, a breeder and racing owner from Midway, Kentucky, and he was as pleasantly surprised as Benjamin was shocked. Bidding on behalf of himself and a partner, Wells Hardesty of Chicago, Walden had been prepared to go to the $500,000 price Benjamin had predicted with a view to immediately forming a syndicate that would get him and Hardesty most of their money back. When asked at a press conference later why he thought he had gotten the colt so cheaply, Walden said that it was probably due to the general awe at the prospective prices that had been kicked around in the media. Everyone was waiting for everyone else, and thus no one but he had dared to proceed. He also conceded that the low price might have been due to the colt's Roman nose and the fact that he toed-in slightly, just like his dam—indeed to the fact that he looked nothing like Secretariat or people's visions of how a Secretariat colt should look. But he stoutly defended the weanling. The toeing-in did not bother him "because I have seen very few athletes, man or horse, with this conformational flaw that couldn't run a hole in the wind. And so what about his nose? The shape of a horse's nose never affected his speed or ability so far as I know."

It was Walden who would name the colt Confidant. He and Hardesty had a syndicate formed to race him before the night was over. Included in the syndicate were E. V. Benjamin's previous partners in the colt.

By November of 1975, all of Secretariat's first sons and daughters had been weaned at the various farms at which they were quartered around the country. One of the last to be taken from its dam was Catesby Clay's chestnut filly out of Spa II. She was developing nicely at Clay's Sunnymede Farm near Lexington and at first glance seemed to have a lot of Secretariat in her. But Clay, an experienced horseman, knew otherwise. She had her sire's color but little of his conformation and indeed had developed a crookedness in one of her foreknees. One of the last foals born, she was nevertheless turning into a fast grower. She had a placid temperament and, once weaned, a hearty appetite. Clay had her scheduled for the following summer's select yearling sale at Keeneland.

Another scheduled for the select sale was Bunker Hunt's Charming Alibi colt who, among the twenty-eight foals, was developing into the horse most like his sire in color, appearance, and physique. Also a late foal, he had sprouted in a few weeks in October into a strapping chestnut specimen with the trademark neck, shoulder, and forearms of Secretariat. If he could be faulted at all it was in the hint of spareness in his hindquarters. Aesthetically, his features were marred by a slight Roman nose, but with four white stockings and a small star on his forehead he looked very much his father's son.

Still another Kentucky-based weanling penciled in for the sales was Warner Jones' chestnut filly out of Jo Dan. Quartered at Jones' Hermitage Farm in Goshen, Kentucky, the filly was one of the better-bred of a number of top-breds but had captured little of Secretariat's conformational purity. "She's a Cosmah (Jo Dan's dam, one of the premier broodmares of the sixties and early seventies) if I ever saw one," said Jones. "It would be nice if she bulked out more like her sire, but with that breeding she's sure to go for top money at Keeneland."

Yet another filly who was in the process of being scheduled for the auction ring was Jacqueline Getty's chestnut out of Windy's Daughter. Getty and her partner had hoped for a colt with a view to racing him in California and then standing him at stud. They had decided, however, that if they got a filly they would sell her. The filly they got was so handsome—a powerfully muscled all-chestnut with no white markings—that they too happily began to think in terms of getting the highest price ever for an auction yearling filly. "The only thing that could stop her from breaking all filly price records is the vestigial prejudice many horsemen have for California breeding in a pedigree," said Jackie Getty. "Out of a mare like Windy's Daughter, with her proven family, I'm sure the horse world is in for some enlightenment finally."

In Florida, the Gilman brothers' roan colt out of Show Stopper was also burgeoning into a mightily muscled and well-conformed yearling. The Gilmans planned to consign him to the following year's other premier yearling sale, the Fasig-Tipton vendue at Saratoga in August. They hoped the colt's conformation and maturity would offset his heavyheadedness and roan coat.

Two other weanlings destined to go on the block at Saratoga as yearlings were Fasig-Tipton auctioneer Laddie Dance's chestnut filly out of Guest Room, and the Firestones' roan colt out of the splendidly bred Exclusive Dancer. Bertram and Diana (Stokes) Firestone had recently married and were in the process of putting together a brand-new stud farm of their own on fourteen hundred acres of rolling open land a few miles from the picturesque Civil War hamlet of Waterford, Virginia, near Leesburg. Sparing no expense, they intended to use some of the money they anticipated receiving for the Exclusive Dancer colt and other yearlings they would sell at Saratoga the following year to help finance the completion of Catoctin Stud, as they called their new Virginia operation. They were also busily establishing a separate stud facility in Ireland and were consolidating their racing stables in England and France, as well as in the United States. When they had gotten married, they agreed that all the fillies they retained from their own broodmares, or purchased for racing purposes, would race in the name of Diana Firestone; the colts would race in Bert's name. By selling the Exclusive Dancer colt, Bert Firestone would not have a first-crop Secretariat to race in his name. With her filly out of Gamba, however, Diana would. That was fine as far as Bert Firestone was concerned. Exclusive Dancer had been bred back to Secretariat following the birth of the colt, was safely in foal, and was due to deliver in April of the following year. With two breeding shares in Secretariat, Bert Firestone was interested in colt foals only for the market. Because he and his wife were building an international breeding operation, they had decided to keep selling the colts they got from Secretariat and to keep the fillies for racing and later breeding.

CHAPTER 9

The Yearlings

Almost half—thirteen of twenty-eight—of the first-crop Secretariats were to be sold as weanlings and yearlings, at auction or by private transaction.

The first yearling to change hands was Walter Salmon's chestnut colt out of his imported mare Fiji II. The buyer of record was California breeder Booth Hansen, who was backed by several wealthy West Coast partners in the unpublicized private $300,000 purchase. They were attracted by the colt's looks and conformation, as well as by the previous produce record of Fiji II and by her immediate pedigree. Fiji II's dam, Rififi, by English *chef de race* Mossborough, had nine foals, four of which had been winners and one a stakes winner. In fact, the stakes winner was Fiji II, who had won Great Britain's Coronation Stakes, a mile race for three-year-old fillies, in 1967. Having shown class as a runner, she had gone on to produce several high-class daughters from a variety of stallions. One was Safety Match, a filly who won a stakes race in England. Another was Fleet Wahine, who won in France and then captured three stakes in England, including the Grade I Yorkshire Oaks.* A third was Pacific Princess,

---

* Because of the proliferation of stakes races in the postwar years, both in America and in Europe, the combined racing industries joined together several years ago to classify stakes races according to their prestige, purses, and class of competition, into three groups or grades. Grade I stakes are

who at the time of the sale of Fiji II's Secretariat colt was beginning to show stakes-winning form as a three-year-old.

Fiji II's Secretariat yearling was maturing into a horse with the
superficial look of his sire, particularly in the face and chest.
Hansen liked his potential, as did his chief partner, California
investor C. L. Occhipinti, and the deal was quickly made. The
colt was shipped to Hansen's farm in California, and Occhipinti
immediately proposed for him the name Acratariat, a coinage
meaning "the best." Whether he would prove the best of Secretariat's first crop remained to be seen, but according to Mereworth Farm manager Ralph Kercheval, "He was the best-looking
of the Secretariats I'd seen in Kentucky and I hated to part with
him."

Throughout the first nine months of their yearling seasons,
thoroughbreds are left pretty much alone. They are generally
handled once or twice a day at feeding time by their grooms—
their hooves picked, their coats brushed and rubbed—to accustom them to human contact, but otherwise are pastured with
other yearlings of the same sex. As they make the transition from
weanlings to yearlings they begin to look like the mature horses
they will grow into, particularly those foaled early in the preceding year. It is during the spring and early summer months of
their yearling seasons that their growth becomes most rapid.
Many professional horsemen are moved to remark in wonder at
this phenomenon. Between the ages of thirteen and fifteen
months, the thoroughbred transforms himself, seemingly over-
night, from a baby into a grown-up horse—"an animal you've
got to watch out for," in the words of one veteran hardboot.
"There's something magical about it. One night, say, in early

---

the most important and prestigious; Grade II stakes, of which there are
many more, are next in class and prestige; and Grade III stakes, which
constitute the majority of stakes races run in a given year, are the least
prestigious. When breeders talk about stakes winners today, they generally
qualify their remarks by saying "he was a Grade I stakes winner" or "she
was only a Grade III stakes winner." Naturally, the most prestigious horses
for breeding purposes are those who have the most Grade I stakes victories
in their racing record. As a three-year-old, for instance, Secretariat started
in six Grade I stakes and won four, placing second in the fifth and third in
the sixth. It is seldom that a horse is ever good enough to compete in so
many Grade I stakes in a single year.

May, you'll put your yearling in his stall and he'll be all nippy and playful and still a bit gangly and you'll feel like you're dealing with a puppy dog that you are in complete control of. The next morning you go into his stall to put a shank on him and you're looking at a grown-up horse who'd just as soon lay back his ears and kick you halfway to Louisville as nuzzle your hand. Suddenly you're dealing with real horseflesh."

Any thoroughbred farm worth its salt is extremely discriminating in the people it employs as yearling grooms. Horses, though domesticated animals, balance on a fine line between tameness and wildness. Their feral instincts are easily aroused during the time they fill out into full-blown yearlinghood. Thoroughbreds have the added factor of "hot blood," which is to say that the instinctive desire to run has long been bred into them to the detriment of docility. Horses are also notorious for the ease with which they pick up unfavorable behavioral habits and lock them into their natures. An impatient or ill-mannered groom is likely to transmit his own habits to the yearlings in his care, and a potentially good racehorse can be ruined as a yearling for racing by anything but the most enlightened and sensitive handling.

Many breeding farms prefer to hire young women to serve as yearling grooms, on the theory that women are temperamentally more suited than men to deal with naturally fractious young horses that are in the process of discovering a sense of their inherent power and competitiveness. This is particularly true of a farm like the Firestones' Catoctin Stud, which breeds not only to sell but also to race. The Firestones planned to sell their Exclusive Dancer colt by Secretariat, it was true. But the filly out of Gamba they intended to retain for racing and, later, breeding. It would be untoward for the Gamba filly to be anything less than a well-behaved specimen when she was ready to be saddle-broken and put into training—which is why the Firestones' horse manager, Frank Leach, assigned his very best groom to her when she was brought from her foaling place in Kentucky to the Catoctin quarters in Virginia. The groom was Sally Marlowe, a graduate of the noted Morven Park Equestrian Center at nearby Leesburg.

The filly had grown into a flashy-looking, brilliant-chestnut yearling with a broad white blaze running the length of her delicate, wide-eyed face and white pasterns above each hoof, the white extending into full stockings on the forelegs. She was alert, was taking on good size and bulk, and showed evidence of moving well. The Firestones decided to name her Oatlands—her first experience in misfortune—after a nearby antebellum estate in Loudoun County that had become an official historical site.

Sally Marlowe cared for Oatlands, as well as the Firestones' gray-roan Exclusive Dancer colt and three other yearlings, with exquisite patience and understanding during the spring and summer of 1976. By the time the Exclusive Dancer colt—eventually to be named Seclusive—was ready to be shipped to that August's Saratoga yearling sale, he was well filled out and properly sassy, but eminently even-tempered. Oatlands, left behind at Catoctin Stud, was the same.

The only sour note for Sally Marlowe came during the spring when the Firestones' racing trainer, Leroy Jolley, stopped by the farm to inspect the yearlings. Jolley, the son of respected veteran trainer Moody Jolley, was thirty-eight and, as trainer of that year's most promising three-year-old colt and filly—Honest Pleasure and Optimistic Gal, both owned by the Firestones—he was at the top of his profession. An opinionated and self-possessed man, he had been singularly unimpressed with Secretariat's potential as a sire after hearing numerous tales during the winter about how the great red horse had failed to stamp his first get with his unique class. Noted within the thoroughbred industry as having one of the sharpest eyes of any for yearling conformation, his judgments were held in great esteem. When he looked at the Catoctin yearlings during his stopover that spring, he was mildly approving of the roan Exclusive Dancer colt. But he scowled when he looked at Sally Marlowe's pride and joy, the filly to be named Oatlands. "Not enough bone for her size," he remarked to Sally. "Wouldn't be surprised if she never raced. Pretty enough to look at, but with those toothpicks between her knees and her ankles she'll never be a runner." Sally had noticed Oatlands' exceptionally thin cannon bones, of course. Sally herself was thin in the calf. "Never stopped me from running fast," she said to Jolley. "You get big as this filly," he retorted with a dry laugh, "and you'd have trouble running for office."

Not far from Catoctin grazed another of Secretariat's first-crop fillies, also a chestnut but without any of his discernible physical features. She was the filly out of Hopespringseternal and for Penny Tweedy, the original owner of Secretariat at whose Meadow Stud she grazed, she was a monumental disappointment. She was "pretty enough to look at," with a fine dished face accentuated by a nose blaze and a sliver of white on her forehead, but she was positively tiny. And she could not even be considered a late foal, having been born at The Meadow on March 4 of the year before. Now, in June of 1976, a full fifteen months old, she was the size of an eleven- or twelve-month-old. Many a fine racehorse has been on the small side; indeed, numerous horsemen prefer smaller horses on the theory that compactness and lightness of weight are racing virtues. But this small? In honor of her extraordinary diminutiveness, Penny Tweedy decided to name her Hope For All—and hoped that there *would* be hope for her pony-sized yearling. With the other mare she had bred to Secretariat—Iberia—having been barren, Penny Tweedy felt that she had been ill served by her beloved red stallion.

Elsewhere in Virginia the situation was brighter. At Paul Mellon's Rokeby Farm, his chestnut colt out of All Beautiful was developing into, in Rokeby trainer Mackenzie Miller's words, "the dead spitting image of Secretariat, the only one I've seen or heard about who that can be said about. It's not just that he's got the same kind of blaze and the three white stockings and the same chestnut shade. In all my travels I have not seen a Secretariat colt or filly that matches the conformation of the big horse like the one Mr. Mellon got. I'm sure he's the only real match in the whole of Secretariat's first crop. And he's only a yearling. Wait until he's two and three. He'll look even more like Secretariat then than he does now."

The colt's dam, All Beautiful, had been the dam of Mellon's most successful horse, 1969 Horse of the Year, Arts and Letters. Mellon, a man of culture as well as wealth and a man with a fine appreciation for human and equine bloodlines, decided to name the yearling colt Debrett. The reference was to *Debrett's Peerage*, the studbook, so to speak, of England's aristocracy.

Raymond Guest was another horseman of wealth who labored over the names he gave his horses. His Secretariat yearling, the chestnut-turned-roan out of the gray Color Me Blue, was forming into a robust specimen despite the lack of his sire's extraordinary physique. He had started out life on the scrawny side because Color Me Blue had suffered from milk worms after foaling him. But once weaned he had filled out fast and by June of 1976 was taking on the proportions of a nicely fattened sales yearling. Guest had it in the back of his mind to race him in France, partly because of the well-known prejudice against roans in the United States. Guest was certain that most professional horse trainers here labored under that prejudice and did not approach the conditioning of roans with the patience or seriousness they brought to other colors. With France in mind, then, he chose the name Sacrebleu for his colt. It was a typically Guestian compound of dam and sire names transposed to French.

Of the twenty-eight Secretariat yearlings, Virginia had five. Seven others were scattered about Maryland, Florida, Texas, and California during the spring of 1976. But the lion's share of the Secretariats was still centered in the Kentucky bluegrass—sixteen. The most notorious of these among local horsemen was Nelson Bunker Hunt's Charming Alibi colt. In March, the chestnut had gone through the sudden transformation from baby to horse and by May he had grown and bulked out, except for his head and hindquarters, into a junior version of his sire. The colt's appearance was dominated by a thick neck, a broad, heavily muscled chest, and powerful shoulders and forearms. He was generously endowed with bone, and with his four white stockings and the traces of white on his face, he looked very much like his father's son indeed. Where he strayed in identicalness was in his head, which was large, heavy, and Roman-nosed. He was also longer in the back than Secretariat, and where the colt's back blended into his rump he was markedly narrower, the relative sparseness of his hindquarters accentuating the bulk of his fore. Some who saw him predicted that he would never be a good runner because of the length of his back and the distance between his fore- and hindquarters—they were too far apart for easy co-ordination. Others disagreed, claiming that he yet had a lot of growing to do and that, as his hindquarters filled out, they would "tuck up nicely" to his fore.

The colt was quartered at Hunt's Bluegrass Farm near Lexington and was being fattened for the Keeneland yearling sale in

July. Also at the farm was the Secretariat chestnut filly that Hunt had bought outright as a weanling from his partner, the Earl of Suffolk, at the November sale the year before. Hunt had decided to keep the filly, send her later in the year to his ranch in Texas to be broken and trained, and then ship her to France as a two-year-old to join his racing stable there. After considering a number of possible names for her, he reserved with The Jockey Club the name Superfast—another of the unfortunate monikers the first crop was being or was about to be tagged with. When one hardened observer of the racing scene learned what Hunt intended to name the filly, he cracked, "Now, there's a name that's guaranteed to ensure that the horse will never run a lick. He might as well call her Great Expectations."

Four other Secretariat yearlings quartered in Kentucky that spring were soon to be shipped overseas. One was Walter Haefner's chestnut filly out of Aladancer, who would be flown to Haefner's stud in Ireland in preparation for consignment to that country's premier thoroughbred auction later in the year.

Another was Stavros Niarchos' bay colt out of Artists Proof, which would be sent first to France for training and then to England for racing. Filling out nicely, although bearing little resemblance to Secretariat, the colt would be named Dactylographer.

The third yearling being readied for shipment to Europe was Jacques Wertheimer's colt out of Gleam II. The colt was to be a gift from Wertheimer to his wife, who would name him Sociologue.

The fourth Secretariat being prepared for an overseas flight from Lexington's airport was Tadao Tamashima's bay colt out of Rotondella. The colt left on May 12, 1976, for Tamashima's Meiwa Stud in Japan, and little would be heard about him again.

By June, the usual sales fever was once again mounting in Kentucky, but this time it was heightened by the knowledge that the Keeneland Association had catalogued seven Secretariat first-crop yearlings for the two-day auction. The first six yearlings were:

• Nelson Bunker Hunt's Charming Alibi colt;
• Tom Gentry's colt out of Levee Night, the mare Gentry had bought in foal at auction in the fall of 1974 from Claiborne Farm;

• Catesby Clay and partners' Spa II chestnut filly;
• Walter Jeffords' My Card chestnut filly;
• Jacqueline Getty's chestnut filly out of Windy's Daughter;
• Warner Jones' Jo Dan bay filly.

The seventh was a surprise. Bunker Hunt had changed his mind and decided to consign the filly he had intended to name Superfast. One had to wonder, however, in the light of future events, whether he really had changed his mind. The filly was not that good-looking. She had nothing of the maturity and stoutness of Hunt's Charming Alibi colt and was lacking in, by American standards, a distinguished pedigree on her dam's side. Yet he put a "reserve" on her of $250,000, which meant that if she did not sell for at least that amount Hunt would get her back.

Because of the presence of the first-crop Secretariats, the 1976 July sale became another national-media event. Newspaper reporters and TV crews poured into Lexington from all over the country, and on the eve of the sale's opening the tension and excitement over Keeneland were palpable. The previous year's sale had gotten some national publicity because two consigned yearlings had been "horsenapped" from their stalls in the dead of night, never to be seen again. The security precautions being taken for the Secretariat yearlings merely sharpened the edge of the tension.

The sale was opened by the gavel of auctioneer Tom Caldwell shortly after 1 P.M. in the afternoon of Monday, July 19. This was the first of four sessions and it was to be preclimactic. One hundred and fifty horses would have to be sold between then and the end of the night session before the first of the Secretariats entered the ring. The Keeneland Association had artfully arranged the catalogue to milk the most suspense possible from the sale. Numerous breeders trying to sell less celebrated yearlings grumbled angrily at the ploy, believing that by focusing all the attention on the Secretariats the auctioneers would cause their horses to bring less money than they otherwise might. "Out of fairness to the rest of us they should have run those seven Secretariats right off from the top," complained one consigner. "Get all the big money spent and then have an auction as usual so that the rest of us would have a shot. As it was, people were failing to bid on a lot of good yearlings hoping that they'd have enough dough left to go after one of the Secretariats."

The first yearling into the ring that Monday afternoon was a sleek filly sired by the top European racehorse-turned-stallion Rheingold. She was from Rheingold's first crop and her pedigree was all but obscure to anyone but the seasoned expert. That she sold for $65,000 to A. T. Doyle, an Irishman who had carved a profitable career for himself as a trainer and bloodstock agent in California, was a sign that money was going to flow during the coming two days.

"Hip No. 2," the second horse in the ring, was a well-muscled chestnut colt by the outstanding American runner and sire Graustark out of a modest mare called Aerielette. The yearling colt was knocked down at $85,000, another good sign.

But then, as the afternoon session wore on, it became evident that many of the horse buyers in the packed auction pavilion were holding back. Of the eighty-three yearlings led into the ring, only four top-bred ones caused figures of $100,000 or more to be registered on the computerized toteboard suspended above the auctioneer's platform. The highest price paid was $136,000 for a colt by the fashionable stallion Hoist the Flag out of a proven producer named Lemon Soufflé. Almost everyone was waiting for the evening session, and even more so for the next day's sessions.

The first night session began shortly after 8:30 P.M. The day's weather had been steamingly hot, and sundown brought little relief. The two Secretariats scheduled to be auctioned toward the end of the session were Jacqueline Getty's handsome filly and Catesby Clay's less comely filly, both chestnuts. The Keeneland people had catalogued the Getty-Blackman filly first in the hope that her sharp appearance and sleek lines would fetch a high sales price—perhaps upward of $250,000. The excitement might then carry over to the Clay filly, which was to follow the Getty yearling into the ring only ten minutes later, and knock her down for more than she was worth on the basis of both her dam's pedigree and her conformation. As Jacqueline Getty debarked from her air-conditioned limousine into the thick heat of the Kentucky evening and pushed her way through the milling crowd in front of the Keeneland sales pavilion, she was nervously thinking in terms of $300,000 for her filly. Following her into the pavilion, Catesby Clay and his partner Howard Noonan were much bleaker in their estimates for their Spa II filly. It was clear from the afternoon session that big buyers were not being beguiled by the fashionability of stallions but were concentrating their money on the degree of black type in the dams and their bloodlines. Spa II had insufficient black type. They could only hope that some rich buyer would be willing to throw financial caution to the winds just to acquire a first-crop Secretariat—any first-crop Secretariat. They felt that they would be lucky to get $100,000 for their filly.

The evening session quickly turned out to be a reversal of the afternoon's bidding, no doubt due to the fact that the catalogue was packed with a number of far more stylish pedigree groupings. Led into the ring were a succession of yearlings by such top-flight and proven sires as Northern Dancer, Exclusive Native, Round Table, Sir Ivor, Buckpasser, Never Bend, Raise a Native, Vaguely Noble (the sire of Dahlia, a half sister to Bunker Hunt's Charming Alibi colt), Graustark, Reviewer, and Damascus. The final-gavel prices skyrocketed as the evening wore on, with several yearlings going for more than $200,000. As the sale approached Hip No. 151, it was getting close to midnight and not a seat was empty. All eyes were on Jacqueline Getty, for No. 151 was her filly. She knew that A. T. Doyle (Tommy to his friends and clients), her California trainer, was going to bid on the filly, but she doubted that he would go over $200,000. Being a good Catholic, she prayed that someone else in the pavilion would shoot for the heavens.

Finally the filly was brought in, her bright chestnut coat gleaming like a freshly minted penny under the spotlights. She pranced alertly on her toes as the handler made quick jerks on her mouth with his shank. As her pedigree was recited by Tom Caldwell's assistant, she whinnied loudly, as if in approval. Caldwell took up the bidding with a call for $150,000. When he got no response he dropped it to $100,000. Suddenly it started and in ten seconds, in $10,000 increments, it was at $150,000.

It hung for a moment at $150,000 and Jacqueline Getty squirmed in her seat. Then someone else came in at $160,000. It was Tommy Doyle, beginning to sense the possibility of a small coup—he knew that Mrs. Getty, a friend and client, was hoping for $300,000. Doyle was raised to $170,000 and he hesitated. Someone else came in at $180,000—was it Jackie Getty?—and he went to $190,000, thinking of the syndicate of friends in his native Ireland he had interested in owning the filly. Oddly, the action stopped. Despite Tom Caldwell's urgings—"Just look at the racing record of her dam, folks, you don't get a chance to get such a filly out of two great racehorses every day"—no one was willing to go to $200,000. The filly, still majestically prancing in the ring, was Windy's Daughter's first foal; despite Windy's Daughter's racing feats, she was an untested producer. The bidding continued to hang at $190,000 despite Caldwell's further pressure, now blatant. Jacqueline Getty knew it was over and scrunched down in her seat. The gavel finally fell and Tommy Doyle owned the filly.

Even the newspapermen in the press gallery were disappointed. The first Secretariat yearling at auction had fallen far below expectations. Secretariat was supposed to break—no, shatter—thoroughbred sales records with his first crop. This was no news story.

"Hang around until tomorrow night," they were told by their colleagues in the racing press.

The advice was well taken. The following afternoon Walter Jeffords' comely chestnut filly out of his good mare and producer My Card sold for $170,000. It did not take long at the final evening session for all the predictions of the real excitement of Secretariat's first crop to come true. The first of the four remaining yearlings to be sold that night was led into the ring shortly after the session opened. Hip No. 279, he was Bunker Hunt's startlingly muscled Charming Alibi colt, and his entrance brought a gasp from the packed house. He was no stranger, since he had been looked over and inspected hundreds of times in the Keeneland stable area during the previous few days. Nevertheless his majestic, mature bearing and the raw power implicit beneath his copper coat as his muscles rippled and fine-edged under the lights made it clear that he was "the horse" of the sale. The only fault any of the knowledgeable horsemen in the pavilion could find with the colt was that he might be a little over at the knees. But it was a minor fault, shared by his famous half sister Dahlia, and it had not prevented her from becoming the leading female money-winner of all time.

The collective gasp at the long-anticipated appearance in the ring of Hunt's splendid colt suddenly transformed itself into a hush as announcer Tom Hammond began to real off the colt's pedigree. The obese Hunt, uncomfortable in the limelight, stared bemusedly at his colt through thick eyeglasses. And then the action began as Tom Caldwell took over in his traditional auctioneer's turkey gobble.

The bidding started at $500,000, the reserve put on the yearling by Hunt, and that in itself brought another gasp. Records had been set in each of the three previous years for a sales yearling. At the 1975 sale a yearling colt by Raise a Native had gone for $715,000, breaking the previous year's record for another Raise a Native colt of $625,000, which had in turn broken the 1973 record of $600,000 paid for the Bold Ruler colt who had become Wajima. When the opening bid on the colt of Bunker Hunt immediately jumped to $700,000, the crowd knew that on this night yet another record would be set. It was simply a question of by how much.

In an instant the $700,000 was nudged to $716,000 by auctioneer Caldwell—an acknowledgment of the previous year's record price and an encouragement to the several bidders. He needn't have bothered, for a call immediately came in for $800,000. It was followed by $900,000. The bidding was so rapid-fire that the electronic toteboard over Caldwell's head was behind almost from the start.

Then came a bid for $1,000,000. Its source was Aaron U. Jones, a wealthy Oregon lumber tycoon and racing man who was representing a syndicate of equally wealthy friends. It was becoming clearer and clearer that only a syndicate would chance such heady prices on an unproven horse. The first seven-figure bid in the history of public horse auctions had been made in less than twenty seconds. It was a milestone and was duly recognized by a wave of cheers, shouts, and applause.

Caldwell paused for a few seconds to let the commotion die. He asked for $1,100,000 and got it without a moment's hesitation. The bidding jumped to $1,200,000 and then to $1,250,000. It continued to climb, to $1,300,000, then to $1,350,000, then to

$1,375,000. It slowed there, as though the various bidders were jockeying for position like a field of horses turning for home.

Caldwell took a bid for $1,400,000, then paused to allow the three different bidders to confer with their potential syndicate partners. "At these prices," he remarked dryly into his microphone, "we can afford to give 'em a little time."

The bidding and conferring continued until a bid of $1,500,000 was reached. And there it stopped. The bid was made by a Canadian named John Sikura, largely unknown to the American thoroughbred establishment, on behalf of a syndicate of several wealthy fellow Canadians he had formed for the purpose of buying the colt. When it was obvious that no one else was going to top the bid, auctioneer Caldwell closed the sale with a "Once—twice—sold!" He banged down his gavel and, bending syntax a bit, then said, "Folks, this colt here is Canadian bound."

The pavilion exploded in noise, startling the oversized yearling and sending him into a nervous flinch. It was a phenomenal, unexpected, and somewhat draining experience. People had anticipated that the colt might bring $1,000,000, maybe a shade more than that. But $1,500,000—it was astonishing! The price was more than twice the previous year's record of $715,000. It was not only the highest price ever obtained at public auction, it was also the largest cash transaction in the history of the thoroughbred industry.

Bedlam reigned. People swarmed around Bunker Hunt shouting congratulations. The Keeneland officials held the colt in the ring for a phalanx of photographers. The media descended on Sikura and the other principals of the syndicate for interviews.

Eventually the sale was called back to order. The $1,500,000 paid for the Secretariat colt was contagious, for there followed a series of further high-money sales on yearlings from other stallions, the highest for $550,000 on another Hunt yearling by Vaguely Noble. And there were still three Secretariats to go.

The next of the Secretariats led in, an hour after the $1,500,000 colt, was Warner Jones' Jo Dan filly. She went to a syndicate for $190,000. She was followed by Tom Gentry's lean bay colt out of Levee Night, and the price on him went to $275,000 before the gavel fell. Finally, as the sale drew to a close, Bunker Hunt's star-crossed filly out of Zest II—the one that had failed to sell as a weanling and that he was going to call Superfast—was led in. The bidding on her was desultory and failed to reach the reserve Hunt had put on her.

It was hard to say whether the hysteria over the Charming Alibi colt's sale had negatively affected the sale of the three later Secretariats or not. Tom Gentry, for one, thought it had—he had been hoping for at least $500,000 for his Levee Night colt—and he was angry about it. So was Warner Jones over the fate of his Jo Dan filly, this despite the fact that Jo Dan was an untested producer and had been unraced. "Didn't matter a bit," he later said. "The filly was worth a hell of a lot more than $190,000. Just look at all that good black type in the second and third dams, Cosmah and Almahmoud, plus the Buckpasser-Tom Fool blood in Jo Dan's sire. No, sir, no way that filly was worth only $190,000."

In any event, it was a record sale not only for Keeneland but for any stallion in history. The seven yearlings from Secretariat had brought in nearly $1,250,000 more than the previous record gross for a single stallion's progeny, which was set the year before when eleven sons and daughters of Round Table earned $1,365,000. Secretariat's gross from seven yearlings was $2,610,000. Moreover, Secretariat shattered the average-per-yearling sales record with a figure of $372,857 for his seven yearlings. The second leading sire of the sale was Vaguely Noble, with an average per yearling of $181,667, a figure attained by virtue of the sale of twelve yearlings.

As in his racing career, Secretariat had proved to be a super-horse as a first-year stallion. It now remained to be seen if he could sustain his reputation. The question of whether he could or not depended on how his first-crop yearlings performed a year or two hence. The final test was at hand.

CHAPTER 10

Initial Training

The Saratoga auctions a few weeks later repeated Secretariat's historic performance as a sire of sales yearlings, albeit on a smaller scale, since traditionally the average prices obtained at Saratoga were considerably less than those in Kentucky.

Three Secretariat yearlings went on the block in Fasig-Tipton's Saratoga sales pavilion—the Gilman brothers' big roan colt out of Show Stopper, the Firestones' Exclusive Dancer colt, also a roan, and Laddie Dance's chestnut filly out of his mare Guest Room. The Gilman colt fetched by far the highest price of the sale, $550,000, breaking the previous record by $200,000. Firestone's roan took down $275,000; the Dance filly, $175,000. Secretariat's average was $333,333, another record, and was almost $200,000 more than the average of the second leading stallion of the sale—Sir Ivor.

All in all, the nine Secretariat yearlings sold at Keeneland and Saratoga had brought an unprecedented average price of $377,778 per horse. Even if the $1.5 million Charming Alibi colt had not been sold, the eight other auction yearlings would have averaged $237,500—still a record-shattering figure. The magic of Secretariat continued to live. But by October, as the sales yearlings and the home-bred horses were being readied for their initial training in anticipation of being turned into race-eligible two-year-olds, their various owners grew more nervous than ever. Would the magic—not to mention their investment judgment—be sustained by any of the horses in the first crop?

Statistically, from any given crop of a stallion's progeny, there will emerge at best only two or three who will prove to be superior racehorses. The owners of the first-crop Secretariats knew this. They also knew that many fine stallions before Secretariat had produced their best sons and daughters from their first crops, while others did not get good horses until later crops. The most that each member of the fraternity of owners could hope for was that he or she would be the lucky owner should anything worthwhile have been produced by Secretariat from his first crop.

In celebration of Keeneland auctioneer Tom Caldwell's closing words upon the sale of the $1,500,000 Charming Alibi colt, the yearling's new owners—the Canadian syndicate—named him Canadian Bound. Bunker Hunt reinvested some of his earnings by buying a share in the seven-member syndicate. The other members wanted him in so that he would be available to advise them on the best course to follow with the colt. Their original plans were to race him in the United States and Canada, something that Montrealer Jean-Louis Levesque intended to do with the Secretariat filly he had gotten from his mare Arctic Dancer. But Hunt had earned the bulk of his thoroughbred millions by racing his best horses in France, where purses were consistently higher than in the United States or elsewhere. He convinced the rest of the syndicate to allow him to oversee Canadian Bound's novice training at his Texas ranch, and then to send him to France to compete under the tutelage of his trainer there, Maurice Zilber. From the very beginning, then, the $1,500,000 colt, expected by many to be the most brilliant performer of Secretariat's first crop, was destined not to be available to the American racing public. Nor was Superfast, the filly Hunt had twice retrieved from the auction ring. He scheduled her for shipment to Zilber's training yard at Chantilly as well.*

With Walter Haefner's Aladancer filly in Ireland (although

---

* Eventually rejected by Zilber as a good racing prospect, Superfast would be returned by Hunt to the United States to race as a three-year-old in California.

she would soon return to the United States after her record-breaking Irish auction sale to another Canadian in September of 1976), with Hunt's two yearlings scheduled for shipment to France, with the Niarchos colt already in France along with the Wertheimer colt, with the Laddie Dance filly (purchased at Saratoga by a partnership) also due to be sent to France, with the Getty filly (purchased at Keeneland by an Irish trainer on behalf of a syndicate) soon to be shipped to Ireland, and with the Tamashima colt long since gone to Japan, American racing fans were left with twenty of the original twenty-eight foals to contemplate as potential performers at United States tracks in the coming year. Given the normal attrition rate brought about by growth problems and training injuries, the public could expect to see at most ten of the twenty run as two-year-olds. But because of fears on the part of several of the owners of injury or failure, the public would in fact see considerably fewer perform in 1977.

The initial training of sound, healthy thoroughbreds usually commences in the early fall of their yearling season. It consists basically of "breaking" the yearlings to the saddle and to the control, through bridle, bit, and reins, of a rider on their backs. Many of the Secretariat first crop were broken and received their novice training at the farms of their owners. Others, whose owners did not have the facilities for such training, were sent to farms that did or to places that specialized in breaking and training for the racetrack. One such place was a compact cluster of barns on a few acres of private property immediately behind the Keeneland racetrack. Owned and operated by John Ward, Jr., a Kentucky hardboot celebrated for his skill and wisdom in training yearlings, the training center had served as alma mater to many fine racehorses, including the durable, popular Forego.†
John Ward's father had started the center in 1947 to accommodate the many new owners who were getting into racing but

---

† Forego was foaled in 1970, the same year as Secretariat, and was roundly defeated by the Triple Crown winner in the 1973 Kentucky Derby, the only race in which the two competed. A gelding, Forego could not stand at stud and therefore continued his career as a runner. In the following years he won enough races to join Secretariat as one of the few earners of more than $1,000,000, indeed becoming the second-place money-earner after Kelso.

did not have training facilities of their own. His father's brother was Sherrill Ward, a veteran racing trainer who had developed Forego and continued in 1976 to oversee his racing career.

Three of the Secretariat first-crop yearlings were sent to the Ward barns in September. The first to arrive, fittingly enough, was the first of the colts to have been sold at public auction. This was the jugheaded bay out of E. V. Benjamin, Jr.'s Chou Croute that had been sold at Keeneland as a weanling to Kentucky breeder Ben Walden and his partner, Chicago financier Wells Hardesty.

"We either had one of the greatest bargains of all time or we'd bought a pig in a poke," said Walden. "Actually, it hardly mattered. Even if the colt was not going to turn out to be much as a racehorse, we figured he would still have considerable value at stud. If he didn't race, or prove a dud, he'd still be able to command a stud fee in the neighborhood of $20,000. If he did well at the racetrack, on the other hand, his fee could go up to as high as $50,000, depending on how well. So we planned to race him from the beginning."

Immediately after their purchase, Walden and Hardesty had syndicated the weanling into nine shares and vanned him back to Walden's Dearborn Farm at Midway, Kentucky. There he was turned out for ten months until it came time for breaking and early training. Some might have thought that a fitting paddock for such a valuable youngster might have been an outdoor padded cell. Weanlings and yearlings, as boisterous as puppies, can injure themselves in untold ways before ever reaching the racetrack as two-year-olds. But the young Secretariat colt, whose name would soon be registered by the Jockey Club as Confidant, was afforded no special care in his preschool months, any more than he was provided with the special security guards one might have expected—given the increasing rash of horsenappings that were taking place in the United States and Europe.‡

"We turned him out with some tough colts," says Walden, "and he got into his share of scrapes. He was even turned out

‡ Not long before, a valuable racemare named Carnauba, owned by Nelson Bunker Hunt, had been kidnapped and offered for ransom in Italy. When Hunt refused to deal with the horsenappers, nothing more was heard of the mare until she was found, scrawny and undernourished, in the stable of an Italian girls' school.

with an Angus bull for a while." The idea was that young horses must learn their lessons in boldness early by fending for themselves in the company of peers and adversaries. "It makes no difference whether a yearling is a $250,000 Secretariat or a $500 plug," Walden said. "Whichever, the youngster who is coddled will show it later, coming up timid when asked to bully his way through a pack in a race. Look at the way Seattle Slew bounced back from all that interference in this year's Kentucky Derby [1977]. He took a terrible beating out of the gate, but by the first turn he was in the lead. You can be sure that it was not just breeding that accounted for that, but the will he developed as a yearling when he was turned out with a pack of other yearlings. Assuming that a horse has the natural speed built into his bones, you can often tell in advance how good he'll be by the way he handles himself in the yearling paddock. I always look for the take-charge yearling. And Confidant was no wilting violet after we turned him out at Dearborn."

And when Confidant arrived at John Ward's training center ten months later, he was absolutely headstrong. He had grown well in the interim, although he would be nothing like Secretariat in size, bulk, or color. His physical resemblance was to Chou Croute—short-backed, thick-rumped, still a bit narrow in the fore, still Roman-headed despite the fact that he had almost grown to his head. But if Secretariat had failed to stamp Confidant with his physical characteristics, he had produced a nicely conformed and sound yearling. And, said Ward, he had passed on to the colt his distinctive personality.

"I think the one characteristic of the three Secretariats we had," Ward reminisced midway through 1977, "and I've heard other people who had his yearlings say the same thing, was that they all seemed to have the same bold, bullish temperament that their father had and weren't as quick to accept the way things were going to be once they got into the first stages of their training. Confidant got to the point where he wanted to be just a bit sultry and petulant. I suspect this came from the Bold Ruler and Nasrullah line, which was always on the tough side. A tougher horse never lived than Bold Ruler, considering all the ailments he had as a youngster. That was the real secret of the success of the blood. Hundreds of stallions can produce simple competitive racing ability. But these boys transmitted that something extra, which I would call pure will. You take two horses of equal racing ability but one that has more ingrained will than the other, and the one with more determination is the one that's going to win time after time. With will goes a bit of temper. It's a trait I like to see in a horse. Most good horses have a touch of temper."

Ben Walden, who made a point of looking at all the first-crop Secretariats quartered in Kentucky as yearlings, agreed. He is known among his fellow horsemen as a man who understands the equine temperament as well as any human being. "The Secretariats I saw all had their own minds," he said, "and they asserted them now and then. But they also had ability. Teaching them to balance their temperament with their native ability is a fine art, like walking a tightrope. That's why I sent Confidant to John Ward. There's no better in the business."

Unlike an older horse's daily training at a racetrack, which amounts largely to conditioning for a familiar athletic task, a yearling's training consists of a working routine entirely foreign to the playful and undisciplined life he has known at home in his paddock. "You can compare yearlings to children of five or six about to be sent off to kindergarten," explains Ward. "You're taking them away from the place they've been raised and all the security routines they've become accustomed to and all the buddies they ran with. It's like having to wean them all over again."

About to embark on the breaking-and-training regimen, the yearlings may be edgy, even volatile during their first few days in new surroundings, but nowhere are there signs of the rough-and-tumble, knock-down battles seen in the dusty corrals of Wild West movies. Breaking, which might more appropriately be called schooling, is a calm, deliberate, progressive educational curriculum in which the young horse is taught in building-block steps to accept the saddle on his back, to balance the weight of a rider, and to respond to his requests in a mannerly fashion.

John Ward's father often said before his death, "There are no mean or unmanageable horses except those made to be mean and unmanageable by the men who train them." The younger Ward carried on that philosophy at Keeneland. "The first thing we do is gain the yearlings' confidence," he says. "Then we teach them the correct thing first, before they can learn bad habits, because the first thing a horse learns is the things he remembers longest, good or bad. In the first few days we try to get their confidence through a routine of gently handling and grooming so that they learn that the people around them aren't going to hurt them. It was the same with Confidant and the other two Secretariats we had as it was with any horse that comes here."

Yearlings broken at the Ward center eventually practice their lessons on Keeneland's track, next door to his barns, but this comes a good six weeks after preliminary lessons begin in the barns. Confidant arrived at Ward's on September 4, and after a few days of routine handling and grooming in his stall and exercise walks around the shed row at the end of a shank, he was ready to take his first step toward becoming a racehorse.

Fitted with a chiffney bit—a round piece of metal less severe than a conventional bit—he was taught to turn both ways in his stall as he walked from corner to corner in a circle. Through this exercise he learned to associate the pressure on each side of his mouth with turning in that direction. The next day the exercise was repeated, since a horse learns best through repetition. Then Confidant, still in his stall, was introduced to the feel of a girth around his belly and a saddle pad on his back. When teaching a yearling to get used to the pressure of a girth, Ward insists on using webbed surcingles rather than elastic or leather girths. This is to eliminate the risk of pinching the yearling's skin, a pinch he might resent the rest of his life and cause him to be difficult to be properly saddled. "The first day we ease the saddle pad on slowly, so they usually pay no attention, it being as light as it is. Then," says Ward, "we slip the surcingle over the pad and fasten it loosely."

While continuing to practice his turning lessons in his twelve-by-fourteen-foot stall, Confidant felt the surcingle tightened a bit more each day. With the first real pressure he humped up and fought it a little. But the reaction was not violent, since the groom holding the chiffney immediately began walking him again to distract him.

At John Ward's barns along with Confidant were the home-bred Guest Room bay filly owned by the Hexters and the chestnut, bent-knee filly out of Catesby Clay's mare Spa II that had been bought at the Keeneland sale for the bargain-basement price of $75,000 by Kentucky coal-company operator Andrew Adams. Adams had recently sold some of his holdings for a reported $20,000,000 and was making his entry into the thoroughbred business with his purchase. Despite her misshapen knee, he had said, "The filly looked just so much like her sire with her chestnut color and white markings that I had to have her and was prepared to go to $200,000 or so to get her." Adams assigned the task of naming the filly to his wife, Reny, and she came up with Sexetary. "At first it was a kind of joke as I played around with possible names," Reny Adams later said. "You know, it is so hard to get a good name registered, since just about every good name you can think of is always taken. But 'Sexetary' began to stick in my mind and after a while I knew I couldn't call her anything but that—she was such a pretty, sexy-looking horse. I'm sort of proud of the name, really."

Many establishment breeders and racing people groaned when they heard about the name. It seemed untoward and somehow cheapening for the offspring of so revered a racehorse as Secretariat. If the filly proved to be a winner of note, it was felt, her accomplishments would be overshadowed by the wisecracks that would descend on her name. "Don't worry," exclaimed veteran breeder Leslie Combs II, "with a knee like she has she'll be fortunate to get to the racetrack." But Adams was determined to get her to the track; he even hoped to see her be the first of the Secretariats to race and win. She had been a late foal, one of the last to be born. Yet by the time she arrived at John Ward's she was farther along in her physical development than Senator's Choice, who was among the first to be born and was physiologically three months older, and Confidant, also a later foal. She was, as well, remarkably mature in temperament. "Secretariat was big and kind," says John Ward, "and this filly Sexetary was a lot like him in spirit, not to mention appearance. She immediately showed she had a lot of sense. She learned fast and showed an eagerness to get on with things without doing the silly stuff most other yearlings get into. I always believed that fillies mature faster than colts, but Sexetary was an exceptional case. The only problem with her was, could she overcome the disadvantage of that crooked knee and really become the racehorse her spirit seemed to indicate she wanted to become? She showed a lot of heart for the business, but you've got to have natural speed to go along with the heart."

By the third day the yearlings at Ward's were accustomed to bit and girth and were led out of their stalls in a group to the enclosed shed row that circled the barn. There they practiced walking in tandem for fifteen minutes a day. Because they were on high-protein rations for growth and had not been getting the exercise they had previously gotten when turned out on their home farms, they overflowed with unused energy. Of the three Secretariats, Confidant became the most fractious during the shed-row walks, jumping and bucking and nipping at his walking mate and handler. "But he was all right on the whole," says Ward, "probably because he had been handled so much before he came here, having been through an important sale. That filly —Sexetary—was downright docile, just as attentive and down-to-business as you could hope."

Senator's Choice, the third of the Secretariats at Ward's, was the opposite of Sexetary and even more bumptious in temperament than Confidant. "Those chestnuts that came from Secretariat seemed to be like him in disposition," said Mike O'Dea, a groom at the Ward training center. "But the bays I seen, colt or filly, was always just the opposite, at least as yearlings. Now that Senator's Choice, it wasn't that she was mean or evil-tempered or nothing, just plain high-strung and hard to handle. Like she took her temper from the name of her mother (Scaremenot). She was just out to prove that nothing any of us human beings did or said to her was going to scare her into doing nothing she didn't want to do. 'Course, she only kept that up for a couple of weeks. Eventually all of them come around, one way or another. I suppose it was because she wasn't in any of the auctions and wasn't getting much handling during all those months in the summer."

When the yearlings at Ward's easily accepted the feel of the tightened surcingle, usually by the end of the first week, Ward and his assistants gently introduced them to the first sensation of weight on their backs. In the case of each of the Secretariats, there were still no bronco-busting exhibitions. With Sexetary, for instance, a small, lightweight rider was merely boosted up to lean halfway across her back while two grooms stood at

Now a gelding, Mellon's Debrett as a three-year-old. Most observers agreed on his resemblance to Secretariat. But the resemblance was purely superficial, since he in no way ran like his father. *(photo courtesy Paul Mellon)*

The first-crop Secretariat bay filly bred by Kentuckian Warner L. Jones out of his mare Jo Dan. A late yearling when this photo was taken, she was named Punctuation and was acquired by Georgia's Dogwood Farm racing stable. Except for an exhibition at New Jersey's Meadowlands, she did not race as a two-year-old and failed to distinguish herself at three. *(photo courtesy Dogwood Farm)*

Oatlands, the chestnut Secretariat filly out of the Firestones' mare Gamba, as a yearling. Too growthy and awkward to race as a two-year-old, and drawing a sinfully low bid when put up for auction by the Firestones, was sent to Ireland in 1978 and had a modest success as a three-year-old before being turned into a broodmare. *(photo courtesy Bertram Firestone)*

Seclusive, the Firestones' first Secretariat colt out of Exclusive Dancer. A roan, he won a three-year-old maiden race at Saratoga on his fourth try in August 1978, and followed this with a victory in an allowance race at Belmont in September. The victim of a serious illness as a yearling, he will probably remain best known as a full brother to General Assembly, the most promising of Secretariat's second-crop colts. *(photo courtesy Rocketts Mill Farm)*

Paul Mellon's mare All Beautiful, a few days before she foaled
Mellon's first Secretariat offspring. *(photo courtesy Allen Studio)*

Seclusive winning his September 1978 allowance race at Belmont Park, Jean Cruguet up. (*photo courtesy Bertram Firestone*)

Jacqueline Getty and partners' Centrifolia winning a stakes in Ireland as a three-year-old before being retired for breeding. (*photo courtesy Jacqueline Getty*)

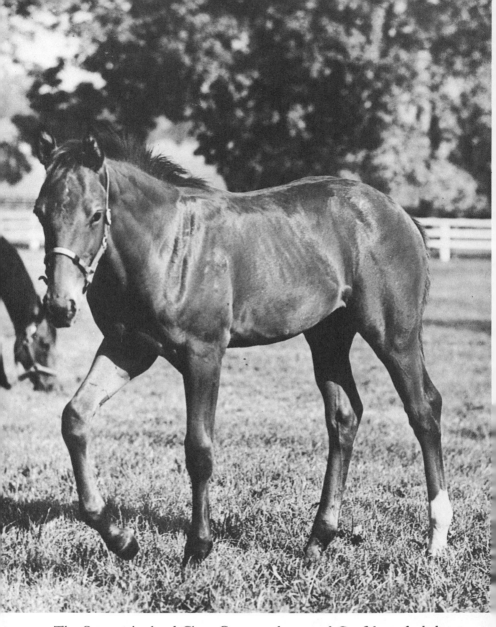

The Secretariat-bred Chou Croute colt, named Confidant, foaled April 1975. *(photo courtesy E. V. Benjamin, Jr.)*

her head in her stall—a procedure called bellying. The rider then slid off and repeated the procedure several times. Bellying occurred over the next three days while the other lessons were continued. Then the filly was led around the shed row with the rider bellied on her back for a few days.

When Sexetary was thoroughly used to the weight, her chiffney was replaced by a conventional bit and bridle, and the rider was able to straddle her without protest. "She jumped once or twice when she was first bellied," recalls Ward, "but by the time our boy straddled her she was accustomed to the sensation of having a weight on her back and made no fuss. It was pretty much the same for Confidant and Senator's Choice."

For a few days the yearlings were led around the shed row by their grooms, who were holding onto a shank, with riders straddling their backs. Then a saddle was added, held in place by a tightened girth. At the end of this period, the grooms with their lead shanks were removed and the yearlings found themselves in the complete control of their riders as they continued to walk in pairs around the shed row. The riders applied bit pressure through their reins—left and right—and the horses responded as taught. Except for an occasional nervous jitter or exuberant buck of hind legs, the yearlings were for all practical purposes saddle-broken. Now began their real education.

It began with jogging—a slow trot—with each yearling learning in the period of several days to further balance its rider's weight on its back. "When Confidant got to jogging," remembers Ward, "it was difficult to get him going. The rider had to do quite a bit of kicking him in the sides, because he wanted to pin his ears back and sulk, to be resentful and fight. This was just the natural juvenile orneriness of most colt yearlings I've dealt with. The two fillies, on the other hand, took to it right away."

Learning to balance the rider's weight—120 or 130 pounds—was one of the most important things the yearlings practiced over the following week. "When they first jogged with weight on their backs they were awkward," Ward says, "especially going around the turns in the shed row. Sometimes they would take the turns too sharply, becoming all out of kilter, while other times they'd not go sharply enough and would end up banging into the wall. At the beginning they were like kids trying to learn how to ride a bicycle."

Elsewhere in Kentucky during September and October, a few of the other first-crop Secretariat yearlings were undergoing similar schooling. At Claiborne Farm, the gray swayback colt owned in partnership by Dinny Phipps and Claiborne, Brilliant Protégé, was in the capable hands of the farm's yearling manager. He was a "growthy" yearling, meaning that he was physically immature in his bone structure and musculature and, as a result, exceptionally awkward and inept. These had been characteristics of Secretariat as a yearling. But unlike Secretariat, Brilliant Protégé was meek and lacking in boldness. Seth Hancock was continuing to predict that he would amount to nothing as a racehorse, and was publicly projecting his disappointment in the gray onto the entire crop. "I'm just not happy with the first crop," he said at the time. "A lot of conformational defects, and few of 'em have gotten much from Secretariat. I'm much happier with what I've seen with this year's foals. More of 'em look like Secretariat, and I believe they'll do much better at the racetrack, if not at the yearling sales."*

But it was beyond the traditional breeding ground of the bluegrass country that most of the Secretariats were being broken and trained. The largest concentration was by then in Virginia. Paul Mellon's chestnut colt Debrett—the one that most people thought was the closest to his sire in appearance, spirit, and conformation—was under tack at Mellon's elegant Rokeby Farm. He too was growthy, however, and Mellon intended to go slow with him, letting him do nothing more than jog until well into his two-year-old season. Many a growthy yearling has been irrevocably injured by the stresses of hard training at too young an age when their cannon bones have not sufficiently hardened and their knees have not yet joined. Mellon was intent on avoiding such injuries to all his horses, but especially to Debrett, and did

---

* During the spring of 1976 Secretariat's second crop had been foaled, and in September and October it was in the process of being weaned. From his second crop he produced forty live foals from covers to forty-four mares, several of whom had been the dams of first-crop horses.

not intend to put him on a racetrack for hard conditioning until he was at least 2½ years old.

Raymond Guest felt the same way about Sacrebleu, his roan colt out of Color Me Blue. The colt was training nicely and showed a high-spirited, inbred eagerness to run once he was introduced to the training track at Guest's Powhaten Plantation in Virginia. But Guest's chief trainer, Patrick Graham, was under strict orders to go easy on the roan, who despite his color bore a strong physical resemblance to his sire and in Guest's words "continued to have a willing, charming personality." Guest planned to keep him out of hard training until the end of the two-year-old season, "and then see what we've got as a three-year-old prospect."

Eastward at Penny Tweedy's Meadow Stud, her undersized chestnut filly, Hope For All, continued to lag behind the farm's other yearlings in physical development. She was broken and put into light schooling nevertheless, although it was likely that she would not get to the races as a two-year-old, if at all.

Nearby was Rocketts Mill Farm, to which the roan colt out of Bert and Diana Firestone's Exclusive Dancer, sold the previous August at Saratoga for $275,000, had been brought. Rocketts Mill, a historic farm that had fallen into disrepair during the Depression, was purchased and refurbished by thoroughbred enthusiast Edward C. Stevens after he quit his job as a sales executive in 1966 to go into the horse business. Stevens quickly established the farm as a thoroughbred training center, much like John Ward's at Keeneland. Using his sales skills, he persuaded a number of prominent owners to send horses to him for pretrack schooling and conditioning. Thereafter he moved into breeding and racing, mostly by forming syndications, and at the 1976 Saratoga yearling sale he put together a syndicate of sixteen members, including Bert Firestone, to buy Firestone's roan.

No sooner did the colt arrive at Rocketts Mill in late August, ready to start training, than near-tragedy struck. He was afflicted by a severe case of salmonella poisoning and was saved from death only by the ministrations of Dr. Daniel Flynn of the Georgetown Veterinary Hospital in Charlottesville, Virginia, where he spent six weeks recovering. Given the name Seclusive, he was returned in good health, although still thin and weak, to Rocketts Mill in late October and was finally broken. "If his will to run," said Stevens, "is as strong as his will to live, he's going to be one devil of a runner."

Virginia was now the home of another of Secretariat's roans—the oversized Show Stopper colt sold for $550,000 at Saratoga by the Gilman brothers. The colt was bought by a syndicate headed by James A. Scully, a former sportswriter who had made a small fortune in thoroughbred syndications and whose biggest coup had been the syndicated purchase of Wajima as a yearling in 1973 for the then-record $625,000. The Scully syndicate, which included among its five partners Mrs. Daniel Evans of Virginia, Spendthrift Farm of Lexington, Kentucky, and Aaron U. Jones of California, sent the expensive yearling to veteran horseman L. Clay Camp's Glenmore Farm in Keswick, Virginia, for breaking and schooling. By October, the colt, who was named Grey Legion, was broken and in light training. Like most of the other Secretariats to be broken that fall, he would be withheld from further formal instruction by mid-November and turned out to do more growing. Serious race training would resume in February of the following year, with the colt, assuming he remained healthy, to be sent to the racetrack in April. Grey Legion was scheduled to be placed under the tutelage of the well-known and popular racing conditioner Laz Barrera, a Cuban who had reached the apex of his training career the year before when, under his tutelage, Bold Forbes won the Kentucky Derby and Belmont. A great deal was expected of Grey Legion, as might have been evident by his sales price, which was the second highest of the first-crop yearlings. Not only did he have Secretariat's breeding and size—by November he was already sixteen hands high and, in Clay Camp's words, "built like a supple tank" —but also his dam, Show Stopper, was a full sister to champion racehorse and sire Raise a Native.

The last of the yearlings in training in Virginia was Diana Firestone's Oatlands, the somewhat delicate chestnut filly out of her mare, Gamba. Both of the Firestones were "stall muckers"— skilled riders and handlers who involved themselves directly in the breaking and schooling of their own horses. Indeed, once Oatlands was broken early in October amid the riotous early-fall foliage of Catoctin Stud, Diana Firestone was mounted on her back almost daily, schooling her in turns and figure-eights and jogging in pairs over Catoctin's small training track. Trainer Leroy Jolley's remark of the previous spring still seemed prophetic, however, despite the filly's pliability and apparent eagerness. She showed no unsoundness, but her lightness of bone forced Diana Firestone to be cautious with her. She had cannons and flattened pasterns similar in configuration and delicacy to the fabled Ruffian's. Some racing people had claimed that Ruffian had broken down during her match race with Foolish Pleasure the year before because it was the first time she had ever really been pressured to run at full effort and her defectively flat pastern, hyperextended, had simply exploded from stress.

Not a great distance from Catoctin, at Alfred Vanderbilt's Sagamore Farm in Maryland, the home-bred colt out of Vanderbilt's mare Cold Comfort was well along in his training. Named Cold Reception, he had grown to a good size. But Vanderbilt, like many of the other home breeders, intended to go slowly with him and did not expect to put him on a racetrack until midsummer of the following year. Cold Reception was spirited and game as he jogged daily over the Sagamore training track, even a bit hard to handle. He had filled out splendidly in his shoulders and chest, great slabs of muscle rippling sinuously beneath his sable brown coat. There was no doubt that up front he had inherited his sire's qualities. But in his hindquarters he was narrow and light, unlike Secretariat. This worried Vanderbilt, for the colt did not have the look of raw power that Secretariat had had as a yearling.

One of the handsomest of the yearlings was training in Florida. Tete a Tete, the Tartan Farm colt out of Arrangement, was of good size and was coal black. John Nerud, Tartan's president and racing trainer, did not seem terribly fond of him, however. "He's a big son-of-a-gun and good-looking, but lazy as a pig," said Nerud in November of 1976. "Awkward, hard to train, can hardly get out of the way of his own feet. I've seen plenty of horses like him before." But Nerud is famous for his sense of humor and surprise. "I'll tell you, though," he said in the next breath, "he may take some time but he's gonna be a good one. He's gotta grow into himself, so he probably won't do much as a two-year-old. But watch out when he's three. I'm looking for him to be a Derby horse."

Another of the Secretariats broken in Florida was fast-food king Dan Lasater's filly out of his mare Aphonia. Named Messina, she was "a tough little girl, well-muscled and built for distance," according to Lasater. One of the midfoals, she had matured early and was "stepping out nicely" in her initial jogs at Lasater's farm in Ocala, showing "good, crisp action and a sense of what she's been put on this earth to do. She's not the prettiest filly you'd want to see, but she looks as though she's going to have ability."

Lasater raced a large stable with divisions at various tracks around the country, and he intended to put Messina to work early. Many horse owners have misgivings about sending two-year-olds into hard training early, for many tend to buck shins and suffer other annoying bone and tendon ailments in their legs that not only put them out of action for a time but also often ruin them as future racers. Not Lasater. He ran his operation strictly as a business and was not going to let the fact that Messina was a Secretariat deter him from putting her to the earliest possible use. "The way I figure it," he said, "if she bucks her shins or hurts herself in some other way she's no different from any other horse. She'll be showing that she's got a weakness and then we'll have to treat it and lay her off for a while. A lot of young horses get through their first hard training with no problems, however. But you never know which is going to come through and which isn't unless you test all of them. If a horse has the weakness as an early two-year-old, she's likely to have it still if she's held back until later. If this filly's going to have trouble up front, she's going to have it whether she's started early or late. I'd just as soon she have it early instead of late. Let her get it out of her system so's she can get down to the business she was bred for."

The term "bucked shins" comes from the appearance of the shin when a horse is struck by the ailment. The shin "bucks" outward, forming a convex swelling on the front of the cannon bone that is accompanied by fever, tenderness to the touch, and acute pain. The condition is an inflammation of the periostum, the tendinous sheath that covers the cannon bone. It occurs most often after a young horse has been run fast his first few times. It usually develops initially in the left front shin, due to the fact that a horse in hard training (or in a race, for that matter) runs counterclockwise. As the horse leans into left-handed turns, undue strain is put on his left foreleg rather than being divided equally between the two forelegs, as when he is running straight. The condition does not develop suddenly, but is progressive. As pain begins to infiltrate the left shin, the horse will transfer much of his weight to his right leg, and the same inflammation will begin to develop there as well.

The treatment for bucked shins consists of the application of counterirritants and heat to promote blood circulation which gradually ameliorates the inflammation. The healing process generally takes about six weeks, after which the horse has to be started all over again in training, beginning with easy walking exercises. It is usually another four or five weeks before he can be breezed.

Bucked shins and other minor leg ailments were not a major concern during the breaking and initial training period of the Secretariat yearlings. As the colts and fillies progressed through their jogging and steering exercises and began to gain a familiarity with the tracks at which they were being schooled, few extraordinary stresses were put on their forelegs. And after each daily training session their legs were hosed down with cold water to prevent swelling and inflammation, then snugly wrapped in bandages to trap their skin heat and promote optimum blood circulation.

Another of the yearlings to train well early was Jean-Louis Levesque's bay filly from Arctic Dancer. Levesque, the French-Canadian, liked to give his horses French names. Because he and his son Pierre thought that the filly was a special asset not only of theirs but also of Canada's, they decided to honor her by giving her a name that would be symbolic of their country. It was for this reason that they chose Feuille d'Erable, the French term for the Canadian national emblem, the maple leaf. All of French Canada, they hoped, would follow the filly's career with a sense of national pride. Moreover, the leader of the intensely political French separatist movement in Canada's Quebec Province was René Levesque. By naming their filly after the Canadian emblem, the intensely loyal racing Levesques, *père et fils*, were also able to show their countrymen that they were not to be confused with the other Levesque—the one who was seeking to divide Canada.

Feuille d'Erable showed signs of early maturity, as did many of Levesque's horses with Native Dancer blood on their dam's side. She schooled easily in the barn and went about her trackside lessons in a more businesslike manner than most yearlings. She was high-spirited but pliant, and when it came time to start slow gallops, she surprised Jean Laclerq, her exercise rider, with her fluid motion.

Several days of galloping—a furlong, then two, then three—brought the end to the initial training period for the yearlings.† Back at John Ward's facility at Keeneland, Confidant, Senator's Choice, and Sexetary made their first gallops late in October, shortly before winter started to settle over central Kentucky. "On the track, the Secretariats were taught to stand and then jog off quietly," says Ward. "At first we were simply teaching them that the track was not a place to be frightened of but a place to look forward to. The two fillies took to it nicely, but the first few times the colt, Confidant, went over he got upset. Once we got them galloping he would look around a lot and wouldn't gallop smoothly. He was a little slower than the others. All of them do that at first, but he just kept on and on and wasn't quite sure he wanted to be doing what he was supposed to do.

"We had to keep him a little longer than the other two. Then, all of a sudden, he finally figured it out and you could see the change in a couple of days. He started galloping like he was supposed to, and he even tried to get strong a couple of times. He'd try to pick it up and lay on some speed, particularly when he was galloping with another yearling. Eventually he got where he'd go down to the training track and just be proud that he was doing it. He finally accepted the whole thing."

That was the point at which Confidant's training stopped. "When he showed the sign that galloping on the track was what

† In racing terms, a gallop is not a top-speed gait but is equivalent to what most people familiar with other types of horses would call a canter. A gallop can range from slow to fast, but it is never a gait that brings a racehorse to full speed. This, in training terms, is called a breeze.

he wanted to do, that he wanted to run, that was the time to give him his diploma and put him up for the winter. Anything from that point on would have been too much repetition and would have made him dull. That's the way it is with all yearlings. Once you got them knowing what they are there to do, which is run, then you should winter them over without any more training and let them do some natural growing and filling out. They're not going to forget what they learned, and the following spring, when they're ready to go back into hard training for the races, they'll remember what they learned."

When Ward had first seen a number of the Secretariats, his expert horseman's eye had winced. "Looking at them in the sales and at some of the others on the farms around here, I was very skeptical about them. They didn't give the appearance of being athletic animals. They looked clumsy and not quite put together, the way you like to see a racehorse built. After the first three or four weeks of working with the three I had, I still held my belief. I figured Secretariat just hadn't done it as a sire. The colt and two fillies—they just didn't move like athletes.

"But once they got to galloping and got their dispositions channeled properly, they were very impressive in their change. It began to appear to me that they were going to be very determined animals on the racetrack. Once they got used to moving, they didn't let anything bother them. They showed me that they had the determination you look for in a classic horse. They're not cowards in any way. They have the potential, and their foundations are solid. Whether they live up to their potential is something else. That's what makes this business such a gamble."

CHAPTER 11

The Two-year-olds

On January 1, 1977, all the first-crop Secretariats officially became two years old and thus eligible to begin racing. Physiologically, however, only one by that date had been alive for a full two years. She was the chestnut filly bred by Walter Jeffords and purchased at the Keeneland select yearling sale the summer before by thoroughbred neophyte Robert Kluener for $175,000. Kluener, who had made his personal fortune as a contract manufacturer and supplier of tools for Sears, Roebuck and Co., had made the purchase to mark his entry into the racing world as an owner. He had determined that by getting a Secretariat he would be giving himself every advantage possible in launching his new career. The filly was so pretty that Kluener was sure he had gotten the best of the lot available for purchase, and he was thrilled to be among the select group of first-crop Secretariat owners.

But beauty does not make a racehorse. What Kluener didn't know was that inside the filly's forelegs and pasterns were structural weaknesses that would discourage her from digging her hooves into the ground with sufficient grip to provide the thrust any horse needs to run fast.

The name Miss Secretariat was unfortunate, since it was sure to attract extra attention and would inevitably draw unfair comparisons if, as a performer, she failed to measure up to the standards set by her illustrious namesake. As it would turn out, the struggle of Miss Secretariat to succeed would be one of the more frustrating ones of the entire crop.

After having her broken in Kentucky, Kluener cast about for a trainer to guide Miss Secretariat's racing career. Intent on making a quick name for himself in the "big leagues" of racing—the New York circuit—he approached several successful and well-known public trainers.

A public trainer is one who operates his own stable and trains a number of racehorses for two or more owner clients on a fee basis per horse, plus a percentage of the winnings of each horse. A private trainer is one who trains under contract for a single owner, usually a large stable that the owner has maintained for many years. Several of those who would be training first-crop Secretariats were private trainers, since they were under exclusive contracts to stable owners who had home-bred sons and daughters of Secretariat and intended to add them to their racing stock. But public trainers were far more numerous than private ones, and there was considerable competition among them to get their hands on those of the Secretariats that were going to be available. One of these was Phil Johnson, a respected and financially successful veteran of the New York-Florida racetrack circuit. It was he whom Robert Kluener chose to handle Miss Secretariat.

Johnson, a garrulous, nervous, white-haired man in his fifties, was at first reluctant to take on Kluener's Secretariat filly, mainly because of her name, but also because he knew that owner Kluener, new to racing and somewhat naïve in his expectations, might make his life more harried than it normally was by his expectations for the filly. Johnson went to some lengths to deflate Kluener's hopes, explaining that Miss Secretariat's celebrated ancestry and the fact the Kluener had spent so much money for her were no guarantees that she would be successful. Once Johnson was confident that Kluener was ready to take a sensible approach to the filly, he agreed to take her on.

Johnson had facilities in the horse country of Aiken, South Carolina, where he "wintered" horses he did not intend to take to Florida after the New York tracks closed down for the winter, where he "layed up" injured or overraced horses, and where he trained clients' two-year-olds that he introduced into his stable each year.* It was to Aiken that Kluener shipped Miss Secretariat in February of 1977. There she was put into light training, picking up with the long, easy gallops she had learned to do the previous October in Kentucky. The oldest of the Secretariat foals, she would be ready to begin breezing for short distances within the month as Johnson set out to build up her muscle, co-ordination, and wind.

The conditioning of a novice racehorse is a long, drawn-out affair requiring patience and perseverance on the part of the trainer and his aides. Many people ignorant of the process—not a few of them first-time owners such as Robert Kluener—find it difficult to understand why a horse cannot simply be trained for a week or so and then sent to compete in races. What they fail to appreciate is that although horses are bred to be racing athletes, they must first be taught the fine skills of the game they are born to play. The basic skill is maintaining their balance while running at full speed with jockeys on their backs. Some horses, especially those that physically mature early or are naturally well balanced in their various anatomical parts, are precocious and pick this up quickly when they are started on their two-year-old training. Most, however, are still far from full growth at this stage, or are still unbalanced in their anatomical parts, or are "growthy"— their frames almost of mature size, but their joints and connective tissues are not yet fully developed. These horses find it difficult to adapt to easy balance early on, and must be drilled on a regular, repetitive basis until they are able to run easily and without missteps or stride-breaking lunges. When a horse racing at full speed does something that causes him to break his stride, he will usually lose a minimum of five lengths on the horses he is competing against, and often will be totally discouraged from trying to regain the lost ground by virtue of the interruption in his concentration.

After learning to run in balance, a horse must learn to co-ordinate the physiokinetic skills that produce raw speed. Most

---

* Actually, starting in 1977, New York racing did not close down but continued racing at Aqueduct Racetrack throughout the winter. Like many of the other established New York trainers, nevertheless, Johnson continued to transfer his stable to the Florida tracks, Hialeah and Gulfstream, during the winter.

early-spring races for two-year-olds are no more than five furlongs in distance—five-eighths of a mile—and are thus pure sprints. The distances are kept short to reduce the chances of fatigue stresses on the youngsters' still-developing leg bones, tendons, and other tissues. The most consistent winners of such races are those who possess the edge in raw speed. Thoroughbreds are bred for speed, of course, and when a group of similarly built two-year-olds start out there is actually very little natural difference among them in the speed they are capable of. The principal components of speed, however, are muscle and co-ordination. Some horses, through their genetic influences, naturally possess more in the way of muscle dynamics and anatomical co-ordination than others. The early conditioning of thoroughbreds is designed to develop and expand the dynamics and perfect the co-ordination so that those possessing these innate attributes will be able to fully realize them and thus gain speed superiority.

A third basic skill is consistency, and the primary components of this are determination, concentration, and energy. Most healthy thoroughbreds possess the necessary energy to consistently run at their maximum speed over a distance of ground. Concentration can be taught, although it is more of an intangible. The ultimate intangible, however, the most important and hardest skills to instill in a young horse, are determination and a will to race consistently at maximum speed. When the three are fully synthesized, and superior muscle dynamics and co-ordination are present, the result is usually a superior racehorse.

Horses cannot be shamed or intimidated, as humans can, into consistently performing at the top of their potential. They can only be taught, and the superior racing trainer is the individual who is blessed with a generous amount of luck and an enormous fund of expertise in instilling and bringing out the best in a horse. If the horse is genetically incapable of running as fast as or faster than other horses, he will certainly never amount to much. If he has the natural capability, the superior trainer will develop it and hope that the intangibles of consistent desire and concentration will accompany it. It usually takes from three to six months for a trainer to learn what kind of a runner, barring injury, a novice two-year-old will make, and to bring out that horse's full poten-

tial. Many a trainer will ruin a potentially good horse by bringing him along too fast. Others will produce the same result
by going too slow with the same horse. There are no hard-and-
fast time rules in training a two-year-old for a racing career, except the rule that it should take from three to six months of carefully thought-out conditioning to make a colt or filly fit to race.
Notwithstanding how the horse performs, the training process
will continue through further racing and interim conditioning
until he has fully developed his physical and spiritual potential,
wherever on the scale of excellence and time that might lay.
Secretariat lost his first race as a two-year-old, although his
admirers retrospectively claimed that the loss was caused by the
unexpected interference he met upon charging from the starting
gate. As a two- and three-year-old, on the other hand, Forego
amounted to little as a racehorse; it was only at four and beyond
that he began to fulfill his natural potential. He was not a "classic" horse in the sense that he was able to excel in the classic
three-year-old races. But he became a classic handicap horse
through his domination of the "four-year-old-and-upward" divisions.

Phil Johnson followed the traditional and time-honored
methods of training a novice runner in his approach to Miss Secretariat. Once she accepted the reintroduction of a rider on her
back, she was sent through four weeks of daily long, slow gallops
of up to two miles. This is called "putting foundation" on a
horse. The gallops not only built her stamina and wind, but also
expanded her muscles and refined her balance. At the beginning
of the fifth week she was started on breezes in the company of
several other horses—sprints of two furlongs or a quarter of a
mile. At first the breezes were "slow." Almost any thoroughbred
can run a quarter of a mile in twenty-four seconds. She was initially breezed in twenty-eight seconds. Her slow breezes were
gradually stepped up in distance over the next few weeks to
three and four furlongs, or half a mile. Once a two-year-old can
go half a mile without strain in fifty seconds, a trainer will start
to breeze him back at two furlongs in twenty-four seconds,
stepping up to three in thirty-six seconds and four furlongs in
48. This is called "going in twelves" or "getting twelves" in rac-

ing parlance—running at a rate of twelve seconds for each furlong. Any horse that cannot go four furlongs in twelves is not yet ready for more intensive race conditioning.

Phil Johnson put Miss Secretariat through her initial twelves from a running start, which is to say that her exercise rider "set her down" into her breezing or sprint pace from a gallop. By mid-March it was time for her to learn the rudiments of the starting gate.

This was a time when fourteen of the twenty-eight first-crop Secretariats were in serious training. Besides Miss Secretariat, Ben Walden's Confidant was breezing lightly every three days at Keeneland racetrack under the tutelage of trainer Bob Dunham, who had trained his dam, Chou Croute. Coal baron Andrew Adams' My Card filly Sexetary, yet another auction purchase, was in training with public conditioner Dave Kassen at the same track. Sexetary, the last foal to be born, was maturing so quickly that it appeared indeed that she would be the first of the Secretariats ready to race.

Helen Hexter's filly Senator's Choice was beginning to breeze lightly at the end of March, as was Syntariat, the lean, slightly awkward-looking Levee Night colt purchased by Texas oilman Mike Rutherford at Keeneland for $275,000 on behalf of a syndicate called Big Horse Stable. Warner Jones' filly from his mare Jo Dan, bought at the Keeneland yearling sale for $190,000 by a syndicate represented by Dogwood Farm of Atlanta, had been named Punctuation and was being conditioned in Florida by New York trainer Jack Weipert. Brilliant Protégé, the Claiborne-Phipps gray colt out of Irradiate, was with Miss Secretariat at Aiken and was being handled by the Phipps family trainer, John Russell.

Alfred Vanderbilt's Cold Reception was with Vanderbilt trainer Elliott Burch in Florida. (Burch had ended his association with Paul Mellon to train for Vanderbilt.) Also in Florida was Mellon's Debrett, who was proving almost impossible to train because of his fractious temperament. There too, at Tartan Farm in Ocala, was the big black colt Tete a Tete. By early April, he was being schooled to the starting gate but was still manifesting a laziness in running that confounded Tartan's chief, John Nerud.

A recent arrival in Florida was Jean-Louis Levesque's filly

Feuille d'Erable. She was with Levesque trainer John Sharp and had begun to show such willingness that Sharp and his aides nicknamed her "Running Fool." Given the frequency with which she would eventually race in the coming months, the nickname was appropriate. Yet another filly training in Florida was Dan Lasater's Messina. She too showed a seriousness of purpose that augured well for Lasater's plan to race her early and regularly. She would soon be sent to one of the several trainers who worked for Lasater in his far-flung racing operation, the taciturn Dave Vance.

All in all, the Secretariats making the fastest progress were the ones that had been sold as yearlings, which lent credence to the old horseman's axiom that the auction yearlings that sell best are those that carry with them the potential of early maturity to go with speed in their pedigrees. Nevertheless, several sales yearlings were not doing so well. Most notable among them was Grey Legion, the Gilman brothers' Show Stopper colt who had been sold at Saratoga for $550,000 to the syndicate headed by Jim Scully. X rays had shown that his knee joints had not fully formed, so he was not extended beyond slow gallops during the spring—a big disappointment to trainer Laz Barrera, who had hoped to get him in New York during the summer and develop him into a Triple Crown candidate.†

Another of the first-crop Secretariats that had been sold as a yearling and was still far from serious training was Seclusive, the Firestone-bred colt that had been bought by Rocketts Mill Farm's Ed Stevens at Saratoga and was stricken with salmonella poisoning shortly thereafter. And Acratariat, the colt picked up privately by California's Booth Hansen from Walter Salmon early in 1976, was also showing signs of late knee maturity. Finally there was Secala, Secretariat shareholder Walter Haefner's former filly out of his mare Aladancer. She had been sold the previous September at the Goffs' yearling auction in Ireland for a record $288,000 to western Canadian Carlo von Maffei and reimported to the United States to train in California under the aegis

† Barrera's disappointment was assuaged by the knowledge that he already had another Triple Crown candidate in his barn named Affirmed. The chestnut son of the fashionable stallion Raise a Native had shown extremely early brilliance in training and, as it would happen, would fulfill his two-year-old potential splendidly during 1977 under Barrera's guidance.

of Tommy Doyle. She too showed signs of late physical maturity and would be restricted to a regimen of slow gallops over the summer at Doyle's training ranch near Santa Anita racetrack, outside Los Angeles.

Such other Secretariats as the Firestones' Oatlands, Will Farish's recently named Romantic Season, Penny Tweedy's Hope For All, and Raymond Guest's Sacrebleu would also be held back from serious training in the spring of 1977. Each owner was a member of the Secretariat syndicate, as were several others who intended not to race their first-crop Secretariats until the fall. And each possessed second-crop Secretariats that had recently become yearlings and that each intended to consign to the 1977 summer auctions. By not giving their first-crop horses a chance to fail, they hoped to sustain the sales value of their second-crop yearlings. Two nonsyndicate owners who had purchased first-crop yearlings and were planning to start racing them in April and May reported having been approached by second-crop syndicate owners with requests to wait until after the 1977 summer sales. One of these was Andrew Adams, whose Sexetary had come to hand rapidly during March under trainer Dave Kassen and who had announced that the filly would run at Keeneland's pre-Kentucky Derby meeting. The indignant Adams rebuffed the attempt to persuade him to hold off.

Ironically, one of the last-born of Secretariat's first crop was ready to run, whereas the first-born, Miss Secretariat, was nowhere near a race. During one of her stepped-up breezes at Aiken in March she had taken a misstep lunging from the starting gate and had cracked a sesamoid bone in her left front ankle. She had to be taken out of training until midsummer.

PART III

The Racehorses

CHAPTER 12

Sexetary

It was only the third race of a Saturday-afternoon program at Keeneland, but the excited buzz thickening the warm air and the mass of perspiring human bodies mobbing the saddling paddock made it seem like the Kentucky Derby. The date was April 16, 1977. The record crowd of more than 22,000 was there plainly because of the continuing public fascination with Secretariat and to bear witness to something that resembled a vital moment in history. For this was the day, and the third race was the race, that the first of the great horse's children would run.

With the breakdown of Miss Secretariat, his oldest, in South Carolina, the honor of being the first fell to Sexetary, among the youngest of his first crop. For the human-drama potential of the event, no better horse could have been chosen, despite her unfortunate name. Although a filly, she bore a striking resemblance in color and markings to her father. There was the famous white star on her forehead blending into a sliver of blaze that ran halfway down her face. And there were the white stockings—four instead of three—setting off the burnished copper coat and tail. She had more than a hint of her sire's massive chest and forearms, and her rump rounded out with a nice suggestion of power. When she was led into the saddling paddock twenty minutes before post time of the third race by groom Ned Suter, the mob

pressing against its railings broke into a loud applause. So popular
was she, although most onlookers had never seen her before and
she had not yet set a competitive foot on a racetrack, that the
crowd had already bet her down to 1 to 2 odds to win. The betting was mostly sentimental, however, part of the history-making
character of the day. Had she been any other horse she probably
would have gone off at 15 to 1 or more. Her works in the weeks
leading up to her debut had indicated nothing in the way of in-
cipient brilliance. In the *Daily Racing Form*'s "Latest Workouts" chart, her breeze times were no better than those of hundreds of ordinary horses.

This was partly by design, according to Dave Kassen, Sexetary's trainer. Kassen was an ex-jockey who had started a career
as a public trainer six years before and had forty-odd horses in
his stable for various small-time owners. In his training career he
had won only two stakes races and was considered by his peers as
a competent if not gifted conditioner of racehorses. One of the
reasons he got Sexetary was because her owner, Andrew Adams,
could find no one of more stature to take her on. Most of the
top-flight trainers who might have wanted a first-crop Secretariat
took one look at her offset right knee when she went through the
Keeneland sale as a yearling and put her out of mind.

When Kassen got Sexetary in December of 1976, still as a
yearling, he took her to Miami's Hialeah racetrack and added her
to the stable of horses he was training there for the winter. Because owner Adams was intent on being the first to race a Secretariat offspring, Kassen rushed her along, despite the fact that she
was physiologically the youngest of the crop, and that her knee
remained crooked. Surprisingly, she took willingly to the training and under Kassen's careful handling avoided injury. Moreover, as she went through two weeks of long gallops at the beginning of January, her knee began to straighten out. What had
happened was that after she had been born, one side of her knee
had grown faster than the other, putting the joint out of kilter.
The daily regimen of gallops forced the underdeveloped side to
catch up, and within just a few weeks the faulty knee was close
to normal.

At the end of January, Kassen began breezing Sexetary once a
week at an eighth of a mile, accelerating the pace each successive

week. She did not show remarkable speed during February, but she demonstrated maturity in all other requisites of a racehorse, including concentration and a willingness to run. "She was just like her old man," says Kassen. "Secretariat was big and kind, and so is she—one of the few of the Secretariats I've seen not only to look like him but also to have his temperament. And the filly had a lot of sense. She was easy to train, never did anything silly or ornery. She did whatever you asked of her."

In March, Kassen stepped Sexetary up to two- and then three-furlong breezes, trying to coax twelves out of her. Having moved his stable back to Keeneland, his home track, he put a four-furlong work into her on the second day of April, getting 50 seconds—not quite even twelves. Five days later, running her against another horse, he put four furlongs into her in 49⅕ seconds. A fifth of a second is considered the equivalent of a length in a race—Sexetary had improved by four lengths. Hassen told Adams that when the filly could get four furlongs in an even 48 seconds, she would be ready to race. A few days later she went four in 48⅖ seconds. Kassen wanted to put two more works into her to try to get those 48. But the impatient Adams had learned that Keeneland had carded a "Maidens Special Weights" race for the following Saturday, April 16. He insisted that Kassen enter her.

Except for the feature race on a given racetrack's daily program, which is usually a stakes, or allowance event, the bread-and-butter contests are claiming races. Most horses who are making their racing debuts, or who have already made their debuts but have never won, are eligible only for "maiden" races. Most maiden races are claiming events. However, there are always a number of maiden horses stabled at a track—those that have either not yet raced or have raced and not won—that are worth too much money to their owners to enter in maiden claiming races. A typical maiden claiming event at Keeneland has its claiming price—the price at which one owner can acquire another's horse—in the $5,000 to $10,000 range. The first-crop Secretariats were worth countless multiples of those amounts, even if they had never before raced. Sexetary, for instance, although at $75,000 the lowest-priced yearling to have been sold, was worth upward of $100,000 in the total cash Andrew Adams had put into her and possibly an additional $100,000 in her immediate potential. To enter a $300,000 horse in a $10,000 claiming race would clearly be folly, since every other owner on the grounds would instantly seek to claim her no matter how she performed.

To give owners a chance to test intrinsically high-priced horses without having to worry about losing them to the claim box, the nonclaiming maiden race was invented and was given the title "Maidens Special Weights." Such races are programmed relatively seldom on a racetrack's card, but they are scheduled often enough at certain times of the year to give owners and trainers of valuable horses a chance to race them without the worry of losing them to another owner. Once a horse wins a maiden race, whether claiming or nonclaiming, the next step up are allowance races, in which the purses are more generous and the claiming system does not operate. The Keeneland April meeting has traditionally been the debut occasion for many an expensively bred two-year-old. As a result, the daily cards usually contain at least one Maidens Special Weights race.

It was in such a race that Dave Kassen had entered Sexetary on Saturday, April 16. He would have liked to have another two weeks to put some further foundation on her, but he had not yet reached the point in his training career at which he could dictate to his clients when and where their horses would run. "And anyway," said Kassen's assistant Dale Bender at the time, "the way she's trained, she shows a lot of promise. She's in perfect shape and has just as much a chance of winning as any other filly in the race."

Kassen was more circumspect about her chances the morning of the race, which was scheduled for 4½ furlongs—a little over half a mile. "She's trained good," he said, "but I think she'll be a little better going farther. She has good speed, no doubt about it, but so far she hasn't shown that she's quick. Her daddy was the same way as a youngster, so I'm not expecting anything great. This is a race for the quick filly, the kind that can get up to full speed in a furlong and carry it the rest of the way. I'm afraid Sexetary will need a quarter mile just to get in gear. Then it might be too late for her to catch up."

Sexetary became excitable in the saddling paddock, no doubt

spooked by the unaccustomed shouting and sound of applause. She reared, yanking groom Suter's chain shank taut and almost lifting him off the ground. She was admirably dry, though, failing to break out into the washy sweat that drains the energy from so many horses before a race. Of course, having never raced before, she had no reason to turn to suds.

She was a handsome sight as she pranced and tossed her head while being saddled. She looked the picture of a racehorse, and once jockey Donald Brumfield was on her back she stepped out alertly on her circuit of the walking ring. Out on the track she jogged smoothly, her head held high, through the post parade.

The filly had schooled well to the starting gate and when she was loaded into the first stall she entered without protest. The six-horse field arrayed against her—all two-year-old fillies seeking their first win—was impressive neither in blood nor in previous works. Not a few wizened bettors muttered that the race was a setup to make the first of Secretariat's runners look good. Anticipation rose over the crowd as the last horse was loaded into the gate, situated on the far side of the track.

There was a pause as the red starter's flag was raised. Then the gate doors sprung open with the clanging of the bell. Sexetary broke sharply and sprinted into the lead down the track's backstretch as the field approached the first and only turn. She showed a quickness of foot after all. She held the lead around the turn and into the top of the stretch. As the closely bunched field straightened for the two-furlong dash to the wire, however, a filly named Hot Commodity quickly moved up to challenge. Brumfield laid his whip on Sexetary, and those who had bet on Secretariat's blood waited for her class to show. Instead, Hot Commodity pulled away and Sexetary began to fade, badly. By the time she reached the finish line she was fourth, beaten soundly by another filly called Set a Limit, who had overtaken Hot Commodity to gain first place. Sexetary earned $325 for her fourth-place finish.

A pall fell over the crowd for the rest of the afternoon. Stone-faced Donald Brumfield was roundly booed during later races, as though the fans held him to blame for the disappointing debut. Asked for a comment on the filly, Brumfield was defensive and sullen. "Don't blame me," he said, although he knew well in advance that he would be blamed if Sexetary failed to make a race of her first start. "She just got outrun today, lost her fire on the turn. If she was by any stallion but Secretariat, nobody would've cared. No reason to condemn her or praise her. She's just another horse, that's all."

Kassen complained that Brumfield had unnecessarily rushed Sexetary out of the gate to get the lead, thus using her up too early. But then he said, "Listen, I didn't send her out there expecting she would win. She got a good race under her, and that's the important thing. In his first start, her daddy was fourth, too. So she's right on schedule."

What Secretariat did after his first start was legendary. Sexetary would not race again for five months. A few days after the race Kassen moved her, along with the rest of his stable, to New Jersey's Monmouth Park for that track's summer meeting. A few days later, in her first hard work, she developed a splint on her right shin and Kassen was forced to lay her off for three months.

Shin splints are as common to young racehorses as bucked shins and are brought about by similar traumatic stresses. Splints are bony growths that usually develop on the insides of the front cannon bones. The inflammation and pain render horses *hors de combat* for lengthy periods. Treatment is similar to that for bucked shins, and even after the lameness disappears a horse cannot be run hard for several months. By the time Sexetary was ready to go back into training in early August, she was still the only Secretariat offspring to have started a race in the United States. Yearlings from Secretariat's second crop that had been consigned to the summer auctions had brought prices considerably lower than those of the first crop the year before, although his average still remained far above that of any other stallion. It was now time for more of the first-crop colts and fillies to test the waters. There could be no excuse for holding the fit ones back any longer.

As several of the other two-year-olds were being trained up to their first races, Kassen was patiently bringing Sexetary back to form. By September, most maiden races had been stretched out to six furlongs, or three-quarters of a mile, and Kassen pointed her toward a race at New Jersey's new Meadowlands track in late September by drilling her at that distance on several occasions throughout the month. The best time she could make was a minute and fourteen seconds, which was two seconds more than even twelves for the six panels. Yet she was fresh and her works were steady, and when she was announced for the race—another Maidens Special Weights—she was marked down once again as the favorite in a twelve-filly field, this despite the fact that most of her opponents had a number of six-furlong starts to their credit.

A day before the race, however, Sexetary came back from a three-furlong "blowout" breeze limping, and Kassen was forced to remove her from the lineup. Her shin was feverish again, although there were no new splints or signs of bucking. He rested her for two weeks, and when she appeared healthy again he began to gallop her slowly at Meadowlands, whence he had moved his stable at the end of Monmouth's summer meeting. He started working her once more with a six-furlong breeze out of the gate on October 22, and a week later he sprinted her four furlongs. In neither work did she evince speed, but neither did she show any further signs of shin tenderness. She was on her toes the morning after the October 29 work, and Kassen decided to keep her in the six-furlong maiden race he had entered her in the following evening.

It was again a third race, on the October 31 Meadowlands card. Although her previous works were not impressive and rumors about her potential unsoundness were rife, Sexetary was sent to the post as the favorite once more, this time because Kassen had managed to secure the services of jockey phenom Steve Cauthen. The filly broke sharply from the seventh post position and moved alertly under Cauthen to second place in the first furlong. The second favorite in the race was a filly called Hit Woman, and she took the lead from the start. As the field pounded down the backstretch to the turn, Hit Woman began to draw away, first by six, then by eight lengths, with Sexetary dropping back into third place and being replaced by Indyson, a long shot. They raced that way around the turn and into the homestretch, with Indyson moving up to challenge Hit Woman. In the last furlong it was a duel between the two, with Hit Woman fending off the challenge to win. Sexetary crossed under the wire a tired third, and her "show" finish was only by virtue of the fact that the six horses trailing were even more fatigued than she.

That was basically it for Sexetary as a two-year-old. She was entered in another six-furlong nonclaiming maiden event November 15 after a fast five-furlong work the week before, but Kassen scratched her when the tenderness in her shins reappeared. After the Meadowlands meeting closed, Kassen moved his stable to Hialeah in Miami for the winter. Sexetary became a three-year-old on January 1, 1978. A series of speedy short works in January indicated that the filly could run with any horse for two furlongs but could not sustain her speed. As she matured as a three-year-old, and if she stayed healthy, she might develop some staying power. But it was unlikely. Many veteran horsemen agreed that she had been raced too early and that this was the reason for her leg problems. After she was scratched from a race at Hialeah on February 14, little hope was held out for her future as a runner. Her total winnings had been $1,425, which barely covered her feed bill.

CHAPTER 13

Brilliant Protégé

The disappointment in Sexetary was tempered by the fact that she had been the product of one of the "cheaper" breedings and, with her suspect knee, had not been expected to achieve a great deal anyway. One of the offspring of which more was expected was Brilliant Protégé, the steel-gray colt owned in partnership by Dinny Phipps and Claiborne Farm, out of Phipps' fine mare Irradiate.

By mid-1977 Irradiate had proved herself a superior producer and was on the verge of achieving "blue hen" status. Commendably blooded, she was a daughter of the champion racemare High Voltage, who had been sired by *chef de race* Ambiorix, and her own sire was the incomparable Ribot. As a filly she had won nearly $50,000 in purses before an injury put an end to her racing career. Sent to stud by her owners, the Phippses, in 1970, her first mating was to Secretariat's sire Bold Ruler in the next-to-last year of his illustrious stud career. From that breeding Irradiate had produced the fine racing filly Celestial Lights, who won $133,000 for the Phippses between 1973 and 1975. Two years later she was bred to the almost-winner of the 1969 Triple Crown, Majestic Prince, and produced for the Phippses a colt they named Majestic Light. By 1977, at four, the powerful Majestic Light was on his way to amassing winnings of $650,000 before being retired; he would miss by a whisker being voted Grass Horse of the Year. Also coming to form in 1977 as a three-year-old was Fluorescent Light, the colt Irradiate produced by Herbager the year after Majestic Light's birth. Fluorescent Light was Irradiate's nursing foal when Dinny Phipps first bred her to Secretariat on one of the Claiborne free seasons in 1974—the breeding that produced Brilliant Protégé. With such a distinguished producing record already behind her, Phipps and Seth Hancock felt justified in holding out high hopes for Brilliant Protégé, which may have accounted for Hancock's acerbic remarks about Secretariat's first-year performance at stud. Delivered into the world with his pronounced swayback, Brilliant Protégé was only one of several of the first-crop Secretariats to be born with less-than-perfect conformation.

A swayback is not a fatal deficiency, however. Many fine race-horses have been swaybacked ₍to one degree or another. John Russell, the Phippses' English-born racing trainer, did not think that Brilliant Protégé's back would be a factor in his success or failure. He was more concerned about the colt's physical immaturity when he took possession of him in Aiken, South Carolina, during the early winter weeks of 1977. Russell, like most English trainers, was cautious about working two-year-olds hard and preferred not to see them race at all. He believed that such young horses' bones, joints, and connective tissues were insufficiently formed to withstand the rigors of hard training and that they should not be raced until they were three. The Phippses, although in agreement with him in principle, were on the other hand bastions of the eastern racing establishment and felt duty-bound to support and promote two-year-old racing. They struck a compromise with Russell: He could condition their two-year-olds in a deliberate manner and would not hurry them. However, he was expected to have at least a few of the youngsters in their large stable ready to make their debuts during the annual August New York Racing Association meeting at Saratoga, the busy and ultrasocial outpost of the family's thoroughbred empire.

Brilliant Protégé had been broken at Claiborne Farm in the fall of his yearling year and, upon turning two in January, was transferred to the Phippses' training quarters in South Carolina for further schooling. Since he would be racing in Dinny Phipps' name, trainer Russell picked him up during the Phipps stable's trek back to Belmont Park from Florida in mid-April. Settled into a stall in the Phippses' Belmont barn with thirty-two other horses, Brilliant Protégé soon became a favorite of Russell's grooms and exercise riders. "He was like a big baby when I first got him," said ex-jockey Eddie Merced, the young man who worked for Russell and who would become the colt's regular exercise rider. "The first couple of times we took him out to jog under tack, he was awkward and unco-ordinated. When we started to gallop him in May he was a bit better and had a stride a lot like his mamma, Irradiate. I knew he was a Secretariat, but he didn't feel like I imagined a Secretariat would feel in his gait. And then, the first time Mr. Russell put a work into him, a two-furlong breeze, I was sure he wasn't going to be another Secretariat. His action wasn't smooth, and he didn't really want to run. He was lazy."

"He was as green a horse as I've seen when I first got him," concedes Russell. "Had a nice personality, although he always seemed to be homesick in his stall for someplace else and used up a lot of energy whinnying and pacing."

The colt, despite his color, looked more like his sire every day as he passed the months of June and July working out on the Belmont training track in the early mornings. His black mane and tail set off his gray coat nicely, and with his white-blazed, dished Secretariat face and powerful arched neck, he appeared every inch a racehorse. "The trouble was," said Russell, "he needed an awful lot of pushing to be made to feel like a racehorse. He'd go out and train nicely enough, but it was hard to get him to extend himself. That didn't discourage me, though. We had two of his half brothers in the barn, Majestic Light and Fluorescent Light, and they were the same way as two-year-olds. That was definitely the Irradiate blood, late-maturing. I had no expectations that this colt would be another Secretariat. If he could develop as well as Majestic Light, I'd be more than happy."

Russell pushed Brilliant Protégé gently but firmly during the early summer at Belmont, giving him long gallops and throwing in an occasional hard three-furlong work against the stopwatch. The colt remained ungainly, breaking slowly from the starting gate and taking an inordinate amount of time to gain his stride.

Russell moved the Phipps stable to Saratoga for the annual 1977 August meeting and began to train Brilliant Protégé up to a race. On the morning of August 5 he sent him on a five-furlong breeze—the colt's longest to date—from a gallop, and the gray turned in a markedly unimpressive time of 63 seconds. An average time would have been 60 seconds flat, a good one 58 seconds. With every fifth of a second on a timer considered the equivalent of a length for distance, it meant that at 63 seconds over five furlongs, had Brilliant Protégé been in a race, he would have lost to an average horse by 15 lengths and to a brilliant one by 25.

Russell remained undiscouraged. He knew the colt was still immature and that breezing alone against the clock was not a true measure of his ability. Many a horse runs sluggishly when he is not in the company of other horses, particularly when he has never raced. Nevertheless, Russell knew that the colt had a way to go yet. He would have liked to hold him back for another two or three months, but pressure from the press at Saratoga was forcing the Phippses to show their hands. Except for Sexetary's single race at Keeneland in April, by August no other Secretariat offspring had started in the United States. Speculation was strong that there was something wrong with the majority of the first-crop horses and that owners were holding back until the completion of the Saratoga yearling sales in mid-August for fear that any further poor performances would reduce the sales value of the second-crop yearlings. As chairman of the New York Racing Association and the nominal owner of one of the first-crop Secretariats, Dinny Phipps was a prime target of the journalistic heat. Once the Saratoga sales were over, he implored John Russell to push Brilliant Protégé toward a race.

On the morning of August 15, Russell put jockey Angel Cordero up on the colt and had him breeze Brilliant Protégé four furlongs. Cordero's instructions were to take him up to the Saratoga track's half-mile pole at an easy gallop and then to set him down around the turn and down the homestretch to the finish line in an all-out effort. Russell wanted to learn if the colt could get the half mile in 48 seconds or less—48 being an acceptable time for the distance.

Brilliant Protégé got the distance in 49 seconds flat, a full five lengths behind the average. His furlong fractions were 11⅘, 11⅖, 12⅘, and 13 even. Analyzing the work, Russell could see that once under steam the colt could move, but that he tired rapidly after his initial speed effort. "He's bred for distance," he grimly told Dinny Phipps, "and he looks as though he's only going to be useful as a distance horse." Nevertheless, if Phipps wanted to race him at Saratoga, he would have to start him in a maiden sprint. Consulting the Saratoga condition book* for the final two weeks of the meeting, Phipps spied a two-year-old Maidens Special Weights event scheduled for Saturday, August 27, the last day of the meeting. "Let's point him for this one," he said to Russell.

On August 22, Russell again sent Brilliant Protégé out for a hard work with Cordero aboard. Russell asked for five furlongs from the starting gate in under 58 seconds, with a sixth "eased up" in an additional 13 seconds. This meant that Cordero would race the horse out of the gate, down the backstretch, and around the turn at full tilt, gradually easing him up as they came into the homestretch and letting his momentum carry him the additional furlong. The race they were pointing for was to be a six-furlong affair. If Brilliant Protégé, who had never breezed six, could get five around a turn in 58, and get the additional furlong in a tiring 13, he would be in shape to go a full six the following week in 71 seconds. The track record for the distance over a fast surface was 68 seconds. Seventy-one seconds, however, would put Brilliant Protégé in contention, provided that there were no exceptionally precocious two-year-olds entered in the race. And Russell had neither seen nor heard of any such horses at Saratoga that August likely to run the distance in less than 71 seconds.

Cordero got Brilliant Protégé into the gate easily that crisp August morning after a mile warmup jog. When the stall doors sprung open the colt broke slowly. The time for his first furlong was 13⅖ seconds. Once under way, though, he began to close the gap on the desired 58 seconds, getting the second furlong in 12 and the third in a surprising 11 seconds. Three furlongs in 36⅖ seconds—a respectable showing from a gate start. But then the gray began to tire. He took the fourth panel at the top of the turn in 11⅘ and slowed to 12⅖ through the final furlong for a total time of 60⅗. That morning ordinary horses were clocking 57s and 58s for the same distances over the fast track. Brilliant Protégé, under a hard, whippy ride by Angel Cordero, was a

* A condition book contains the schedule of races and their conditions for the following weeks, and is printed by a racetrack's management mainly to let trainers and owners know what races are available for their horses.

good ten to fifteen lengths slower than the "platers" that made up most of Saratoga's equine population.

Notwithstanding the disappointing work, Russell entered him in the ninth and last race of Saturday, August 27, the final day of the Saratoga meeting. On Friday Russell gave Brilliant Protégé an unclocked two-furlong "blowout" over the training track under the guidance of his regular exercise rider, Eddie Merced. During the afternoon he brought the colt to the main track's tree-shaded saddling area to school him to the crowds. It was Brilliant Protégé's first exposure to masses of people, and he reared and whinnied incessantly, provoked by the excitement that rippled through the crowd when the news spread that he was one of Secretariat's offspring.

Saturday dawned cool and clear over the Saratoga stable areas. It was getaway day and there was little training being done. Most of the activity centered around the loading of dozens of huge horse vans that would transport most of the remaining horses back to Belmont Park, Aqueduct, and other racetracks in the East. The atmosphere was that of a carnival closing up. By noon there were less than a hundred horses left on the grounds, most of them scheduled to run that afternoon.

The eighth and feature race of the day was the Champagne stakes that pit the nation's two top juveniles—Alydar and Affirmed—against each other. Brilliant Protégé's race followed. Normally, the final race on a track's program—especially the final race of the last day of the meeting—is of interest to only a handful of hard-core bettors, with most of the day's crowd heading for the parking lots after the feature. But on this day hardly anyone left after Affirmed won the Champagne. Everyone knew that a son of Secretariat would be making his first start in the ninth race. The saddling area and paddock were jammed as the gray was led, whinnying fiercely, through the throng.

All of the ten horses in the race were two-year-old non-winners, and four, including Brilliant Protégé, had never started before. The most experienced was Innocuous, a well-bred chestnut trained by the Firestones' trainer, Leroy Jolley. Ordinarily he would have been the program favorite, followed by a bay colt called Golden Reality, based on previous races and works. But the favorite for this event was the unraced Brilliant Protégé, who was without any remarkable work times. Once again the normally hard-bitten oddsmakers had given way to sentiment.

Not the regular Saratoga horseplayers, though. They took one look at the nervous Brilliant Protégé in the paddock and bet him down to second favorite, installing Golden Reality as their first choice as the horses went to the track for the post parade. The jaunty Angel Cordero was up on the gray colt, while Steve Cauthen rode a weedy bay colt called Shove. Shove was from the first crop of Riva Ridge, Secretariat's Meadow stablemate in 1972 and 1973. The irony of the two colts racing against one another was not lost on the crowd.

The starting gate for the six-furlong event was positioned at the top of the backstretch, across the infield from the amply filled grandstand. The horses would race three furlongs down the backstretch, sprint two more through the sweeping turn, and pound the final panel through the homestretch to the finish line in front of the stands.

Breaking from post position eight under a shout in Spanish from Cordero, Brilliant Protégé not surprisingly was one of the last horses out of the gate. He was immediately cut off by Shove, who broke from the ninth stall and angled in toward the rail to briefly take the lead. Disconcerted, Brilliant Protégé struggled to find a stride and dropped back to tenth as the twelve-horse field began to string out. He remained tenth all the way down the backstretch as Golden Reality took the lead from Shove and the Riva Ridge colt began to drop back. Approaching the turn, Shove had retreated to fifth, while Innocuous streaked from third place to nudge Golden Reality off the pace. Brilliant Protégé was going no faster, but horses ahead of him were tiring and dropping back so that he moved from tenth to ninth to seventh in midturn. There he stayed as Cordero began applying the whip into the homestretch; when the winner, Innocuous, crossed under the wire seconds later, Brilliant Protégé was still seventh, eleven lengths behind.

The winner's time was 1:11⅕, or 71⅕ seconds, far off the track record for the distance of 68 seconds. John Russell, sitting in Dinny Phipps' clubhouse box, timed Brilliant Protégé in 1:13⅘. He had not tired so much as he had been without speed, said Cordero afterward. He had raced greenly, first getting out of the gate slowly and then failing to respond to Cordero's whip, as though content to stay where he was. On the basis of his first race, no one would venture a guess as to what kind of a horse the colt would turn into. Russell's hopes, however, reservedly bright at the beginning of the day, began to fade. He now wondered if the swayback indeed had anything to do with Brilliant Protégé's lack of swiftness.

The colt was shipped back to the Phippses' barn at Belmont Park the next day, having come out of the race with no distress or injury. Theoretically, with a race behind him, he should begin to train more alertly. A week later Russell breezed him at Belmont and he got a very slow five furlongs. A few days later he went six in 74 seconds from a galloping start, slower even than his Saratoga race. Russell nevertheless entered him in another maiden for two-year-olds at Belmont on September 14.

Breaking slowly again, this time from the fourth stall, Brilliant Protégé raced tenth in a thirteen-horse field to the turn. As several other horses tired in the turn, he moved up to sixth, then fourth at the top of the stretch. He stayed there during the dash toward home, finishing seven lengths behind the long-shot winner, El Lagarto. Brilliant Protégé raced the six furlongs in 1:13⅖, two-fifths of a second faster than he had at Saratoga. It was hardly the improvement Russell had hoped for, and the trainer now began to think of taking him off the track for a while and saving him until he turned three.

As it happened, Brilliant Protégé did not run again as a two-year-old. Russell shipped him to Santa Anita racetrack in Southern California with the rest of the Phippses' stable at the beginning of 1978 and began to train him as a grass racer. Midway through his three-year-old season, he had still failed to place in a race.

CHAPTER 14

Feuille d'Erable

When Jean-Louis Levesque's Canadian trainer, John Starr, heard what Levesque had called his Secretariat-Arctic Dancer filly, he joked to his assistant about the difficulties American track announcers would have in pronouncing her name. "Fool Derabbel was the name I expected to be hearing in Florida and Kentucky for the next few years," he later said. "There was no way those American announcers were going to get it right. I even suggested in a humorous way to Mr. Levesque that he send the filly to France. That way she'd get her proper recognition."

The proper pronunciation was Fuh-eeyuh Deh-rabbluh, but it took a person accustomed to French to say it properly. Not even Starr could manage it, and it worried him. "Who ever heard of a great horse with an unpronounceable name?" he complained.

"If the horse turns out to be a great one," shot back Levesque's son Pierre, "her name will no longer be unpronounceable."

If not a great filly, Feuille d'Erable certainly appeared to have the potential to be a notable one when Starr added her to his stable after returning to Canada from the 1977 spring race meetings in Kentucky. Levesque raced his horses in Canada during the summer, mostly at the Port Erie and Woodbine tracks at Toronto. He sent his stable, with Starr in charge, to the fall meeting at Keeneland in Kentucky, then on to Florida to compete at Gulfstream and Hialeah for the winter. In the spring Starr brought the stable back to Kentucky for the Keeneland and Churchill Downs meetings, and then moved back to Canada. Feuille d'Erable had already undergone some intensive conditioning by the time Starr got her. After stumbling over her name for a while, he took to calling her, with admiration, "Running Fool." Thanks to Levesque's policy of putting his horses to work early and regularly, a running fool she would turn out to be.

Nevertheless, she had problems. A mature, well-formed bay, Feuille d'Erable did not hanker for the starting gate. She was ready to race by June. But because she refused to train from the gate, Canadian racing stewards would not permit her to be entered in a race. In Canada, as in the United States, a horse may not start in a race until it has trained satisfactorily three times from the gate. Starr spent much of July and August breezing her from gallops and schooling her to the gate. Her breezes reflected speed and ability, but any time she got near a gate she became fractious.

By early August Starr had settled her down. The second problem, however, he could do little about. When the filly breezed, she had a habit of furiously swishing her tail. Her work times, 36 seconds for three furlongs, 61 for five, might have been better had she not expended so much energy on her tail.

Despite this, Feuille d'Erable breezed five furlongs in a better-than-ordinary 58⅕ seconds on August 14 at the Fort Erie racetrack. Starr decided that she was ready for her first start and entered her in a five-furlong maidens race August 20.

The filly finished sixth, having raised a ruckus in the gate and gotten a slow start. With her tail spinning, she made up some ground on the turn but tired in the stretch to arrive at the wire six lengths behind the winner. In view of the fact that the company she had raced against was markedly undistinguished, it was an inauspicious beginning. At least Brilliant Protégé, finishing seventh a week later in his first race, would have raced against some hardy pedigrees.

Starr sent Feuille d'Erable back to the post at Fort Erie a week later, on August 28, in a six-furlong maiden. This time she did not tire despite another slow start. She made up ground on the turn and chased the leader, a filly named Kelly's Invader, to a close second-place finish.

By September, the first-crop Secretariats had four races to their credit. Sexetary had been fourth in her only race months before. Brilliant Protégé had been seventh in his debut. And Feuille d'Erable had finished sixth and second, the first of the crop to get a share of purse money.

Her third start, on September 10, was another maiden sprint, this one for two-year-old fillies bred in Canada, at Woodbine, over six furlongs. In her previous race she had gotten six furlongs in 1:13, or 73 seconds, a marked improvement over her first start but certainly no black-type performance. Yet because she would be going against even lesser company than before, Starr expected a win. So did the crowd, which sent her off the favorite.

Feuille d'Erable was surprisingly calm in the gate for this race. She broke well from the tenth position and gained the lead over the eleven-horse field going into the turn. Coming down the stretch to the wire she began to tire, but under hard whipping by her jockey, Jack Kelly, she hung on to outlast the fast-approaching Favorite Tune by half a length.

Secretariat finally had his first winner. It was a Pyrrhic victory in most American observers' eyes, however, since it occurred in Canada against a field of minor-league horses; it was no measure of class. On the other hand, many "class" horses had broken their maidens, as the saying goes, against even less formidable company.

Having broken her maiden, Feuille d'Erable was now an allowance horse. This meant that in order to avoid claiming races, she would be eligible only for allowance events in which her competition—other well-bred winners—would be tougher. She needed little in the way of training now; her almost-weekly routine of racing took care of that. Starr decided to begin stretching her out in order to test her ability at greater distances. To do this, he entered her in an allowance race at Woodbine during the last week in September, another contest limited to Canadian-bred horses. She led most of the way but could not stay the seventh furlong, fading to finish third despite being the bettors' favorite.

Starr put her back into another allowance on October 10, this one at 6½ panels. Again she led most of the way, only to die in the last sixteenth of a mile to barely hold onto second place, losing to Favorite Tune, the filly she had edged in her only victory. Feuille d'Erable was beginning to show herself as a three-quarter-mile sprinter—a contradiction of her breeding—and Starr began to despair of her ever developing into a classic-race contender as a three-year-old. But at least she was proving durable, which was a tribute to the soundness in her pedigree.

Before the end of the year the filly had raced four more times, all of them allowance sprints at Calder Race Course in Miami, where Starr wintered the Levesque stable. Having lost her form as a result of the trip south in mid-November, she finished out of the money on all four occasions. Her total share of purses for 1977 was a shade over $7,000, enough to pay her feed and training expenses but not the harbinger of a brilliant future.

The filly had a surprise in her, though. She mildly astonished the discouraged Starr by finishing third—and a strong finish it was after running half the race under a strong hold by jockey J. P. Souter—in an allowance race of over a mile. The date was January 5, and Feuille d'Erable had just officially become a three-year-old. Starr, believing that the distance had put a good measure of stamina in her, entered her in an identical race nine days later at Calder. She finished third again after having led the field for most of the distance. In a mile-and-an-eighth allowance on January 26 at Hialeah she was third again, rallying well after being rated by Souter for half the going.

Starr decided that the filly definitely performed best under a hold for a certain distance, to be then let out into the fast closing sprint she seemed capable of. But, he also thought, she could accomplish this better at shorter distances. He therefore selected as her next outing at Hialeah a seven-furlong allowance on February 17. Jockey Souter was under firm orders from Starr to rate Feuille d'Erable for the first four panels—run her behind the leaders under an energy-saving hold—and then to set her down into a closing sprint coming out of the turn into the homestretch.

Souter broke the filly from the fourth stall of the starting gate and followed instructions perfectly. He settled her into seventh place in the nine-horse field going down the backstretch and got her to relax. Gliding into the turn, he squatted low into the saddle and hit her twice with his stick. Feuille d'Erable leaped forward and began to pass the field. At the top of the homestretch she was third. Midway through the straight she passed the two leaders and flashed home the winner by almost two lengths. It was a classically run race and, although the time was unremarkable, the filly showed competence and ability at the distance. Moreover, she was the first of the Secretariats to have won two races. While unable to prove herself a stakes-quality horse, she had at least saved her sire from complete embarrassment as a freshman sire.

Starr continued the filly on a regimen of one allowance race every seven to fourteen days through March. She reeled off three straight third-place finishes against tougher company than she had faced in her February win, earning a total of $11,510 in purse money for the first three months of 1978. But then her rigorous schedule began to take its toll. She showed nothing in three races in April, and Starr decided to give her a rest. The likelihood of her coming back from it with more speed and racing ability was slim. Even Pierre Levesque was disappointed, although the filly had earned her way. "With her breeding," he remarked, "we had hoped to get a champion, but at this moment my father and I have little hope for much more improvement. It would be wonderful if she could win a stakes or two during the summer. However, to be realistic, I think what we've got here is a fairly nice allowance filly. We'll continue to race her into the fall, and then we'll probably retire her and breed her."

By 1978 Kentucky Derby time, Feuille d'Erable had proved to be, if not the brightest of Secretariat's first offspring, at least the most durable. She had raced seventeen times in her brief life, had won twice, and had finished in the money on nine other occasions. She was clearly not of championship caliber and it was doubtful that she would even distinguish herself with a stakes win. But she was indeed a running fool.

CHAPTER 15

Cold Reception and Syntariat

Alfred Vanderbilt, long a nabob of the eastern racing and breeding establishment, had not had a horse worthy of entry in the Kentucky Derby since the time his magnificent charger Native Dancer was "robbed" of a win in the race. When Vanderbilt sent his stakes-winning mare Cold Comfort to Secretariat in 1974, his earnest hope was that he would get a colt that, four years later, would carry his colors to Churchill Downs. He knew that it was an unrealistic dream, that no Derby horse has ever been bred to order; yet he refused to deny himself the hope.

When Cold Comfort foaled a colt—a late foal—in 1975, a further installment was paid on the dream. As the colt grew into yearlinghood, Vanderbilt decided to name him Cold Reception and to nominate him for the Derby, making the first of several payments required to keep a horse eligible for that classic of classics. And when the yearling became a two-year-old, Vanderbilt was sure he had a horse of Derby potential.

Officially registered as "dark bay or brown" in color, Cold Reception was more of a rich seal brown verging on black. He was thick-set through the chest and bold of neck, but narrow in the flanks, giving him the look of a greyhound. Except for his chest he did not have much of his sire in him physically, but he was still a very handsome-looking young horse indeed. During his initial yearling training at Vanderbilt's Sagamore Farm he displayed a fine co-ordination and way of going, unlike many of the Secretariats who were clumsy and ungainly, and he gave himself heartily to his first gallops.

Vanderbilt was sure that, if not a classic horse, he had a sure stakes performer in Cold Reception. He worried about the lightness of his hindquarters but hoped that several months of conditioning and competition would muscle them out. Cold Reception was bred to be a distance horse and looked like one. Vanderbilt resolved to go slowly with him, not exposing him to the rigors of hard race training until the fall of the two-year-old season. His plan was to get two or three races into him in the late fall in New York and, if he showed well, to start him on the road to Churchill Downs in May of 1978 by developing him in Florida during the early months of his three-year-old season.

Vanderbilt, in conjunction with his trainer Elliott Burch, stuck to the plan throughout 1977. It did not take Vanderbilt long to learn that Cold Reception was not a Derby horse, however.

Cold Reception first saw a genuine racetrack in August of 1977 when he was shipped to Saratoga to join Burch's stable. Burch galloped him easily for the first two weeks and schooled him to the starting gate and paddock. In the meantime Vanderbilt was busy syndicating the eager, well-behaved colt among several of his friends, thereby recapturing most of the cost of his share in the Secretariat syndicate. Burch first breezed Cold Reception toward the end of the Saratoga meeting and the colt reeled off a very promising 36 seconds for three furlongs—promising because it was his first hard work.

Vanderbilt and Burch had no wish to introduce the colt to competition at Saratoga, however. They shipped him back to Belmont Park at the end of August, and Burch spent the month of September putting more long gallops into him in the mornings. He then began to point him for a six-furlong Maidens Special Weights race on the closing day of the fall meeting at Belmont in mid-October. On October 1, Burch gave Cold Reception his first hard work at the six-furlong distance and the colt turned in a time of 75⅗ seconds. This relatively slow clocking was deliberate; Burch had ordered the exercise rider not to push his horse. Once the colt "knew" the distance, Burch would begin putting some speed into him.

He did so four mornings later, sending Cold Reception five furlongs in $60\frac{2}{5}$ seconds out of the gate. Now the colt was ready for real speed effort, and on October 8, with his rider ordered to use a whip, he turned in a four-furlong sprint in a sharp $47\frac{3}{5}$ seconds, which meant that he was skimming twelves. Cold Reception could run, Burch decided. The question now became: Could he carry his speed for six furlongs?

The last day of the Belmont fall meeting was one in which the racing secretary tried to get all the best horses out. It was a day of several featured stakes races, including the Hopeful Stakes for two-year-olds, in which the two top juveniles—Alydar and Affirmed—would again meet to decide two-year-old championship honors.* The race immediately preceding the Hopeful was the maiden that Burch and Vanderbilt had chosen for Cold Reception's debut. When the two got a chance to examine the rest of the field entered in the event—most well-bred first-time starters like their colt—they elected to withdraw. In training, Cold Reception had evinced a dislike for racing in a crowd of horses and tended to shrink back rather than bully his way out. This was a fault of temperament that Burch hoped to correct. But, he judged, this race's high-quality field might all too easily intimidate the Vanderbilt colt and thus reinforce the bad habit.

The next race available to the colt was at Aqueduct on Saturday, October 22, against genetically less formidable but more experienced opposition. Burch entered him. Partly because his short training breezes had shown speed, but more so because he was such a handsome son of Secretariat, the crowd sent him off as the favorite. The colt broke well from the gate under jockey Mike Venezia and sprinted sharply with the leaders for three furlongs, reeling off fractions of about eleven seconds for each. But he had used himself up by the fourth panel, struggling through the closing two to finish a soundly beaten seventh in a twelve-horse field. Venezia reported later that the crowd around him entering the turn had killed the colt's spirit. The jockey opined that Cold Re-

* Affirmed lost to Alydar but still would be named best two year-old of 1977. His rivalry with Alydar would continue through 1978.

ception was physically capable of winning the race, but that his will to do so had been compromised by his dislike of the traffic. "He felt strong and I thought he had plenty of run left. But once he let those other horses pass him with all the bumping that was going on, he just didn't want to catch up."

Burch entered him in another maiden ten days later, this time with Ron Turcotte, who had gained fame as Secretariat's regular rider five years before, in the saddle. The race was at seven furlongs, and Turcotte's orders were to rate Cold Reception and then send him to the leaders at the top of the stretch. The eleven-horse field broke evenly, and Turcotte "took back" Cold Reception and let him race in the middle of traffic. Having experienced a crowd once, the colt did not spook and instead paid attention to business. He was in fifth position at the top of the homestretch as the field spread out, and Turcotte put the whip to him. Racing wide, he almost caught the second horse, Ivanhoe, at the wire. His third-place finish earned him $1,200, and it was a promising effort. "This is definitely a distance horse," Turcotte told Vanderbilt.

But in order to get into a distance race with competition he was able to deal with, Cold Reception would first have to win a maiden at six or seven furlongs. Elliott Burch consequently went looking for the right race, one in which he would not be over-matched. He entered the colt in an early November maiden event but then scratched him when the lineup of horses appeared over-laden with capable sprinters. Burch found another six-furlong two-year-old contest for him on November 19, however; on the basis of Cold Reception's last performance, the colt went off as the favorite once again.

This time the colt appeared that he would justify the odds. Under Eddie Maple, his third jockey in three starts, he rated nicely through the first two furlongs and then moved handily to the lead through the third. He left the three-eighths pole at the top of the turn with a length's advantage over the second horse, Ring of Truth, and further opened his lead at the top of the stretch. Maple brushed him with his whip as the field started on the last furlong and a half to the wire, then gave him three sharp raps as he felt Cold Reception begin to labor. Unseen by the jockey, a long shot called Tyrannical, who had been laying well off the pace, at the beginning of the turn, suddenly began to move. He streaked from tenth to fourth place around the turn and drew a bead on Cold Reception at the top of the straight. Down the straight he pounded under strong whipping by jockey Jacinto Vasquez, gradually edging in toward the rail-running Cold Reception and overtaking him. He caught the tiring Vanderbilt colt in the last fifty yards and had a head on Cold Reception as they bobbed across the finish line. Alfred Vanderbilt, watching with Burch from his box in the Aqueduct clubhouse, slumped in disappointment. The Kentucky Derby looked farther and farther away.

Burch was angry at jockey Maple, castigating him for having put the colt into the lead too early. Maple defended himself by saying, "But he wouldn't rate. He wanted to run today, he wanted to get out of that bunch on the backside. I had to let him go or else he would have quit and dropped out of contention altogether."

Cold Reception, despite the stresses on his legs brought about by his fatigue, came out of the race sweating profusely but sound. His next outing was another six-furlong maiden at Aqueduct on December 3, a week after turning in a very slick 34⅘-second training breeze over three furlongs a few days before—the fastest time any Secretariat offspring had run the distance. The colt could run, Burch told Vanderbilt. It was just a matter of conditioning him to go at the leaders when he was rated for most of the distance in a race. He still did not like to run at other horses, although he had the ability if not used up early. He preferred to hang back and let the tide of front runners carry him along. The only way he might go after the leaders was if he felt pressure from horses behind him.

On December 3, he broke well and immediately responded to Maple's rein restraints, dropping back into fifth place and holding that position to the turn. As the tightly bunched leaders flattened out into the straight, Maple urged his colt to go after them. To a degree he did, moving from fifth to fourth to third in a few bounds and with a great burst of acceleration. But then, as he approached the two leaders midway through the straight, he hung. Maple applied the whip but could get nothing more out of him. He was four lengths ahead of the fourth and fifth horses and did not feel the requisite pressure from behind. He swept smoothly across the line in third place, almost catching the failing second finisher, Roman Reasoning, who had suddenly started to "back up" after a stretch duel with the winner, Bold Voyager.

At the end of the Aqueduct fall meeting just before Christmas, Burch shipped his stable to Hialeah in Florida. Once settled in he immediately put Cold Reception to work, breezing him hard for longer and longer distances. To win a maiden race, the colt would have to be conditioned to lead from start to finish, even though he was not sprint-bred. Burch interspersed the five- and six-furlong breezes with hard two-mile gallops to build up Cold Reception's stamina.

The colt's first race as a three-year-old was over six furlongs at Hialeah on February 17, 1978. This time Maple broke him on top and set a fast pace. Several horses challenged Cold Reception on the turn but he just ran faster. Coming toward home he was three lengths the better of the field, and Maple began to worry about his fading. He faded only a little in the final half furlong, however, hanging on to win the race and finally break his maiden. His winning time was 71⅖ seconds, better than average for the distance.

Vanderbilt began to think Kentucky Derby again, but trainer Burch discouraged him. "He's a nice colt, but it's going to take a long time to get him up to the classics distance [of ten to twelve furlongs]," he said. "He has to run on the lead—it's the only way he likes to race. His win today took a lot out of him and I'm going to have to rest him for a couple of weeks before I begin stepping him up. He'll never be able to run more than a mile wire to wire by the spring."

Cold Reception did not race again in Florida. He came off his win uninjured but a physiological wreck from the effort. He went off his feed for a few days, caught a coughing sickness that further debilitated him, and did not begin to recover and regain weight until the beginning of March. Burch brought him back to New York with the rest of his stable at the end of the month to prepare for spring racing at Aqueduct and Belmont. Cold Reception turned in a pair of good breezes at Belmont Park during the first week in April and appeared on his toes. Burch thereupon entered him in an allowance race at Aqueduct scheduled for April 12.

It was a historic race after a fashion, for also entered was another of Secretariat's first-crop offspring, Syntariat. It was the first time two of Secretariat's children would compete against one another.

Like Cold Reception, Syntariat had been withheld from serious training until midway through his two-year-old season. The bay colt, who had been bred by Seth Hancock and then sold *in utero* to Kentucky market breeder Tommy Gentry when Hancock consigned his in-foal mare Levee Night to the Keeneland November sale in 1974, and who had been resold by Gentry at the 1975 yearling auction to a syndicate headed by Texas oilman Michael Rutherford for $275,000, had never been as impressive-looking as Cold Reception. Syntariat looked even less like his sire and lacked the flashy appearance of the Vanderbilt colt. Yet from the moment he was put into hard training at Saratoga in August of 1977, he impressed all of his connections as a horse of promise. His principal virtue lay in his agility. During several early-morning breezes at the upstate New York track he wasted no time getting into running gear. Of the eight Secretariats in training there, he quickly rose to the top in terms of potential racing class in the eyes of the clockers.

Rutherford, in whose name Syntariat would race, had assigned the colt to trainer Steve DiMauro, a public conditioner who the year before had succeeded Lucien Laurin as the trainer of Penny Tweedy's Meadow Stable horses. DiMauro went easily with Syntariat on his return to the fall Belmont meeting in New York and then took him to Santa Anita with the rest of his stable for the winter. Rutherford had decided not to race the colt until he was a three-year-old, since so many top-notch two-year-olds had come to the fore in the fall. The conventional wisdom was that many of these juveniles would not hold their form after they turned three. They would fade into obscurity, leaving the door open for several unraced two-year-olds to take their place and possibly race their way into Kentucky Derby contention. Rutherford expected Syntariat to be in the forefront of the three-year-olds who would come to hand in the early months of 1978. His principal reason for choosing DiMauro as the colt's tutor was the job the large-beaked trainer had done with Wajima, the record-priced yearling of 1973 who had been prevented by early injuries from realizing his superhorse potential and did not begin to sparkle until well into his three-year-old season.

Syntariat trained sharply in California during December of 1977, turning in some scintillating early-morning breeze times. Although by the beginning of 1978 there were several first-crop Secretariats at Santa Anita, he appeared to be the only one who was race-ready.

The presence of the Secretariat offspring was testimony to the increased prestige of California racing. Several New York-based stables that would ordinarily have wintered at the Florida tracks had gone instead to California to take advantage of the considerably larger and more frequent stakes purses at Santa Anita and Hollywood Park.

Syntariat was the first of the Secretariats to start in California. He raced well in his debut, a 6½-furlong maiden, but was deliberately "saved" under orders from DiMauro and finished out of the money. His debut was for experience only and so that DiMauro could get a line on his form over the distance. Satisfied that the colt was capable of a speed effort without injuring himself, DiMauro entered him back in another maiden on March 11. This time, over a slow, sloppy track, Syntariat led from start to finish to win easily by six lengths. The distance was again 6½ furlongs, and his time—77⅗ seconds—was remarkable under the execrable racing conditions.

Thus was the colt's racing record one win in two starts as he prepared to meet Cold Reception in the April 12 allowance at Aqueduct—the first time two Secretariats would compete. DiMauro had returned his stable from California two weeks before. Syntariat had worked sharply twice over the Belmont Park training track and once at Aqueduct and was, in racetrack parlance, on his toes. Cold Reception seemed likewise on the muscle, and on the day of the race the bettors were hard put to decide between the two as the favorite.

It was a sunny spring New York afternoon as the two colts

were paraded once around Aqueduct's tiny paddock. The small
weekday crowd looked on in fascination. Cold Reception, prancing under jockey Jacinto Vasquez, looked much more the impressive of the two, while Syntariat, thin and gangly beneath
rider Angel Santiago, plodded about placidly. Alfred Vanderbilt,
comparing the Rutherford colt to his own, pondered once again
the vagaries of breeding luck. Although his horse was more impressive to look at, he knew, on the basis of Syntariat's recent
work times, that Rutherford's horse would probably win. Syntariat had shown in his works for the race the three prerequisites of
class—speed, consistency, and will. Cold Reception had shown
only the first with any regularity.

The crowd finally installed Syntariat as the favorite, with Cold
Reception close behind in the odds. At the end of the six-furlong
race, the Vanderbilt colt would not even be near. As the gate
doors sprung open, Syntariat sprinted to an immediate three-
length lead and held it along the backstretch and around the turn.
Racing easily, he opened it to five lengths down the straight to
the wire, walking off with his second win in three starts. Cold
Reception, in the meantime, ran into his usual traffic problems.
Under hard urging from Vasquez he moved from last to third
down the backside but wanted to go no farther, apparently
disliking the clods of dirt flung into his face by Syntariat
and Dr. Sam Scher, the second horse. Cold Reception veered
wide out of the turn and lost interest in the homestretch after
making a brief effort to escape being caught by the fourth horse
in the seven-horse field. Cold Reception crossed under the wire
nine lengths behind the easy-striding Syntariat, finishing fourth.
Moments later, when the two "brothers" returned to the weigh-
out scales to be unsaddled, Syntariat was composed and not
breathing hard. Cold Reception was puffing wildly, his coat
awash with foamy sweat.

That night, Alfred Vanderbilt withdrew his nomination of
Cold Reception for the Kentucky Derby. It was too late for the
jubilant Michael Rutherford to think about the Derby for Syntariat, but he spoke about how "This colt's going to win some big
ones later this year, just like Wajima did." This despite the fact
that Syntariat had not yet raced more than 6½ furlongs.

But that was the nature of racehorse ownership: hope and optimism. "Class always shows," said Rutherford, referring to Syntariat's pedigree. From the colt's performances up to that point, he had reason for optimism. Of all the Secretariats, only Syntariat had thus far demonstrated class.

CHAPTER 16

The Others

Of the twenty-three other first-crop Secretariats, twelve have, as of this writing in the fall of 1978, never been tested in competition.

The pretty chestnut filly bred by Jacqueline Getty out of Windy's Daughter and sold at auction to an Irish syndicate is today in Ireland under the tutelage of celebrated trainer Vincent O'Brien. Named Centrifolia, she suffered from a series of minor leg ailments late in her two-year-old season and was not ready to race until she was three. As a three-year-old, she has won two minor stakes races in Ireland. She will soon become a broodmare.

The big gray Gilman brothers' colt sold at Saratoga in 1976 for a record $550,000 for that vendue, named Grey Legion, has only lately been considered mature enough to be put into hard training. Whether he will accomplish anything late in his three-year-old season remains to be seen. It is likely that he won't, since he still lacks agility. Indeed, he is almost musclebound.

The Jo Dan filly bred by Warner Jones, sold to a Georgia syndicate as a yearling at Keeneland, and called Punctuation has been in intermittent training since midway in her two-year-old season. Due to a succession of bucked shins, splints, and other minor but nagging equine ailments, she has never officially raced. However, she won an unofficial exhibition race during the ceremonial opening of the Meadowlands racetrack near New York in the fall of her two-year-old season. Her competition was, to be kind about it, second-rate. Her trainer, Jack Weipert, remains optimistic, however.

One of the saddest ironies of the Secretariat syndication remains Hope For All, the diminutive chestnut filly bred by Penny Tweedy for the Meadow Stable. Like Syntariat, she came under the tutelage of trainer Steve DiMauro and turned three while DiMauro had her in California. Her works have been unimpressive and she has evinced an almost uncontrollable temperament. She has not raced.

Another sad case is that of Oatlands, the comely chestnut filly out of Gamba for whom Bert and Diana Firestone had such hopes. After being trained for several months by Leroy Jolley, their conditioner, the blunt Jolley advised them that she would never amount to anything on the racetrack. As a consequence they sent her to auction as a two-year-old in a Horses of Racing Age sale at Belmont Park in October of 1977. There they experienced the final rub. Having cost in excess of $250,000 to breed, raise, train, and maintain, she brought a high bid of only $50,000, which fell far short of the reserve the Firestones placed on her. They got her back as a result, and since Jolley wanted nothing further to do with her, they sent her to Ireland. In the bargain they incurred the ire of several other Secretariat syndicate shareholders for risking her at sale. From their viewpoint, the paucity of the money offered for Oatlands automatically deflated the value of future Secretariats they would be putting up for sale.

Oatlands finally got to race in Ireland. She won one contest in six starts before being retired to the broodmare band at the Firestones' Gilltown Stud in County Kildare.

The Firestones' other first-crop Secretariat, auctioned as a yearling at Saratoga to the syndicate headed by Ed Stevens of Virginia's Rocketts Mill Farm for $275,000, and named Seclusive, recovered from his salmonella affliction and managed to train nicely for a while in the fall of his two-year-old season. But then he bucked his shins in Florida and had to be rested by trainer Mike Hernandez for two months. Hernandez put him back on the track as a three-year-old in March of 1978, but he could do little more than gallop him up to the time of the Kentucky Derby. Nevertheless, according to Hernandez, he was "a racy-looking colt and we expect him to achieve a stakes victory before the year is over." During the late spring and early summer of 1978, Seclusive went to the post three times and was beaten on all three occasions. But then he finally won a maiden race at Saratoga in August, and he followed this with an allowance victory at one mile in September at Belmont Park. Since then, however, he has failed to sustain his promise.

Despite the only modest successes of their first two Secretariat offspring, no one is weeping for the Firestones. A year after producing Seclusive, their mare Exclusive Dancer dropped a second foal by Secretariat. Another colt, the Firestones named him General Assembly. As a two-year-old in mid-1978 he showed exceptional promise, impressively winning several important stakes before being beaten by a nose in the Cowdin Stakes by another top two-year-old, Calumet Farm's Tim the Tiger. He then came in second to two-year-old Horse of the Year Spectacular Bid in the Laurel Futurity. Despite these two late-season losses, General Assembly is expected to be a contender for the 1979 Kentucky Derby.

Hernandez might have been whistling in the wind, as fellow New York trainer Bob Dunham conceded he himself had been doing when he received Confidant, the bay colt out of Chou Croute whom Kentucky breeder Ben Walden had bought on the cheap from E. V. Benjamin, Jr., as a weanling at Keeneland late in 1975. "This colt's going to go places," Dunham said at Saratoga in August 1976 after putting him through a series of slow gallops just before the Fasig-Tipton sale of second-crop Secretariats. After the sale, back in New York, Dunham worked Confidant four furlongs at a breeze and the colt promptly developed sore shins. "Still growthy," Dunham said. "But with his breeding we'll get him into some of those early three-year-old sprints in Florida and then you'll see how he'll fly." As of October 1978, Confidant, still plagued by tender shins, had not raced.

Another exquisitely bred Secretariat colt not to have started in a race at midthree was Debrett, Paul Mellon's chestnut out of the mare All Beautiful. He is still destined to be given a stern trial on the racetrack rather than be salvaged for stud duty, however, because late in his two-year-old season he was gelded. This came as a large surprise to many observers. One of the very few offspring to have inherited his sire's appearance and conformation, Debrett, even unraced, would have been worth a king's ransom as a stallion. But Paul Mellon does not believe in breeding untested horses. So when Debrett's coltish temperament proved too unruly for the racetrack at two, Mellon ordered him castrated. Once the horse's sexuality was removed, he gradually settled down and began to train with concentration and willingness. "This horse has just got too much potential to let him go through life without having raced," said Mackenzie Miller, the new trainer of Mellon's Rokeby Stable. "He probably won't be ready to make his first start until midsummer. But he's such a powerful son-of-a-gun that it wouldn't surprise me if he became the next Forego."* So far, he has given no indication that such a happy outcome is even a remote likelihood.

There are others among the first crop who not only haven't raced but who also have for all practical purposes disappeared from sight. Tadao Tamashima's colt, shipped to Japan as a yearling, was not even thought of as a racehorse. Instead, Tamashima started breeding him to Japanese mares when he was two. His first foals were born this year, making Secretariat perhaps one of the quickest equine grandfathers in history.

Will Farish's bay filly out of Ran Tan, which he eventually named Romantic Season, has done little in the way of serious training, Farish having decided to save her for breeding purposes. Nor has Reportage, the nicely formed chestnut colt out of Crimson Saint owned by Texas breeder Roger Braugh and acquired as a result of his purchase of Mrs. Dupont's 1974 breeding right in the Secretariat syndicate. Braugh's acquisition was a once-in-a-lifetime opportunity, and he has been extremely cautious with the colt for fear of losing him for the stud.

And Secala, the chestnut filly out of Walter Haefner's Aladancer whom Haefner sold at auction in Ireland as a record-

* The venerable, huge Forego had been gelded as a three-year-old because of his faulty racetrack manners. A poor performer in that year of Secretariat's glory, and ineligible for later stud duty, he went on to become a legend in his own right as a racer during the next four years.

priced yearling to Italian-Canadian magnate Carlo von Gaffei and who was returned to this country to train under Tommy Doyle in Southern California, has seen no action due to slowly closing knee joints.

Of the remaining twelve members of the first crop, all were racing or in training at the time of this writing, but none had done much to advance their father's reputation as a sire. The most disappointing of all was Miss Secretariat, perhaps because she tried the hardest and accomplished the least.

Miss Secretariat, the first-born, had recovered from her cracked sesamoid bone and was back in Phil Johnson's barn at Belmont Park in July of 1977. He took her with him to Saratoga in August, after building her up with long gallops, and started his heavy work on her again there. Throughout the month she breezed every fourth morning but was unable to get a distance from three to five furlongs in anything close to even twelves. The best she worked was five furlongs in sixty-two seconds on a day when average horses were getting the distance in fifty-eight. She was twenty lengths behind the average.

Johnson insisted that the slow works were deliberate—he wanted to bring her along carefully so as not to risk another ankle mishap. But back at Belmont in September, when he asked her for more speed and concentration, she showed no improvement. She still could not put together a breeze of twelves. Johnson nevertheless entered her in a six-furlong maiden race for two-year-old fillies at Aqueduct in mid-October. But when he tried to sharpen her for the race a few days before with a five-furlong breeze at the Belmont track and she turned in a sluggish sixty-four-second clocking, he scratched her.

Another work on October 28 over the fast Belmont training track in 63 ⅖ revealed little improvement in her ability. But Robert Kluener was pressuring Johnson to get the filly into a race. The harried trainer thereupon entered her in another maiden contest scheduled for November 1. The race filled with thirteen other smartly bred fillies who had not yet won, several with excellent morning works behind them. Johnson was tempted to scratch Miss Secretariat again—a poor performance would not reflect well on his training abilities—but Kluener insisted on going. So she went.

Breaking slowly from the seventh gate-stall under French jockey Jean Luc Samyn, the rangy red filly never got in the race. She struggled down the back side in last place and only managed to move up in the last furlong because three other horses running in midfield tired badly and "stopped." She finished eleventh, beaten by thirteen lengths. Samyn described her effort by saying, "She went well enough but she was just out for a gallop. She really didn't try."

His comments were almost identical two weeks later when she started again in a six-furlong maiden and finished last in a field of nine.

Johnson scratched Miss Secretariat from a Thanksgiving Day race and decided to try her at a greater distance in a race carded for December 8 at Aqueduct. She was, after all, bred to stay. Perhaps in a race of a mile or more her plodding pace would catch horses tiring after six or seven furlongs. He prepped her by working her a mile twice during the two weeks before the race. Her clockings were less than impressive.

The December 8 race was at a mile and a sixteenth. As before, the filly remained in last place as the nine-horse field swept around Aqueduct's mile oval. At the top of the stretch her speed remained constant while the leaders turned on the gas for the run home. A couple of horses ahead of her eventually tired and she managed to get under the wire in seventh place. But she was beaten by fifteen lengths.

On January 2, 1978, the day after Miss Secretariat turned three, Johnson tried her back at six furlongs in the hope that her previous test might have sharpened her for a speed effort. It was to no avail. The filly continued to show no taste for competition and ran what had by now become her usual race. She dawdled along ninth in a ten-horse field and finished in that position in an extraordinarily slow time over a fast track.

Shortly afterward Johnson moved his stable to Florida. Miss Secretariat did not run there but had one more race at Aqueduct in March of 1978, again performing dismally. Johnson finally counseled owner Kluener to forget the filly as a racehorse and to instead think about exploiting her broodmare potential. The dejected Kluener assented. He had not made a penny back on his $200,000 investment in the horse, and he would not realize any money for at least two more years, when she started dropping salable foals. Such were the fortunes of wealthy men who tried to break into the racing business with expensive, one-shot yearling purchases. Secretariat was no longer a happy name around the Kluener household.

Nor did Secretariat's name sit any better with the infinitely more experienced horseman John Nerud, the chief operating officer of Florida's Tartan Farm and the trainer of its racing stable. He had grown to like his big black first-crop Secretariat colt, Tete a Tete, enormously. "A terrific personality," he said, "and you couldn't ask for a kinder, more willing horse in the morning." Which meant that Tete a Tete trained well; indeed, he reeled off a handful of sparkling clockings in his initial morning works at Saratoga in August of 1977 after recovering from bucked shins suffered in his earlier training. "But in the afternoons he's a bum. Just a big old horse that don't ever want to try."

Nerud had hoped to put a race into the Arrangement colt at Saratoga but didn't want to start him out in too-fierce company. Almost every two-year-old maiden race at the ancient track that August filled out with the class of the East, so Nerud held Tete a Tete out until he could get more speed into him. Yet his morning works indicated that he was ready to run: four furlongs in 47 seconds on August 14; four in the same time out of the gate a few days later. Nerud decided to wait until he returned the Tartan forces to Belmont Park in September.

On August 30, back at Belmont, Tete a Tete clocked 35⅕ seconds in a three-furlong breeze out of the gate—not a black-type move but an indication that the big, menacing-looking colt was ready. He followed this with a four-furlong dash over a heavy rain-soaked track in 48, a definite black-type work considering the conditions. Nerud was pleased. Arrangement, Tete a Tete's dam, had been a good runner in the mud, and he seemed to have inherited that favorable trait. Of course, Secretariat could run well over any surface. Nerud entered the colt in a Maidens Special Weights on September 17 at Belmont for his first start and prayed for rain.

Rain he got. And mud. Despite the conditions, Tete a Tete finished next to last, fifteen lengths behind the appropriately named winner, Flying Duck. Nerud was perplexed. True, his colt got off to a slow start, but he never made an effort to move up on the field once he was in gear. Jockey Patrick Day blamed it on the divots of mud thrown in Tete a Tete's face by the horses ahead of him. "It's one thing to breeze alone in the slop in the morning," he remarked. "It's another to race in it in the afternoon when you've got all that muck coming back at you. This colt was just confused. He couldn't put his mind on the task."

For his next start Nerud selected another six-furlong maiden test on October 1 at Belmont, this one with a different jockey, Jacinto Vasquez. Nerud instructed Vasquez to try to break Tete a Tete fast, snatch the lead, and hold it throughout. The colt had breezed four furlongs in 47⅕ seconds a few days before over a fast track. If he could hold that speed for six, he had a very good chance of winning the race.

Vasquez followed orders. He got the black colt out fast and had him vying for the lead down the backside with two others. They went the four furlongs in 46⅕ seconds, the fastest Tete a Tete had ever run the distance. But he had nothing left. Around the turn he began to tire badly, dropping back to sixth place and ambling home an exhausted seventh, a good eleven lengths behind winner Cloud Forest, an undistinguished two-year-old colt.

Nerud scratched Tete a Tete from his next scheduled race on October 15 after seeing the better class of horses he'd be competing against. He decided to lay him up until he was three and then try him again. He sent the colt back to Florida for two months on the farm, and then put him back into training at Hialeah in January of 1978. The handsome black son of Secretariat again showed a willingness to run in the mornings. But he remained lackluster in the afternoons. With no in-the-money finishes to his credit as a three-year-old, he ran his last race prior to the time of the 1978 Kentucky Derby, when Nerud returned his Tartan Stable string to New York in the spring. It was another six-furlong maiden event at Aqueduct on May 1. Tete a Tete raced ninth for most of the going in a nine-horse field, managing to finish eighth after one of the leaders "died" at the top of the stretch.

John Nerud could have died as well. "One of these days maybe he'll catch on," he said of Tete a Tete after the May 1 race. "It may take him till he's ten years old, but we'll keep running him till he does. I'll tell you this: Any son of Secretariat who doesn't win a stakes isn't gonna be worth a plugged nickel at stud so long as the old man is alive. Maybe Mr. Mellon had the right idea having his colt cut. If Secretariat can't produce runners, his children aren't likely to."

By November of 1977 it had become clear that Secretariat's first crop was not going to amount to much as two-year-olds. And if their two-year-old form was viewed as a harbinger of things to come, they would probably remain disappointments at three—at least those racing in this country.

The situation with the offspring that had been sent abroad was not much brighter. Canadian Bound, the $1,500,000 yearling, had made his debut in a mile-and-an-eighth test in France on September 19 and was sent off as the heavy favorite. A giant in stature by then, he had been patiently trained up to the distance (French races tend to be run half a mile longer than equivalent American ones) by Maurice Zilber, Nelson Bunker Hunt's expert European conditioner. The competition was not considered particularly keen for the big red Secretariat-like colt—if anything, he was even more impressive-looking than his sire—and Zilber was as confident as the bettors of an easy maiden victory.

Ridden by top jockey Freddy Head, Canadian Bound rated well through the first six furlongs, being saved by Head for the stretch run over the grass course. Going into the straight, Head began to urge the colt on, and Canadian Bound responded by moving up on the four tightly bunched leaders and catching them with a furlong to go. But he did not have enough stamina to sustain the preplanned charge and sweep to the lead. Instead, tiring with the others, he became engaged in a five-horse duel over the final furlong to see which could hold on longest. A few yards from the finish Canadian Bound finally gave out; conceding the race to a long shot named Captaine West, he finished second, a shade in front of the other three horses.

Zilber was understandably disappointed, having trained the colt to the mile and a quarter in exemplary times. "He ran well," he said, "but I'm puzzled why he tired at the end. He has never done that in training. I expected him to go by those other horses on his last furlong and win easily. At least I think he tired. Perhaps he just enjoyed running alongside the others and didn't want to leave them behind." Zilber nevertheless left no doubt that he expected Canadian Bound to emerge as a top horse in France in 1978. But by the fall of 1978, he had not run again.

Another Secretariat handled by Zilber was State Room, the chestnut filly sold at the Saratoga yearling auction by her breeder Laddie Dance for $175,000. She had suffered a similar fate in her first start in France, tiring in the last furlong and finishing well back in the field. In her second race, in October, she showed improvement, almost hanging on over a mile to be beaten slimly. But she too, as of this writing, has not run again.

But the big news from Europe concerned Dactylographer, the bay colt Stavros Niarchos had acquired by buying his dam, Artists Proof, in foal to Secretariat at auction from syndicate member Zenya Yoshida. Dactylographer was sent to race in England in the name of Niarchos' son Philip after being broken and schooled in France. Trained by the top English conditioner Peter Walwyn, he just missed winning his first start early in September of 1977, but then came back to win a maiden race at Ascot later in the month. The race was called the Sandwich Stakes. Nevertheless, the American Jockey Club did not accept it as a genuine stakes race, since it carried no more significance than a maiden race at an American track.

But the splendidly proportioned colt would not be denied a genuine two-year-old stakes. He was sent out on October 22 to win the William Hill Futurity, a Grade I stakes of one mile, by a neck. His victory earned him $74,745, putting a solid dent in the $385,000 Niarchos had paid to get him, and made him eligible for Great Britain's classic races for three-year-olds in 1978. Nevertheless, British racing handicappers were not optimistic about his three-year-old potential, rating him well below other two-year-old prospects at the end of 1977. His two wins came against second-rate competition, was the consensus.

Dactylographer, being prepared for entry in England's most prestigious race for three-year-olds, the June 1978 Epsom Derby, ran his first race of the new season in May—a minor stakes. He finished well out of the money and has not competed again.

It would take considerably longer for Secretariat to get his first stakes winner in the United States. When he did, it would be a filly.

Messina was the name given by syndicate shareholder Dan Lasater to the first-crop filly produced by his mare Aphonia. The young and personable fast-food millionaire had devised the mating of Aphonia to Secretariat based on his reasoning that "Aphonia was a winner at three and she was the dam of two top runners. But even more important, her dam was Gambetta, who was also the dam of the great champion filly Gamely. I was breeding the best I had to the best performer from the best bloodline in the world. Being relatively new to the breeding world, I had to follow its oldest axiom. You can say I was only mildly disappointed in what has happened so far."

Lasater said this after Messina, a blocky, medium-sized bay, had failed to win or place in her first two starts as a two-year-old in Florida during November and December of 1977. Conditioned by Lasater trainer Gordon Potter, she had spent the preceding spring in California but had bucked her shins during a morning work in preparation for her debut there. She was sidelined during the summer, recovering at Lasater's farm at Ocala, Florida, and was then put back into training at the Calder Race Course in Miami. She trained well during October, and Potter entered her in a six-furlong maiden race on November 9. Like several of the Secretariats before her, she raced greenly, exhausting herself as she tried to run away from her rider in the backstretch, and she finished well to the rear of an unremarkable field.

Sent back to a second maiden event over the same distance on December 7, she finished sixth after showing some speed to the top of the stretch and then tiring.

Potter decided that Messina needed more conditioning and spent January building up her stamina so that she could sustain her speed. When he moved his division of the Lasater stable to its regular springtime milieu of the Oaklawn Park racetrack in Arkansas at the end of January, he entered the filly in another maiden event. This one, run on February 6, a month and a week after Messina turned three, she won.

The Lasater stable was peripatetic, shuttling particularly among the minor-league racetracks of the Midwest. Messina's next stop was the Latonia racetrack, across the Ohio River from Cincinnati. There, on March 4, she was entered in an ungraded "stakes" race.† Going off at 6-to-1 odds, Messina waltzed the six furlongs over a fast track in the agonizingly slow time of 74⅕ seconds to win by ten lengths—a tribute to the tortoiselike mediocrity of her competition.

Her achievement would not get her any genuine black type in a sales catalogue, and her next race—back at Arkansas' Oaklawn Park—would do little more to enhance her reputation. Potter sent her to the post in a genuine stakes contest, the $50,000-added Magnolia at six furlongs, on March 15. Messina expressed her natural short-distance speed down the backside, sharing the lead with considerably higher-quality company that she had faced at Latonia. But she tired at the four-furlong pole and straggled home an exhausted seventh in the field of ten.

As of the spring of 1978, Messina had put together two wins from five starts for total earnings of about $10,000. Discouraged, Lasater retired her and sent her to be bred to Exclusive Native, hoping to sell her in foal at a fall auction and get a top price. She was entered in a sale at Ocala, Florida, in September 1978 but then had to be withdrawn. It was found that she was barren.

Messina was clearly the best of the fillies to have raced, although Feuille d'Erable's Canadian connections might have argued that claim. On the whole, however, the fillies out of Secretariat's first crop were a monumental disappointment. And none

† An ungraded stakes is any race called by a track's management a "stakes" that has a total purse of less than $25,000. Many second-echelon tracks, in order to attract crowds, call a race a stakes that at a major-league track would be nothing more than an allowance event.

reflected the futility their trainers experienced with them more than did Senator's Choice, the bay out of Helen Hexter's mare Scaremenot.

Senator's Choice grew up to be sleek and narrow and was sent to New York trainer Mike Freeman in the early summer of her two-year-old year. Freeman, headquartered at Aqueduct, trained her steadily up to six furlongs and thought about putting her in a maiden when he moved to Saratoga in August. At the upstate New York track he continued breezing her at six furlongs every five days, and although her clockings improved each successive morning, she could never get the distance in twelves. He decided to wait.

Back at Aqueduct in September, he gave her full-tilt work from a gallop at four furlongs and she managed to get the distance in 47⅖ seconds—the first time she showed a hint of speed. Immediately thereafter Freeman wrote her down for a six-furlong maiden at Belmont. But he scratched her when the field turned up with what he considered to be too much class. He found another maiden for her a week later and this time let her go to the post.

It was the same story as with so many of the other Secretariats. Senator's Choice broke poorly under the gifted Steve Cauthen and ran a distant last down the backside. She gained little ground around the turn despite Cauthen's stern urging, and managed to finish a badly beaten eighth only because four horses in front of her quit and gave her the spot.

Senator's Choice did not race thereafter at two. She spent the winter of 1977 in Florida with Freeman but showed little desire or ability to run. She did manage to come back in the summer of 1978 to capture a maiden against undistinguished competition, but quickly faded again. She has since been retired to Kentucky and will become a broodmare.

Another failure in the filly ranks was Superfast, the Nelson Bunker Hunt chestnut who was bought back twice by Hunt from auctions. Hunt sent her to France as an early two-year-old, but when it became apparent from her mediocre training times that she was not suited to European distances, he returned her to the United States and installed her in California. She finished fourth in her debut over six furlongs at Hollywood

Park as a three-year-old, and then came back a few weeks later to finish fifth in her second try. She revealed little promise of future brilliance in either race.

The prospects for the colts in the first crop of performers were not much brighter than those of the fillies. Only Dactylographer in England and Syntariat in the United States showed promise of coming to useful hand by the time of the three-year-old summer classic races in 1978, but neither appeared a good bet to qualify for such prestige events. There was one colt, however, who remained somewhat of an enigma. He was Raymond Guest's blue roan Sacrebleu, whom Guest had gotten by buying Color Me Blue, his dam, in foal at auction.

Like most of the other Secretariats being conditioned to run as late two-year-olds, Sacrebleu looked nothing like his sire. Yet he had grown into a lean, well-balanced, and extremely racy-looking horse. Patrick Graham, Guest's trainer, brought him along slowly through the fall of 1977 after bucked shins had brought a stop to his training during the summer. His morning works were not impressive, but the colt was willing and, in Graham's view, would definitely have finishing speed if not used early in a race. It was this philosophy that Graham applied as he trained the colt up to his first start on December 21, 1977, at Laurel Race Course in Maryland. Graham had worked Sacrebleu at four furlongs a few mornings in August at Saratoga before his shins became afflicted. In November and December, stabled at Maryland's Bowie racetrack, he breezed the recovered roan at five and six furlongs in preparation for his first race.

December 21 arrived gray, cold, and sleety. By race time the track was a sea of slop. The race was a seven-furlong event for maidens, and the field was undistinguished in pedigree or value except for Sacrebleu and one other horse. Laurel was, after all, a minor-league racetrack but for two or three days a year. Under instructions from Patrick Graham, jockey John Adams took Sacrebleu in hand at the start of the afternoon's first race and reserved him third, within easy striking distance, down the backstretch. The colt rated obediently, thanks to Graham's training, running smoothly and not fighting Adams' hold. Coincidentally, the pace setter was Beaver Power, a son of Riva Ridge.

Sacrebleu continued to move confidently around the turn, oblivious to the barrage of mud shrapnel in his face. At the top of the stretch Adams hit him twice and he took off, sweeping into the lead in a few bounds. Adams hit him once more in midstretch when the colt seemed to want to dally, and Sacrebleu spurted ahead again, opening up a six-length winning lead to the wire.

The roan was in fact the first of Secretariat's initial crop to have won a race in the United States. Feuille d'Erable had won earlier in Canada and, of course, Dactylographer had won in England. Sacrebleu won so easily that at the time he seemed the best of the lot. Ten of Secretariat's first crop had raced, only two had broken their maidens, and just one had won a stakes (Dactylographer). Compared to what the offspring of several other first-year stallions had achieved, most notably Roberto and Secretariat's fine racing rival Sham, the statistics represented a dismal first-year performance at stud.

Patrick Graham confidently predicted that Sacrebleu would rescue Secretariat's reputation during the first few months of the three-year-old season, and might even race himself into the Kentucky Derby. But his confidence was misplaced. Believing the colt, bred for distance, would race even more authoritatively at a mile, Graham entered him in an allowance a week later. Sacrebleu, going off as the favorite, duplicated his performance of the week before by attacking the leaders at the top of the straight and earning the lead. But this time he was in against better company. He held the lead to the start of the eighth and last furlong, then tired to fade and finish third. He came out of the contest with a recurrence of sore shins and has not been able to run since.

Raymond Guest subsequently sold Sacrebleu in a private transaction. "I hope I shall not regret this last matter," he said plaintively on a recent occasion.

Epilogue

The 1978 Kentucky Derby became history on May 5, 1978, Affirmed putting away sentimental favorite and long-time rival Alydar in as splendid a race run at Churchill Downs since the year Secretariat set his record for the distance. Many were disappointed that at least one of Secretariat's first crop did not make it to the starting gate. Two or three might have been eligible, namely Syntariat, Cold Reception, Sacrebleu, even Dactylographer, had their owners chosen to pay the final entry fees and, in the case of Dactylographer, the shipping costs from England. It is a credit to the owners that they didn't. It would have been a sad spectacle indeed to have seen one of Secretariat's children trying to deal with the likes of Affirmed, Alydar, Believe It, Darby Creek Road, and Sensitive Prince—the outstanding horses of their age-group.

The day after the Derby, Secala, the filly bred by syndicate member Walter Haefner and sold for a record yearling price at auction in Ireland in 1976, broke her maiden at Hollywood Park. Secretariat was thus represented by another low-purse winner, but not even Secala gave promise of salvaging her sire's mediocre stud record. As 1978 moved toward the three-year-old summer classics and major stakes races, it appeared that the burden would fall on his second crop—some of which were just beginning to appear at racetracks around the country—to revitalize Secretariat's memory.

Many great racehorses have produced superior progeny from their first two stud crops. When such a stallion fails to do so, the odds that he will produce an outstanding runner from subsequent crops plummet. The statistical likelihood is that Secretariat will never produce anything remotely equal to himself, not to mention better than himself. That is one of the heartbreaks of thoroughbred breeding. It is possible that someday Secretariat will be remembered not as one of the greatest horses that ever lived, but as one of the biggest disappointments at stud. Yet there always remains a hope. And that's what, despite the heartbreaks, makes the business of breeding so compelling.

Secretariat's second crop, by which I mean just a trio of young horses from that crop, has so far met the challenge posed by the failure of his first. Aside from the aforementioned General Assembly, who won several thousand dollars in purses for the Firestones as a two-year-old and who is considered a top prospect for the 1979 Kentucky Derby and other classics, the great red stallion produced an equally brilliant filly who burned up the tracks of California during the summer of 1978. Named Terlingua, she broke several records in winning stakes races at Santa Anita and Hollywood Park. She was shipped east in the early fall in the hopes that she would shatter the myth that horses who perform well in the West do so only because of the lack of quality competition.

Unfortunately, the myth remained secure. Terlingua failed to distinguish herself in a pair of tough races in New York. Some blamed her inexplicably poor performances on the difference in racing surfaces between West and East, while others were content to refer to the old prejudice about West Coast horses. Nevertheless, Terlingua remains healthy and is expected to find her original form again soon, whether in the East or the West.

A third horse from the second crop to distinguish himself as a two-year-old was Jean-Louis Levesque's Medaille d'Or. Racing in Canada during the early part of his career like Levesque's Feuille d'Erable before him, Medaille d'Or won much more in purse money and is also being talked about as a good prospect for Kentucky in 1979.

Today Secretariat is stabled still at Claiborne Farm and his is the premier stall in the stallion barn. Looking much as he did five years ago, although heavier, he still commands the first attention of visitors as he grazes about his lush two-acre paddock. He remains the proud and beautiful superhorse of his youth. Little does he know, or reflect, his tarnished reputation. And as Seth Hancock recently said with an unexpected show of affection, "The old boy was always his most thrilling when he was coming from behind. He's way behind now, but let's not count him out. I have a feeling he's gonna come from behind one more time."

Since Hancock was proven right in his assessments of the quality of the "old boy's" first crop when they were foals, it is not unrealistic to believe that he may be onto something. We may yet see another Secretariat. Or even better. And that would be a very fine thing indeed.

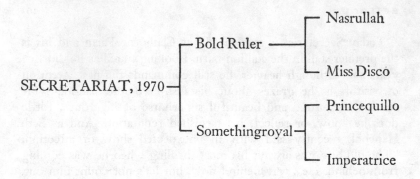

SECRETARIAT, 1970
- Bold Ruler
  - Nasrullah
  - Miss Disco
- Somethingroyal
  - Princequillo
  - Imperatrice

*SECRETARIAT'S first-year foals, their dams, and their dams'
immediate bloodlines:*

ACRATARIAT—*Fiji II*, by Acropolis out of Rififi (by Mossborough)

BRILLIANT PROTÉGÉ—*Irradiate*, by Ribot out of High
Voltage (by Ambiorix)

CANADIAN BOUND—*Charming Alibi*, by Honey's Alibi out
of Adorada II (by Hierocles)

CENTRIFOLIA—*Windy's Daughter*, by Windy Sea out of
Fleet Judy (by Fleet Nasrullah)

COLD RECEPTION—*Cold Comfort*, by Nearctic out of Scar-
let Letter (by Native Dancer)

CONFIDANT—*Chou Croute*, by Lieutenant Stevens out of
Witherite (by Kentucky Colonel)

DACTYLOGRAPHER—*Artists Proof*, by Ribot out of Be Ambitious (by Ambiorix)

DEBRETT—*All Beautiful*, by Battlefield out of Parlo (by Heliopolis)

FEUILLE D'ERABLE—*Arctic Dancer*, by Nearctic out of Natalma (by Native Dancer)

GREY LEGION—*Show Stopper*, by Native Dancer out of
Raise You (by Case Ace)

HOPE FOR ALL—*Hopespringseternal*, by Buckpasser out of
Rose Bower (by Princequillo)

MESSINA—*Aphonia*, by Dunce out of Gambetta (by My
Babu)

MISS SECRETARIAT—*My Card*, by My Babu out of Ace
Card (by Case Ace)

OATLANDS—*Gamba*, by Gun Bow out of Silver Bright (by Barbizon)

PUNCTUATION—*Jo Dan*, by Buckpasser out of Cosmah (by Cosmic Bomb)

REPORTAGE—*Crimson Saint*, by Crimson Satan out of Bolero Rose (by Bolero)

ROMANTIC SEASON—*Ran Tan*, by Summer Tan out of Mehrabi (by Migoli)

SACREBLEU—*Color Me Blue*, by The Axe II out of Nosey Body (by Tom Fool)

SECALA—*Aladancer*, by Northern Dancer out of Exclusive Bower (by Shut Out)

SECLUSIVE—*Exclusive Dancer*, by Native Dancer out of Mock Orange (by Dedicate)

SENATOR'S CHOICE—*Scaremenot*, by Bagdad out of Not Afraid (by Count Fleet)

SEXETARY—*Spa II*, by St. Crespin III out of Pange (by King's Bench)

SOCIOLOGUE—*Gleam II*, by Spy Well out of Not Afraid (by Count Fleet)

STATE ROOM—*Guest Room*, by Hail To Reason out of Little Hut (by Occupy)

SUPERFAST—*Zest II*, by Crepello out of Mary Brandon (by Owen Tudor)

SYNTARIAT—*Levee Night*, by Royal Levee out of Night of Nights (by Johns Joy)

TETE A TETE—*Arrangement*, by Intentionally out of Floral Gal (by Noble Hero)

UNNAMED—*Rotondella*, by Ribot out of Fantan (by Ambiorix)

Mares who did not have foals, or whose foals did not survive:

Barely Even—by Creme dela Creme out of Dodge Me (by The Dodge)

Belle Foulee—by Tom Fool out of Levee (by Hill Prince)

Bright New Day—by Ambiorix out of Break o' Morn (by Eight Thirty)

Broadway—by Hasty Road out of Flitabout (by Challedon)
Iberia—by Heliopolis out of War East (by Easton)
Iskra—by Le Haar out of Fasciola (by Fastnet)
Lady Be Good—by Better Self out of Past Eight (by Eight Thirty)
Natalma—by Native Dancer out of Almahmoud (by Mahmoud)